RADICALS

RADICALS

AUDACIOUS WRITINGS BY
AMERICAN WOMEN,
1830–1930

VOLUME TWO

Memoir, Essays, and Oratory

EDITED BY

Meredith Stabel and Zachary Turpin

UNIVERSITY OF IOWA PRESS, IOWA CITY

University of Iowa Press, Iowa City 52242
Copyright © 2021 by the University of Iowa Press
Foreword copyright © 2021 by Katha Pollitt

ISBN 978-1-60938-768-6 (pbk)
ISBN 978-1-60938-769-3 (ebk)

www.uipress.uiowa.edu
Printed in the United States of America

Cover design by Kathleen Lynch / Black Kat Design
Text design by April Leidig

Printed on acid-free paper

Cataloging-in-Publication data is on file
with the Library of Congress.

For the women who came before—MS

Especially Harriet Tubman, who risked her life for so many—ZT

Contents

List of Illustrations

That every child on earth shall have right conditions to make the best growth possible to it; that every citizen, from birth to death, shall have a chance to learn all he or she can assimilate, to develop every power that is in them—for the common good;—this will be the aim of education, under human management.

In the world of "society" we may look for very radical changes.

—Charlotte Perkins Gilman, *The Man-Made World* (1910)

Foreword

The only nineteenth-century women I remember learning about in eighth-grade American history class were Dorothea Dix, who revolutionized treatment for the mentally ill, and Clara Barton, founder of the American Red Cross. Well, let me be fair. In high school English class, our teacher regaled us with the famous anecdote about Margaret Fuller's announcing "I accept the universe" and Thomas Carlyle's responding: "By Gad, she'd better." I'm sure Susan B. Anthony was mentioned at some point. As for the great nineteenth-century struggles to which so many women devoted themselves—for the vote, education, the abolition of slavery, rights for workers and married women, control of sexuality, access to professions and jobs—you could easily graduate from high school with all As and know very little about any of it. The vote, for example, was something women were "granted," not the victorious culmination of a seventy-five-year-old battle waged by women themselves.

The 1970s women's movement, which gave rise to the revolutionary new field of women's history, changed all that. Today, most educated people know a bit about at least some of the major women in nineteenth-century American history: Susan B. Anthony, Elizabeth Cady Stanton, Harriet Tubman, Sojourner Truth, Ida B. Wells-Barnett. There are scholarly studies, biographies, essays galore. As I write, a statue of Anthony, Stanton, and Truth is going up in Central Park—the first to honor real-life women in that glorious and historic public space where up until now the only female statue was of Alice in Wonderland.

You'll find selections from the writings of many iconic women in this volume. Ida B. Wells-Barnett delivers an exposé of lynching that still scorches, and the activist and educator Mary Church Terrell delivers another. Anna Julia Cooper boldly prefigures intersectionality: "Only the BLACK WOMAN can say 'when and where I enter, in the quiet, undisputed dignity of my womanhood, without violence and without suing or special patronage, then and there the whole *Negro race enters with me.*'" Emma Goldman vigorously attacks the institution of marriage: "The institution of marriage makes a parasite of woman, an absolute dependent. It incapacitates her for life's struggle, annihilates her social consciousness, paralyzes her imagination, and then imposes its gracious protection, which is in reality a snare, a travesty on human character."

Charlotte Perkins Gilman, today most famous for her short story "The Yellow Wall-paper," in which a woman is driven insane by her oppressive marriage, was far better known in her day as a prolific journalist and economist. Her argument that employment for women, especially mothers, was key to their liberation is still a controversial claim (e.g., Mommy Wars): "Women; wives and mothers; are becoming a permanent half of the world workers. In their interest we shall inevitably change the brutal and foolish hardships now surrounding labor into such decent and healthful conditions as shall be no injury to any one. That children should be forced to work for their livings is an unnatural outrage, wholly injurious. That adult women should do it, is in no way harmful, if the hours and conditions of labor are suitable; and they never will be made suitable until overwhelming numbers of working women compel them" ("Maternity Benefits and Reformers"). Gilman's optimism is typical of the women collected in *Radicals*, as of so many nineteenth-century figures. The questions might be difficult, but the answers tended to be simple. What would Gilman make of the fact that most mothers are in the workforce today but we are still waiting for those "suitable working conditions"? Similarly, many suffragists thought suffrage was not just a right that belonged to women as citizens; they also believed women's votes would transform the nation: women would purify the public realm as they purified the home and ensure honest, responsible government and the protection of women and children. It turned out to be a lot more complicated than that. For decades after the ratification of the Nineteenth Amendment, women who could vote were less likely to vote than men, and when they did vote, they often voted like their husbands. Curiously, the major electoral victory of women until almost our own day was achieved before most women could cast a ballot. That would be Prohibition, the Eighteenth Amendment, the culmination of a crusade begun decades before by the formidable Frances Willard, tireless head of the Woman's Christian Temperance Union. Willard's separate spheres ideology sounds terribly antiquated today and not very feminist, but in an age in which middle-class white women were firmly confined to the home, it was rather clever to turn domesticity into a power base for public action—"our great home cause."

The nineteenth century was violent and grim. Black people were enslaved and then forced into subjection. Native Americans were driven off their land, their children sent to boarding schools that sought to extirpate their culture. Millions of women were trapped in desperate poverty, domestic violence, low-wage employment, without even the right to custody of their own children. This collection reminds us that it was also a time of great social and intellectual excitement. Feminism was brewing in surprising places: Frances Willard found liberation in learning to ride a bicycle. Religious women demanded a wider role as church workers, missionaries, and even preachers. Christianity itself could be bent to feminist uses. "And how came Jesus into the world?" asks Sojourner Truth in her speech to the Women's Rights Convention in 1851. "Through God who created him and woman who bore him. Man, where is your part?"

The shortcomings of nineteenth-century feminists are obvious to us today. Some were racists and some were suspiciously eager to control population and "improve" society through sterilization. Gilman in particular had a penchant for taking a sensible idea much too far. An essay that begins in support of rational suicide (she herself committed suicide when her terminal cancer became unbearable) ends up calling for widespread capital punishment and killing off the old and sick. It's worth remembering, though, that racism, classism, eugenics, nativism, hostility to non-Christian religions and cultures, and a penchant for sweeping solutions and quick fixes were not unique to feminists. They were common features of the "progressive" thought of the era.

The women represented in the following pages are an unusually varied bunch: Black, white, Native American, famous and obscure, preachers and teachers and revolutionaries, editors and farmers and activists. They disagreed about many things: about sexual morality, about women and men's true nature, about motherhood, about God, but each in her own way enlarged women's scope of action. Each fought for recognition of women's worth and right to self-determination. And each believed her thoughts were worth setting down in writing for others to read. That in itself was radical. And indeed it still is.

Katha Pollitt
—New York City, August 5, 2020

Introduction

American literature is often read, studied, and taught as if it makes the same basic demands of each reader. Before beginning this anthology, it is important to set aside such an assumption as not only incorrect and useless but dangerous.

Here is what the American literary tradition has always, or anyway up until quite recently, asked of its readers: *Do you have the strength to be an individualist? (Even as I deny the very fullness of your personhood?)*

The first question is all-embracing. It is the inquiry that makes Americans Americans, and as such it is the seed of Americanism in its many forms: Puritanism, republicanism, Unitarianism, transcendentalism, pragmatism, American modernism, intersectional feminism, and more. The second question, on the other hand, is heard only by some. Americans in power, Americans of privilege, Americans unaware of their overrepresentation in culture and politics, do not hear it, nor are they commonly forced to consider it. But many more are. It reverberates, soundlessly inquiring year after year: Can you live a life of fullness, self-determination, love and common bonds—can you be an individualist—when society denies your individuality?

The women of these volumes answer in thunder. What their answers are, you will have to read on to hear and understand. One commonality you may notice is that many of them deny the very premise that individualism precludes collectivism as the foundation of American society. It is a premise that, in the nineteenth and early twentieth centuries—the time span of this anthology—yielded immeasurable suffering. As summed up by Emma Goldman, anarchist and radical par excellence, it is a presupposition that preserves power for the few. "The oft repeated slogan of our time," she writes,

[is] that ours is an era of individualism, of the minority. Only those who do not probe beneath the surface might be led to entertain this view. Have not the few accumulated the wealth of the world? Are they not the masters, the absolute kings of the situation? Their success, however, is due not to individualism, but to the inertia, the cravenness, the utter submission of the mass. The latter wants but to be dominated, to be led, to be coerced. As to individualism, at no time in human history did it have less chance of expression, less opportunity to assert itself in a normal, healthy manner.[1]

In other words, if America is pulsed forward by regular and radical redefinition, it is not the inward-looking but the outward-embracing person who has the deepest soul, is the fullest patriot, and joins what Goldman calls the "non-compromising pioneers of social changes." For that, it takes thinkers who are willing to smash the contradictions that hide beneath social norms, and the women in these volumes are just such iconoclasts.

Today, perhaps more than at any time in living memory, social and cultural upheaval has come to define the American way of life. Even as we write this introduction, in the summer of 2020, the United States is undergoing radical changes of an extremity that hasn't been seen in generations. Though born of tragedy, many of these shifts promise to be uplifting. The murders by police of George Floyd and Breonna Taylor, as well as hundreds of other innocent African Americans just this year alone, have led to worldwide displays of solidarity for the Black Lives Matter movement and widespread activism toward police reform. Likewise, after decades of legal struggle, the U.S. Supreme Court's Obergefell v. Hodges ruling has cemented protections for LGBTQ Americans under the Fourteenth Amendment, protections that have long been suppressed by American employers and legislators alike. At a more local level, communities and regional governments across the country (as well as protest groups, when localities refuse) have been removing Confederate flags and pulling down Confederate monuments, disposing of a longstanding Jim Crow iconography designed to discount the terrors of slavery and enshrine racism in the American public sphere. Finally, as of this writing, the United States is poised to elect its first woman vice-president, having narrowly missed electing its first woman president in 2016. These events—and many others similarly monumental—suggest that the twenty-first century may be one in which radical American voices move the world further toward the good: toward equality, enfranchisement, and essential freedoms protected by law.

As in the twentieth century—when such voices impelled the passages of the Nineteenth Amendment and the Civil Rights Act, the enactment of the New Deal, the near passage of the Equal Rights Amendment, and Supreme Court decisions such as Loving v. Virginia and Roe v. Wade—radicalism is a force for good, not merely an example of fringe individualism or eccentricity. The same is not so often assumed of nineteenth-century radicals. Despite its seismic struggles over slavery, suffrage, and legal enfranchisement, the nineteenth century is an era rarely represented as a time of widespread radicalism in the United States. In particular, the extent to which radicalism surged through the daily lives, thoughts, and writings of American women in the nineteenth and early twentieth centuries is hardly well represented in textbooks or trade volumes today.

Even the word itself, "radical," is all too rarely used to describe early American women's voices, especially the voices of women of color. Worse yet, if early American women's words are represented in collections of history or literature as radical, it is too often in the etymological sense of acting as a root and thus being root-*like*: staid and unmoving, inflexible. Where in the word—or in the anthologies built around it—is the movement, the energy, the color of early radicalism? Where are the works by all those women who, as Zora Neale Hurston says, were busy sharpening their oyster knives?

In this anthology, you will find them. These volumes are perhaps the first of their kind: a full-length collection of radical writings by early American women, with little-known rarities included, voices of color prioritized, and all major genres represented (fiction, poetry, drama, memoir, essays, and oratory). Our selections span from early radical works such as Sarah Louise Forten's antislavery poem, "The Grave of the Slave" (1831), and Sojourner Truth's *Narrative of Sojourner Truth*, a memoir of bondage and liberation (1850), to Angelina Weld Grimké's antilynching sonnet, "Trees" (1928), and Charlotte Perkins Gilman's essay in favor of euthanasia, "The Right to Die" (1935). In between, the reader will discover many lesser-known and unknown texts, most of which, while vibrant and challenging, often go uncollected, crowded out by more commonly anthologized major texts.

In this anthology, we intend to represent the underrepresented. Thus, we include a number of texts that are rarely, or in some cases have never been, anthologized. For example, we include Emily Dickinson's more overtly erotic poems, those usually passed over in favor of other verses that, when taken alone, misleadingly suggest celibacy or a disinterest in sex on Dickinson's part. We include a pair of Kate Chopin's later tales, "An Egyptian Cigarette," her first-person fictional account of smoking pot— originally published in *Vogue*, of all places—and "The Storm," a story so sexually explicit that it did not see publication in her lifetime.

This is also true of Emma Lazarus's "Assurance," an erotic sonnet that her sisters (in their role as literary executors) left out of her posthumous, still standard *Poems*. We have included it alongside three longer, overtly queer poems that have also somehow missed collection, even though they appeared in the widely circulated *Lippincott's Monthly Magazine*. Until only a few years ago, these poems were almost entirely unknown. New to readers, as well, will be Rebecca Harding Davis's "At Noon," a story that until recently lay dormant in the pages of an 1887 issue of *Harper's Bazaar*. Its complex critique of upper-class womanhood almost certainly raised the eyebrows of readers of the *Bazaar*, who were used to the magazine's lighter fare on fashion and ice creams. Today, Davis's tale still has the power to shock.

Indeed, many of the pieces in these volumes are included at the expense of more well-known texts. In these pages, for instance, readers will not find such foundational works as Chopin's *The Awakening*, Lazarus's "The New Colossus" (famously inscribed in the Statue of Liberty), nor Davis's *Life in the Iron-Mills*. In our view, such writings have been so thoroughly anthologized—and rightfully so—that it is time to present more from these women and their peers, especially those texts that typically miss collection for being too uncompromising, idiosyncratic, or hard to categorize.

The poet and scholar Tillie Olsen, herself an important anthologist (and the rediscoverer of *Life in the Iron-Mills*), defines the absence of such readings in modern anthologies as *silences*—"some silences hidden; some the ceasing to publish after one work appears; some the never coming to book form at all." This anthology thus exists to continue the work of Olsen and many other scholars before and since in undoing such silences by amplifying many important works of literature that often go unread and undiscussed.

In these pages, then, you will not find the standard version of Sojourner Truth's "Ain't I a Woman?" with the refrain that yielded its now famous title. Instead, we include Truth's speech as it was first recorded and published, a month after its delivery to the Women's Rights Convention in Akron, Ohio, in May 1851. Truth's original language has a power that its later editing and rewriting by white abolitionists cannot hide. Likewise, you will not find Julia Ward Howe's "The Battle Hymn of the Republic," the unofficial song of the Union during the U.S. Civil War, and perhaps the most famous American lyrics of their day. Instead, we include excerpts from *The Hermaphrodite*, an unpublished novel that is one of the earliest, and certainly the most sensitive of, nineteenth-century treatments of intersex life in America.

Rather than reproduce Gilman's immortal short story "The Yellow Wall-paper," we have collected a number of her lesser-known works, to display her incredible range of style and subject. These include the tale "When I Was a Witch," her political poem, "The Socialist and the Suffragist," excerpts from her feminist utopian novel, *Herland*, and essays such as "What Is Feminism?," "Maternity Benefits and Reformers," and "The Right to Die," which is Gilman's final essay, drafted while she was suffering from inoperable breast cancer and completed shortly before she took her own life with chloroform. Likewise, we have not included Harriet Jacobs's *Incidents in the Life of a Slave Girl*, if only because such a foundational slave narrative is today widely available. Harder to find is Jacobs's "Letter from a Fugitive Slave," her first published work and a powerful response to "The Women of England vs. the Women of America," that infamous defense of slavery penned by former First Lady Julia Gardiner Tyler.

All that said, this anthology is not constructed exclusively from lesser-known writings. Indeed, many of the works will be immediately recognizable to the average reader. From Frances E. W. Harper's "Learning to Read" to Adah Isaacs Menken's "Judith," from Pauline Hopkins's "Talma Gordon" to Emma Goldman's "A New Declaration of Independence," from Margaret Fuller's *Woman in the Nineteenth Century* to Elizabeth Cady Stanton, Susan B. Anthony, and Matilda Joslyn Gage's introduction to their *History of Woman Suffrage*, these texts help form a continually expanding canon of American women's literature, some of whose elements are so unique that they are essentially one of a kind.

Indeed, in some instances we reproduce the only known writings of an author. In such cases, we aim to further popularize what are still underread texts, many of them written by authors of color and some of which were rediscovered only recently. For example, we include long excerpts from Harriet E. Wilson's *Our Nig* (1859), possibly the earliest novel published by a Black woman in the United States, uncovered by scholar Henry Louis Gates Jr. in 1981; *Gifts of Power*, the long-unpublished autobiography and revelations-record of African American Shaker eldress Rebecca Cox Jackson; *Louisa Picquet, the Octoroon*, the memoir of a mixed-race freedwoman and her experiences of sexual and psychological mistreatment as a slave; and Ida B. Wells-Barnett's *Southern Horrors*, a record of lynchings and lynch laws in the Jim Crow South, for which Wells-Barnett received death threats—and, just this year, a posthumous Pulitzer Prize for Journalism.

While many of the women represented in these volumes were professional writers, just as many were not. Cox Jackson was a preacher, Julia A. J. Foote a deacon, Dickinson a gardener and baker, Buffalo Bird Woman a traditional Hidatsa agriculturalist and promoter of matriarchal culture. Others were orators, abolitionists, suffragists, and women's rights advocates, whose active public-speaking schedules precluded their writing as prolifically as they might have liked. And more than a few were political trailblazers: Victoria Woodhull and Belva Lockwood, for example, were the first American women to run for president, Woodhull in 1872 (illegally) and Lockwood in 1884, shortly before she became the first woman lawyer to practice before the U.S. Supreme Court. (Lockwood's life would inspire generations of women lawyers, including the late Supreme Court justice Ruth Bader Ginsburg.) Woodhull's letter "To the Women of the South" and Lockwood's speech on "The Growth of Peace Principles" both appear in this volume, for the first time anywhere since their initial publication. Overall, this anthology exists to re-present—or in some cases, present for the first time—the many beautiful, lesser-known examples of early radical womanhood in America.

It should be noted that some of these words are disputed, and justifiably so. *Womanhood*, for example, may seem obvious enough to need no explanation. But as Margaret Fuller writes at the early date of 1843, maleness and femaleness, which one might expect to "represent the two sides of the great radical dualism," are in fact "perpetually passing into one another." She adds, with a resounding full stop, that "there is no wholly masculine man, no purely feminine woman." It is the Tao-like crux of Fuller's manifesto on empowered womanhood: any gender line, once drawn, will prove porous. Womanhood is no more monolithic than manhood. Because gender is embodied, enacted, constructed, discovered, to be a woman is in some ways a perpetual exercising of individualism—a finding of the self, a learning to "live *first* for God's sake," as Fuller says, and an asking of an ancient question yet again: What *is* womanhood, and what can it be? That so many writers in this volume ask this very question, and not merely for the individual but for the collective, is why we call them *radicals*.

As a term of politics, "radical" is often taken to mean "progressive" when used to describe an attitude of or toward American womanhood—and in that regard, many of the writers included are radical, even by today's standards. Their works, however, are also radical in the second, etymological sense mentioned earlier, of rooting the foundations of their era. All this, added to their vibrancy and unorthodoxy and self-determination, is what makes them implicitly—and often explicitly—*feminist*.

Indeed, all the writings in this anthology may be described as examples of First-Wave feminist thought—to the point that we strongly considered foregrounding the First Wave as this anthology's uniting theme. It will become clearer as you read through these volumes, however, that the First Wave is not the only one represented by these writings. The longer we linger in the writings of the early waves of feminism, the easier it is to see the hallmarks of later waves presaged within them. Chopin's fictions, for example, are pivotal First-Wave texts, depicting the difficulties of living as a white woman without legal enfranchisement, within the straits of traditional gender ideology. Many of her concerns, though—desire, sexuality, work, and autonomy—look ahead to the Second Wave of the 1960s. Perkins Gilman, likewise, continually looks forward to the Second Wave while also forecasting Third-Wave concerns, including reproductive rights, the reclamation of derogatory terms, and sex positivity. Further still, Fuller's *Woman in the Nineteenth Century*, perhaps *the* core First-Wave text in America, posits ideas about gender roles, race, and equal opportunity that resoundingly preecho today's Fourth Wave. Thus, while we might have framed these volumes as a collection of First-Wave feminist thought and life—and they certainly are that—they are more broadly a celebration of the timeless expressions of radical womanhood, whose continuity has no obvious interval.

Doubtless, to represent advances as "waves" is, in the symbolism of history, to sacrifice complexity for intelligibility. History *is* sequential, of course. Event succeeds event like swells in the ocean, and this is true enough of the waves of woman's advancement. But on what shore do they break? Where do they end? Consider the First Wave, whose crest, arguably, is 1920, the year of the ratification of the Nineteenth Amendment enfranchising white women voters. Its "conclusion," however, does not arrive until at least 1965 (the year the Voting Rights Act finally ensured the vote for Black women voters in the South), if not much later—or even at all, considering current and very real erosions of voting rights in many states. Similarly, while the Second Wave women's liberation movement may appear to be consigned to the 1960s and 1970s, in reality it is hardly concluded, thanks to twenty-first-century legislative and judicial assaults on reproductive rights. The Third Wave is subject to similar attacks. All this is to say that the waves of feminism, represented (or presaged) throughout this anthology, are not only a historical sequence of steps made toward equality, equity, and justice but also a chaotically beautiful, back-and-forth system, a roiling confluence of waves passing, crashing, and receding through the others, reinfusing, eddying, and surging forward again.

To further complicate things, the texts in these volumes will occasionally present readers with contradictions of philosophy or intent between and among avowed suffragists, women's rights activists, and abolitionists, many of whom were comrades, to say nothing of the contradictions to be found within the writings of any single author. For scholars of the writings of early radical women in the United States, this may come as no surprise, but for students it will almost certainly be startling. It is the shock of what lawyer and critical race theorist Kimberlé Crenshaw has termed "intersectionality," the combination of overlapping and interrelated elements of identity—such as race, class, gender, sexuality, and physical ability—whose interaction yields unique injustices for some, unique blind spots to (and benefits from) injustice for others.

Thus, among the authors collected in these volumes, cross-purposes inevitably arose, many of them traceable to the political and social leveraging exerted by nineteenth-century and early twentieth-century white feminists. While their contributions to literature and law are unquestionable, we endeavor in these volumes to counterbalance their voices with a greater proportion of writings by underanthologized Black feminists, Native feminists, and Asian American feminists, many of whom were writing for their lives and the lives of their families and communities, often at the risk of being harassed, slandered, dispossessed, disenfranchised, or killed.

At that, not every text may seem all that radical or even feminist by contemporary standards. Julia A. J. Foote and Rebecca Cox Jackson, for example, chiefly recount their conversions to Christianity and calls to preach. Buffalo Bird Woman counsels the reader in the clearing and planting of land. These women, however, document working their way toward access to power, speech, and an audience. They promote morality, independence, and matriarchy. And they out-think, out-pray, and out-philosophize their male gatekeepers all along the way.

Their writings are also deeply human. The works included in *Radicals* are records of the vanguard of a new era, but they are also, regardless of time period, the original efforts of powerful artistic minds. Hence, we include excerpts from Pauline Hopkins's *Of One Blood*, a novel of alchemy and the undead, and Amelia E. Johnson's *Clarence and Corinne*, a traditional romance novel. In an era when many of the writers represented were legally considered property, had few or no voting rights, and led lives in which reading and writing were seen as privileges of the free and wealthy, simply publishing one's words was an assertion of autonomy and selfhood. Thus, to write for pleasure and enjoyment, beyond any effort to prove one's humanity to disbelieving others, was a radical act all its own.

One and all, these were women of genius and audacity, and as Adah Isaacs Menken writes, "this very audacity is divine."

NOTE

1. See Goldman's "Minorities versus Majorities," *Anarchism and Other Essays* (New York: Mother Earth Publishing Association, 1910), 75–84.

A Note on the Text

Generally, we maintain all variant spellings, vernacular English, typos, and errors, as they appeared in the original versions of texts. For readerly ease, we do not use [*sic*]. In a few cases, when the meaning of a passage is altered or unclear due to an original typo, we have silently amended it.

While we standardize a few minor typographical elements—such as converting single quotation marks to full quotation marks and removing spaces before colons and semicolons—we largely maintain those elements of nineteenth-century typography that, while nonstandard today, were common for the period, such as midsentence exclamation and question marks (e.g., *American Mothers! can you doubt that the slave feels as tenderly for her offspring as you do for yours?*).

RADICALS

Buffalo Bird Woman
(Waheenee / Maaxiiriwia)

ca. 1839–1932

BUFFALO BIRD WOMAN (Hidatsa: Maaxiiriwia, also called Waheenee) was a Hidatsa woman who was born in Knife River, North Dakota, and lived the majority of her adult life on the Fort Berthold Reservation. She never learned to speak English and used traditional Hidatsa agricultural methods throughout her life. Her son, Edward Goodbird, arranged for ethnographer Gilbert Wilson (1868–1930) to conduct interviews with their family between 1907 and 1918. These formed the basis for Wilson's doctoral dissertation, *Buffalo Bird Woman's Garden* (1917). It compiles information from Buffalo Bird Woman about agricultural techniques as well as Hidatsa history, origin myths, and cultural practices. In 1921, Wilson published *Waheenee: An Indian Girl's Story, Told by Herself*, which he had transcribed.

From *Buffalo Bird Woman's Garden, As Recounted by Maxi'diwiac (Buffalo Bird Woman) of the Hidatsa Indian Tribe (ca. 1839–1932)* (1917)

CHAPTER II. Beginning a Garden

Turtle

My great-grandmother, as white men count their kin, was named Atạ'kic, or Soft-white Corn. She adopted a daughter, Mata'tic, or Turtle. Some years after, a daughter was born to Atạ'kic, whom she named Otter.

Turtle and Otter both married. Turtle had a daughter named Ica'wikec, or Corn Sucker; and Otter had three daughters, Want-to-be-a-woman, Red Blossom, and Strikes-many-women, all younger than Corn Sucker.

The smallpox year at Five Villages left Otter's family with no male members to support them. Turtle and her daughter were then living in Otter's lodge; and Otter's daughters, as Indian custom bade, called Corn Sucker their elder sister.

It was a custom of the Hidatsas, that if the eldest sister of a household married, her younger sisters were also given to her husband, as they came of marriageable age. Left without male kin by the smallpox, my grandmother's family was hard put to it to get meat; and Turtle gladly gave her daughter to my father, Small Ankle, whom she knew to be a good hunter. Otter's daughters, reckoned as Corn Sucker's sisters, were given to Small Ankle as they grew up; the eldest, Want-to-be-a-woman, was my mother.

When I was four years old, my tribe and the Mandans came to Like-a-fishhook bend. They came in the spring and camped in tepees, or skin tents. By Butterfly's winter count, I know they began building earth lodges the next winter. I was too young to remember much of this.

Two years after we came to Like-a-fishhook bend, smallpox again visited my tribe; and my mother, Want-to-be-a-woman, and Corn Sucker, died of it. Red Blossom and Strikes-many-women survived, whom I now called my mothers. Otter and old Turtle lived with us; I was taught to call them my grandmothers.

Clearing Fields

Soon after they came to Like-a-fishhook bend, the families of my tribe began to clear fields, for gardens, like those they had at Five Villages. Rich black soil was to be found in the timbered bottom lands of the Missouri. Most of the work of clearing was done by the women.

In old times we Hidatsas never made our gardens on the untimbered, prairie land, because the soil there is too hard and dry. In the bottom lands by the Missouri, the soil is soft and easy to work.

My mothers and my two grandmothers worked at clearing our family's garden. It lay east of the village at a place where many other families were clearing fields.

I was too small to note very much at first. But I remember that my father set boundary marks—whether wooden stakes or little mounds of earth or stones, I do not now remember—at the corners of the field we claimed. My mothers and my two grandmothers began at one end of this field and worked forward. All had heavy iron hoes, except Turtle, who used an old fashioned wooden digging stick.

With their hoes, my mothers cut the long grass that covered much of the field, and bore it off the line, to be burned. With the same implements, they next dug and softened the soil in places for the corn hills, which were laid off in rows. These hills they planted. Then all summer they worked with their hoes, clearing and breaking the ground between the hills.

Trees and bushes I know must have been cut off with iron axes; but I remember little of this, because I was only four years old when the clearing was begun.

I have heard that in very old times, when clearing a new field, my people first dug the corn hills with digging sticks; and afterwards, like my mothers, worked between the hills, with bone hoes. My father told me this.

Whether stone axes were used in old times to cut the trees and undergrowths, I do not know. I think fields were never then laid out on ground that had large trees on it.

Dispute and Its Settlement

About two years after the first ground was broken in our field, a dispute I remember, arose between my mothers and two of their neighbors, Lone Woman and Goes-to-next-timber.

These two women were clearing fields adjoining that of my mothers; as will be seen by the accompanying map,[1] the three fields met at a corner. I have said that my father, to set up claim to his field, had placed marks, one of them in the corner at which met the fields of Lone Woman and Goes-to-next-timber; but while my mothers were busy clearing and digging up the other end of their field, their two neighbors invaded this marked-off corner; Lone Woman had even dug up a small part before she was discovered.

However, when they were shown the mark my father had placed, the two women yielded and accepted payment for any rights they might have.

It was our Indian rule to keep our fields very sacred. We did not like to quarrel about our garden lands. One's title to a field once set up, no one ever thought of disputing it; for if one were selfish and quarrelsome, and tried to seize land belonging to another, we thought some evil would come upon him, as that some one of his family would die. There is a story of a black bear who got into a pit that was not his own, and had his mind taken away from him for doing so!

Turtle Breaking Soil

Lone Woman and Goes-to-next-timber having withdrawn, my grandmother, Turtle, volunteered to break the soil of the corner that had been in dispute. She was an industrious woman. Often, when my mothers were busy in the earth lodge, she would go out to work in the garden, taking me with her for company. I was six years old then, I think, quite too little to help her any, but I liked to watch my grandmother work.

With her digging stick, she dug up a little round place in the center of the corner; and circling around this from day to day, she gradually enlarged the dug-up space. The point of her digging stick she forced into the soft earth to a depth equal to the length of my hand, and pried up the soil. The clods she struck smartly with her digging stick, sometimes with one end, sometimes with the other. Roots of coarse grass, weeds, small brush and the like, she took in her hand and shook, or struck them against the ground, to knock off the loose earth clinging to them; she then cast them into a little pile to dry.

In this way she accumulated little piles, scattered rather irregularly over the dug-up ground, averaging, perhaps, four feet, one from the other. In a few days these little piles had dried; and Turtle gathered them up into a heap, about four feet high, and burned them, sometimes within the cleared ground, sometimes a little way outside.

In the corner that had been in dispute, and in other parts of the field, my grandmother worked all summer. I do not remember how big our garden was at the end of her summer's work, nor how many piles of roots she burned; but I remember distinctly how she put the roots of weeds and grass and brush into little piles to dry, which she then gathered into heaps and burned. She did not attempt to burn over the whole ground, only the heaps.

Afterwards, we increased our garden from year to year until it was as large as we needed. I remember seeing my grandmother digging along the edges of the garden with her digging stick, to enlarge the field and make the edges even and straight.

I remember also, that as Turtle dug up a little space, she would wait until the next season to plant it. Thus, additional ground dug up in the summer or fall would be planted by her the next spring.

There were two or three elm trees in the garden; these my grandmother left standing.

It must not be supposed that upon Turtle fell all the work of clearing land to enlarge our garden; but she liked to have me with her when she worked, and I remember best what I saw her do. As I was a little girl then, I have forgotten much that she did; but this that I have told, I remember distinctly.

Turtle's Primitive Tools

In breaking ground for our garden, Turtle always used an ash digging stick; and when hoeing time came, she hoed the corn with a bone hoe. Digging sticks are still used in my tribe for digging wild turnips; but even in my grandmother's lifetime, digging sticks and bone hoes, as garden tools, had all but given place to iron hoes and axes.

My grandmother was one of the last women of my tribe to cling to these old fashioned implements. Two other women, I remember, owned bone hoes when I was a little girl; but Turtle, I think, was the very last one in the tribe who actually worked in her garden with one.

This hoe my grandmother kept in the lodge, under her bed; and when any of the children of the household tried to get it out to look at it, she would cry. "Let that hoe alone; you will break it!"

Beginning a Field in Later Times

As I grew up, I learned to work in the garden, as every Hidatsa woman was expected to learn; but iron axes and hoes, bought of the traders, were now used by everybody, and the work of clearing and breaking a new field was less difficult than it had been in our grandfathers' times. A family had also greater freedom in choosing where they should have their garden, since with iron axes they could more easily cut down any small trees and bushes that might be on the land. However, to avoid having to cut down big trees, a rather open place was usually chosen.

A family, then, having chosen a place for a field, cleared off the ground as much as they could, cutting down small trees and bushes in such way that the trees fell all in one direction. Some of the timber that was fit might be taken home for firewood; the rest was let lie to dry until spring, when it was fired. The object of felling the trees in one direction was to make them cover the ground as much as possible, since firing them softened the soil and left it loose and mellow for planting. We sought always to burn over all the ground, if we could.

Before firing, the family carefully raked off the dry grass and leaves from the edge of the field, and cut down any brush wood. This was done that the fire might not spread to the surrounding timber, nor out on the prairie. Prairie fires and forest fires are even yet not unknown on our reservation.

Planting season having come, the women of the household planted the field in corn. The hills were in rows, and about four feet or a little less apart. They were rather irregularly placed the first year. It was easy to make a hill in the ashes where a brush heap had been fired, or in soil that was free of roots and stumps; but there were many stumps in the field, left over from the previous summer's clearing. If the planter found a stump stood where a hill should be, she placed the hill on this side the stump or beyond it, no matter how close this brought the hill to the next in the row. Thus, the corn hills did not stand at even distances in the row the first year; but the rows were always kept even and straight.

While the corn was coming up, the women worked at clearing out the roots and smaller stumps between the hills; but a stump of any considerable size was left to rot, especially if it stood midway between two corn hills, where it did not interfere with their cultivation.

My mothers and I used to labor in a similar way to enlarge our fields. With our iron hoes we made hills along the edge of the field and planted corn; then, as we had opportunity, we worked with our hoes between the corn hills to loosen up the soil.

Although our tribe now had iron axes and hoes from the traders, they still used their native made rakes. These were of wood, or of the antler of a black-tailed deer. It was with such rakes that the edges of a newly opened field were cleaned of leaves for the firing of the brush, in the spring.

Trees in the Garden

Trees were not left standing in the garden, except perhaps one to shade the watchers' stage. If a tree stood in the field, it shaded the corn; and that on the north side of the tree never grew up strong, and the stalks would be yellow.

Cottonwood trees were apt to grow up in the field, unless the young shoots were plucked up as they appeared.

Our West Field

The field which Turtle helped to clear, lay, I have said, east of the village. I was about nineteen years old, I think, when my mothers determined to clear ground for a second field, west of the village.

There were five of us who undertook the work, my father, my two mothers, Red Blossom and Strikes-many-women, my sister, Cold Medicine, and myself. We began in the fall, after harvesting the corn from our east garden, so that we had leisure for the work; we had been too busy to begin earlier in the season.

We chose a place down in the bottoms, overgrown with willows; and with our axes we cut the willows close to the ground, letting them lie as they fell.

I do not know how many days we worked; but we stopped when we had cleared a field of about seventy-five by one hundred yards, perhaps. In our east, or yellow corn field, we counted nine rows of corn to one *na'xu*; and I remember that when we came to plant our new field, it had nine *na'xu*.

Burning Over the Field

The next spring my father, his two wives, my sister and I went out and burned the felled willows and brush which the spring sun had dried. We did not burn them every day; only when the weather was fine. We would go out after breakfast, burn until tired of the work, and come home.

We sought to burn over the whole field, for we knew that this left a good, loose soil. We did not pile the willows in heaps, but loosened them from the ground or scattered them loosely but evenly over the soil. In some places the ground was quite bare of willows; but we collected dry grass and weeds and dead willows, and strewed them over these bare places so that the fire would run over the whole area of the field.

It took us about four days to burn over the field.

It was well known in my tribe that burning over new ground left the soil soft and easy to work, and for this reason we thought it a wise thing to do.

SOURCE

Buffalo Bird Woman's Garden, As Recounted by Maxi'diwiac (Buffalo Bird Woman) of the Hidatsa Indian Tribe (ca. 1839–1932), edited by Gilbert Livingstone Wilson. Originally published as "Agriculture of the Hidatsa Indians: An Indian Interpretation," *Bulletin of the University of Minnesota*, Studies in the Social Sciences no. 9, 1917.

NOTE

Chapter opening photo: Buffalo Bird Woman hoeing squashes with a bone hoe, ca. 1917. From *Buffalo Bird Woman's Garden, as Recounted by Maxi'diwiac (Buffalo Bird Woman) of the Hidatsa India Tribe (ca. 1839–1932)*, edited by Gilbert Livingstone Wilson. Originally published in 1917 as *Agriculture of the Hidatsa Indians: An Indian Interpretation*, a PhD thesis by Gilbert Livingstone Wilson.

1. Illustrations and figure numbers have been omitted throughout this selection.

Jennie Collins

1828–1887

JENNIE COLLINS was born into a poor white family in Amoskeag, New Hampshire, and worked in the cotton mills to support herself starting at age fourteen. She became one of New England's leading female labor reformers, abolitionists, humanitarians, and suffragists, founding the charity Boffin's Bower in Boston in 1870. The Bower was a place for working-class women to socialize, learn new skills, and obtain food, housing, and employment when they needed it. Collins gave lectures on child labor, the eight-hour workday, and better wages and working conditions for women, and spoke at the 1870 convention of the National Woman Suffrage Association. In 1871 she published *Nature's Aristocracy*, her treatise on the dangerous levels of wealth inequality in the United States, and became one of the first working-class American women to publish a volume of her own writings.

Woman's Suffrage (1871)

Woman's Rights.—Woman's Sphere.—Using the Talents
which God gave her.—History of the Suffrage Movement
in America.—Margaret Fuller.—Why the Rich do not
want the Ballot.—Who need it.—Conclusion.

I.

The exact meaning of the word "rights" has never been definitely settled, and the expression *"woman's* rights" only serves to render its import more vague and complicated than when standing alone. You want your "rights." I want my "rights." White men want their "rights," and black men want their "rights"; but in the whole list there is nothing so indefinite as woman's "rights." Men and women stare at each other with an expression of nothingness, whenever the subject is mentioned. "What *can* woman want more than she has got?" Some venturesome wights, who seemed to think that an unmeaning or foolish reply is better than none, have made good Pope's remark, that

"Fools rush in where angels fear to tread,"[1]

by making some of the following statements: "Women want the right to go to the polls with the men," "They want to go to war," "They wish for the chance to rule," "They desire to be placed in positions for which they are unfitted," "Woman wants to vote merely because she has not had the privilege," "Woman is discontented in her proper sphere," "She wants the right of doing man's work," "She wants to oblige her husband to do the housework while she devotes her attention to the farm, the factory, and the warehouse," "She wishes to perform impossibilities," &c., &c. The more absurd and impracticable the proposition the more convinced have these buffoons been that it was just what the women the most desired.

"Woman's rights," however, have never been defined, and never can be defined in any one or any series of books. The needs of one woman are not the wants of another, and the desires of one class can find no sympathizers in any other class. They can unite on no certain remedy as applying to every class, because there are no certain wrongs that apply to the whole sex. Some are blessed with everything they desire; others have nothing. Some are forced into higher positions than they can fill; others are far below their natural station. While one is favored, another is slighted; and oftentimes that which makes one happy makes another miserable.

It cannot be supposed that there is a remedy for all the wrongs which women suffer; but the measure which seems to promise the greatest results is that of Woman's Suffrage. By this means women are placed on a political equality with men, and have nearly an equal chance with them of receiving a recognition of such natural talent as they may happen to possess. The agitators demand *universal freedom*. I do not believe that the thinking women of to-day desire or expect the passage of laws which will *oblige* them to do man's duties. They demand the liberty to do that for which Nature seemed to have intended them when she endowed them with intelligence and bodily vigor. No human law can change their

physical stature or enlarge the size of their brains; but the absence of re-
strictive laws may afford them an opportunity to cultivate their brains
and strengthen their physical stature. Neither do I think that laws or their
consequences could ever make women as a class the mental equals of
the men as a class. But when there are women, as often happens, with
brains as large, with minds as strong, and with physical stature as enduring, as can be found in the ranks of men, I would not suffer a law to exist
which prevented such a person from occupying an equal place with the
men of her ability. I would open the whole stage to free competition from
every class, and award the crown to the successful ones without regard
to age, sex, or nationality. *No law should prevent the use of a single talent
which God has given to man or woman.* The woman whose tastes take her
to the bedside of the sick, with her who feels that she has the ability to
defend the right upon the rostrum, should be protected and encouraged.
If there were found in the ranks of women some who were able and willing
to shoulder a musket or accept the position of a sea-captain or police-
officer,—as absurd as it seems at first thought,—I would not deny them
the privilege. The few women that have been soldiers, sailors, and detectives have no more "brought disgrace on their sex" than the tailors,
hospital nurses, and bakers have injured the fair fame of the men. It needs
no argument, however, to establish the truth of the axiom which recog-
nizes the propriety of doing that for which one is best fitted; and woman's
suffrage will serve no other purpose but that of giving equal opportunities to those equally endowed.

II.

The Woman's Suffrage movement is the outgrowth of civilization, and is
also the more immediate result of a recent retrograde movement among
the political and social leaders of enlightened society. In the earlier ages of
the world physical strength determined the superiority, and women with
the weaker classes of men were held in bondage. But little attention was
paid to mental qualifications for leadership, for muscle was the master.
In that field woman had her "rights," and we often read in history of Ama-
zonians like Boadicea, to whom were accorded leadership on account of
their physical power. Then came the age of chivalry, when, for the lack of
other causes of contention, the lovers of bloodshed and war agreed upon
assuming a protectorate over the weaker sex; each man looking upon the

whole class as his immediate charge. After endless quarrels and murders in attempting to do for woman what they would not let her do for herself, the men gave up the task, and woman relapsed into her former obscurity and servitude. But the advance of civilization, while it rejected the idea of serving woman merely because she was the "weaker sex," increased man's respect for her gentleness and natural kindness of disposition.

The Pilgrim Fathers, when they came to America, did not hesitate to bring their wives and children with them across the stormy sea; but they were, nevertheless, so far advanced that they respected and honored true womanhood. Years passed, and this respect increased, until the men of New England gave to their wives and daughters the lightest and neatest part of the family labor, considering the house and its keeping more fitted to their ability, while the men undertook to perform all the out-door work, which required physical strength and endurance. It was done as an equitable division of labor, and among other duties the men undertook the care of town and colony affairs. There was no intentional injustice, and the woman had no thought of asking a vote for the purpose of protecting rights which had always been accorded to her without question.

There were husbands for all the ladies, and it was a sin and disgrace to be an old maid; hence the men felt that every woman could have a protector, who could defend her in case of any attempted injustice. They meant no evil themselves, and did not surmise that their successors would harbor thoughts of selfishness and wrong. Woman did not feel that she was deprived of any rights, because she had no occasion to exercise them.

The war of the Revolution of 1812, and the campaign in Mexico, left many widows and husbandless maids, and for the time awakened some interest in the rights of women who had no male protector; but as that generation passed off the stage the sexes were again equalized, and comparative harmony restored. The effects of the Mexican war, as slight as it was in the light of subsequent events, had not ceased entirely to be felt in the New England States when the discovery of gold in California, and the unprecedented "Western fever" induced the emigration of a large number of young men from the Eastern States. They could not entertain the thought that the women whom they loved should be exposed to the hardships which they expected to endure, and so they left the women at home while they went out by thousands "to make their fortunes." Thousands never came back, nor sent back for the girls whom they left behind; and a large surplus of female population was found in all the Eastern States at the next census. Then came the war with the South, and tens of thousands went into the field never to return, leaving behind them wives and daughters who had depended solely upon their support. The soldiers fell, and the bereaved women were left without protectors: and with but a very little means of sustenance. Then it was that frail women, placed at the head of families, were obliged to pay taxes on their little homes, according to assessments the justice or injustice of which they had no political power to question. They were subject to expensive delays by the "red tape" behavior of officials, in whose election, unfortunately, they had no voice; and were obliged to send their children to schools where they had no influence, either with regard to the discipline or the plan of studies. In short, they were obliged to do all of a man's work, and all of a mother's; under the double disadvantage of being physically weak and of possessing no political influence that would entitle them to respect. Many a widow has been slighted and harshly treated when she applied for pension, or tried to do a man's business, because the unprincipled official did not wish to bother with a person who could give him no vote.

III.

When the surplus of women became so great, and it was evident that a large number must either starve or find some permanent employment, there arose the question as to how far a woman might with propriety proceed with a man's work. Thousands must live and die single, and there was no provision made by custom or law for this class of human beings. They must encroach upon the domain before held in exclusive possession by the men. Long before the war this question presented itself, and had been decided by many in favor of clerkships and teaching. In order to obtain any foothold in this exclusive territory, the women were obliged to repeat the action of those who, at the beginning of the factory system, attempted to obtain places in the mills. They accepted anything that offered itself, and took whatever pay was tendered them; which in some instances was exceedingly small. Notwithstanding they knew that their predecessors had received thrice the amount which they received, they never found any fault, so glad were they to obtain anything. Thus a precedent was established which, as it soon passed into custom, could not be broken without the assistance of the law. To this number of poorly paid working-women was added the host of widows and orphans left destitute by the war. The market for woman's labor was crowded to repletion with anxious applicants, and because they were in such sore need the speculating employers refused to pay them more than enough to sustain life. Great fields of labor, untilled and unthrifty, lay all around them, the bounds of which they could not pass, and men were becoming rich on salaries paid for work which women could perform equally as well as the men; but those offices were political offices, and none but voters and controllers of voters could be admitted. Farms were in need of tillage, mills were lying idle, and great enterprises were dormant for lack of man's labor, while the men who should have been caring for them were in offices which women could just as well have filled had they been qualified voters.

IV.

The first great advocate which woman's suffrage found in this country was Margaret Fuller Ossoli.[2] The vast emigration of the men from England, and the sad situation of the women had awakened some enthusiasm there; but, unlike the movement in this country, it had leaders, but no followers. Here there were plenty of followers, but no distinguished leaders. Through all the agitation upon the Woman's Suffrage movement in this country there has never been another advocate of its principles so uncompromising and so purehearted as Margaret Fuller Ossoli.

Her remarkable life and her unswerving fidelity to principle are too well known to the American people to need a repetition here. How she labored and wrote, talked and persuaded; how she pitied the imprisoned "victims of a debased civilization"; how she labored, while in Rome, in the preparation of a history of the Revolution of 1848; and how with her husband, Count d' Ossoli, she was wrecked in sight of land and with her valuable manuscript lost to the world forever,—are facts in the history of America's great and good. She was one of Nature's noblemen, combining the comprehensive mind of Webster with the culture and polish of Everett.

I remember being in attendance one evening on a lecture delivered by a woman upon Margaret Fuller's life, and the speaker, after saying much in praise, summed up her entire speech in the closing words: "Her life was a failure." In the audience, unbeknown to the speaker, sat the mother and brother of the unfortunate genius about whom the words were uttered, and the old lady turned to the brother, saying, "If you do not get up and reply to that lecturer, then I will." But the man needed no urging, and he calmly arose in his seat, and in a clear, sweet, unimpassioned voice said: "The lecturer has said some beautiful things of my sister, but she also states that her life was a failure. Could the life of that woman have been a failure, who was the staff and stay of a widowed mother, who refused advantageous marriage in order to be able to give her two brothers a college education, and who wrote 'Woman in the Nineteenth Century'?" The applause which greeted him showed plainly where lay the sympathy of the audience. Her life was by no means a failure. That great mind, which could sing her little boy to sleep amid the breakers that scattered the wreck, and encourage the sailors to face death when even they were without hope, has left its impression in her writings, and on her disciples who remain. Biographers may call her an "egotist," may assail her as they choose; the time will come when she will be appreciated, and when the great reform, which she almost unconsciously originated, will claim the homage and respect of every civilized nation on the face of the earth.

It was pleasant indeed to find on the sixtieth anniversary[3] of Margaret Fuller's birthday so many able women who were willing to take up the work where she left it.

Such a strong, sensitive, judicial mind as that of Elizabeth Cady Stanton, such eloquence and independence as Mary A. Livermore displays, such culture and originality as marks the efforts of Julia Ward Howe, are just the elements which insure success. Above all this, however, is the faith they have in the cause, and their apparently conscientious behavior.

V.

To-day in New England—and it is only there that women are so numerous as to be at present much neglected or oppressed—there are three great classes of women with whom this question has to do, namely, the aristocratic, the middle, and the working classes. The aristocratic class do not want the ballot, and declare that they "could not be forced to vote"; the middle classes concede that the ballot is plainly a right, but avoid the question, by saying that woman does not need it; while the laborers see in it a remedy for many of their ills, and are anxious to obtain it.

The daughter of an aristocratic family, beginning in infancy, is supplied with every comfort and pleasure which money can furnish. Books, dolls, toys, and pictures fill the hours of childhood; while visits, games, parties, music, and the dull pleasures of a private school return day after day in ever fresh variety as the weeks of girlhood pass. When after seventeen or eighteen years of a happy life have gone, during which time she has never been without devoted and wealthy friends to do her bidding and satisfy every wish, she is suddenly placed in the marriage market by her relatives. A splendid and costly entertainment is provided, and nearly all of the young men and young ladies of her class are invited to participate in the ceremonies of her "coming out." If very wealthy she at once becomes a prize, set up for the best or the richest or the shrewdest or the most noted young man in society. The race begins at once, and although the young lady most concerned may look on with considerable interest, yet she has little or nothing to do with the regulations which are to govern and decide the race.

The young man who has seen the lady and thinks that it is best for him to attempt to win her, calls at her house late in the afternoon. He does not ask for her, however, nor mention the object for which he calls, but sends his card to the young lady's mother, and requests her presence in the parlor. If, during the interview which follows,—when he tries his utmost to be agreeable to the old lady,—the young lady is introduced to him, or encouraged in his presence to converse with him, he concludes that he is regarded with favor.

He asks permission to call again if all parties seem to be "exceedingly pleased," but at each subsequent interview some member of her family is present, until such time as the suitor has become by common consent the betrothed husband. Then a formal engagement is made, the world is notified, and no restraint is placed by guardians upon the movements of the young couple. The young gentleman thinks it to be his duty to wait upon his affianced bride with unceasing care and devotion, and watches her footsteps with the greatest vigilance lest she be annoyed or injured in some way.

Then follows the marriage, the parties, the presents, the tours, and sensations, after which she becomes the mistress of a mansion where her word is law, and where she is ever protected and cared for by numerous hired domestics. In all the journey of life, she holds in her hands the imperial power which money and position supply, is educated to no work, taught to avoid working men and women, and told by all that it is vulgar for a lady to do anything but oversee the servants, receive callers, and stitch upon fancy work. In her presence no man would venture a word upon politics. Such women naturally look upon the idea of going to the polls with a promiscuous crowd of men and women, and having only the same number of ballots that a servant has, as something repulsive and very much to be feared. In their blissful ignorance of the world and its ways, the ballot is a very undesirable thing. They have nothing to gain by it, while it might cause them a great deal of trouble. That they have a duty to perform to those whom it will benefit cannot be impressed upon their minds, because the whole tendency of their education has been to give them the opinion that they are beings higher and nobler than they who work; while in some few cases the lower classes are treated by them as a nuisance to be abated on the first occasion. There are more of those ladies who have no part or interest in the government, and who regard any participation in politics by a lady as an exhibition of coarseness or vulgarity, than there are of "low Irishwomen" who would not understand the meaning of a vote. Either would use the ballot with great awkwardness until the faulty education of the one and the ignorance of the other were overcome by experience and care.

VI.

Omitting any extended notice of the middle classes, who incline toward one or the other of the two remaining divisions as circumstances happen to influence them, and who take but little pains to advocate woman's suffrage, although they all recognize the natural right of every sane woman to the ballot; I will refer to the women who see their degradation, and feel their chains, but cannot escape.

The factory-girl, who enters upon her work when ten or twelve years of age, has none of the friendly care and none of the comforts which the wealthy daughter possesses. She is treated neither with politeness nor consideration. She must go to the agent herself, and without favor or advice, make her own bargain with him. She must hire her own board, buy her own clothes, earn her own money, and attend personally to all her affairs of business, whether they call her to the street, the counting-house, or the parlor. She has no difference shown her there because she is a woman; and she must work as hard and do her task as well as a man, or, like him, be discharged, without ceremony or apology.

Treated in every respect like a man, governed by the same strict rules, and as often obliged to defend her property or character, she receives only about one half of a man's pay, and none of his "perquisites." She is placed in a position where she is exposed to calumny, temptation, and crime; with no weapon to defend herself, and no friends to act for her. Her contact with the world and her experience in affairs of business gives her an independence of character and a knowledge of her rights which, under present circumstances, serves only to aggravate her discontent. She feels the power of the law, and knows full well that many of her trials are due to unjust enactments which she might amend if she had an equal right with the half-witted loafer who is employed to do "odd jobs." If you should ask her opinion about the delicacy of going to the polls to vote, or with regard to the reasons why she would vote for specified measures, she would say that the polls could not be a worse place than those which she is obliged to enter every day, and that she is as able to discuss questions of politics, takes as many papers, and has as much interest in public affairs as any of the men who work beside her.

Factory-girls are always politicians; they must discuss something; and in the absence of fashionable balls, dinner-parties, new styles, and the amusements of high life, they turn their attention to the solid affairs which concern the welfare of State and nation. They see the deceit, double-dealing, and fraud which enter into politics, making men miserable as well as women. They are cognizant of the dangers that beset the nation, and of the measures which would avoid them; but they can only sit and weep while politicians concoct their schemes for plunder and advantage.

VII.

The lady clerks and accountants, who form a large proportion of the women employed in the non-manufacturing towns, are obliged to care for themselves and do their own business. In Massachusetts there are thousands of orphans, both in factory and store, who began very young, and have had no assistance of any kind in providing themselves with the comforts of life. Many began as little "cash girls," and from the time they shrinkingly entered the salesroom for the first time, they have been constantly schooled in the severest trials of life. Engaging in men's business, they became as efficient as men; and although they so unjustly receive but one half the compensation which men would receive, have been successful competitors with them in every mercantile department into which they have been permitted to enter.

I remember a row of little girls who were seated on the edge of the platform during a meeting of the "Dover strikers," and who appeared to me to be too small to be away from home without a guardian. Leaning over so as to call the attention of one of the nearest of the group, I asked her what she could be doing there. "O," said the lisping child, "*I ese on der sthike.*"

Two little girls who had been turned out of employment by a refusal of the other employees to attend to their duties, went into a confectionery shop, where one proposed to purchase some candy; but the smaller one, who was about six years old, advised the elder to save her money, and added: "You know we are on a strike, and there is no certainty about the time when we shall earn any more!"

"I know," said the other independent child, "but the money I've got is my money. I earned it, and I'll spend it as I see fit."

Beginning thus in their youth, and continuing through life in the same course, they become, by force of circumstances, intelligent women, endowed with a large amount of practical knowledge, and its excellent helpmeet, good old-fashioned common sense.

The most favored and at the same time the most abused class of clerking women are those who have succeeded in obtaining situations in government offices. Their pay is usually better than that of many other women, but their weakness and lack of political power exposes them to the insults and despicable chicanery of any political rascal who presumes to attack them. If they had votes to cast, no such assaults would ever be made upon them. There might be political quarrels, jealousy, and hate, but for every actual wrong there would then be the same means of redress which the men have.

A short time ago a member of the United States Congress arose in a branch of that august body, and accused all the girls in the employ of the Treasury Department of crimes which cannot be rehearsed here. Why he should spend his temper, time, and breath in thus accusing the wives of wounded soldiers, the daughters of deceased generals, and virtuous supporters of invalid parents and children, can only be accounted for by the fact that his associations elsewhere had been such as to destroy his respect for women in general, and kill every sense of shame which he might otherwise have possessed. The untruth of his statements was so apparent to all that the people of the country laughed at him, and excused him as the Yankee did the donkey, because "he didn't *know* any better." It may be that some of the government offices employ female clerks whose reputations are not good, and if so, it is the fault of the men who vote and who hold the offices. But this could be said of but very few in the departments at Washington compared with the whole number, and those would not remain in office, and continue to sin if woman had sufficient political influence and the opportunity to meet in Congress the few debauched and unprincipled representatives who keep those disreputable persons there. Neither would those defenceless women, to whom a good name is everything, have been permitted to mourn and weep under the insult, without a single word of defence from among that host of talented lawgivers.

On the evening—I should say, *night*—of the 22d of February, 1870, a great number of the fashionable ladies and titled men gathered at a hall in Washington to celebrate the birthday of Washington; and the description of the event, from the pen of that unrivalled correspondent, "Olivia," found its way over the country in the columns of the Philadelphia Press. O the magnificent equipages and the gorgeous apparel! The most fashionable people of other cities sighed and wondered while they read. It was a ball of the "old school," and unnatural aristocrats were in their glory.

In all that company of diamond-decked ladies it is very doubtful if there was a single one who would not scoff at the idea of woman's suffrage. They had more than their rights, and were satisfied to trail their silks and coquette with their jewelled fans, while thousands in that same city were without a good name, without friends, and without proper sustenance, for the very reason that these ball-goers possessed such a wealth of display.

At that same time the umbrella and parasol girls of New York were on a strike, attempting to obtain a slight approach to a just compensation for their work. One of them seeing "Olivia's" description of the ball, exclaimed as tens of thousands have done before,—

"Oh! why was I born? It does seem as if God cursed the poor and always favored the rich!"

I doubt not that the effect of that display upon the desponding hearts of poor working-girls was the indirect, if not the direct, cause of many of the suicides which followed in such numbers so soon after.

Do you ask if woman's suffrage would remedy these evils? We all know that it would remedy a great many of them; and I doubt not that the knowledge of woman's political principles and the power for good which she would possess has hindered the movement much more than the fear of evil has done. The great and good have never opposed the elevation of society and the advancement of woman; the little and the bad have always done so.

CONCLUSION.

In the inscrutable course of nature, men and women are endowed with special mental and physical qualifications, fitting them for certain stations in a perfect state of human society and unfitting them for others.

In the present condition of the world very few men or women reach the exact station for which they appear to have been designed; while some are so far misplaced as to cause much wretchedness and crime.

So uncertain are we as to the time when, or the place where, great and noble women will be born that the only safe and just plan is to so regulate our laws that all the men, women, and children may have the full advantage of their natural genius.

In order to accomplish this there must be an entire lawful equality between all mankind, and the facilities for mental and physical culture must extend to all alike.

With the aid of such laws and assistance the great will rise to their stations untramelled, while the little will fall to theirs,—making a complete and harmonious whole.

But as we cannot look for perfection nor hope to rid the world entirely of evil, we will not attempt in our weakness to right at once all the wrongs which we find in the world.

For some evils, however, resulting from the unnatural condition of society, we can plainly, unmistakably, see the remedies; one of which is, *practical co-operation* between the laborer and the capitalist, and the other is *woman's suffrage.*

The first will give to working men and women alike the means to assist themselves into the spheres of labor for which they are fitted, will alleviate much suffering, and eradicate much evil. Without it education is a curse to many, as it creates desires which can never be satisfied and leaves them to a poverty, the full misery of which they are sufficiently enlightened to realize.

Woman's suffrage gives to women who are specially gifted the opportunity to assume their proper stations in the political affairs of the nation. It is not expected that many will leave the kitchen, or the parlor, or the bedside, or the desk to assume the badge of office, for few of them are fitted for it. Woman will never rule, or aspire to rule, those who are better qualified for office than she. But there are crimes to prevent, fallen women to raise, poverty to alleviate, ignorant people to educate, and justice to do, which have not been done under the exclusive franchise of the men, and which in all probability woman would accomplish if she had the power that the ballot gives.

Suffrage, taken aside from the good it would accomplish, is due to woman as an act of the simplest justice. She is taxed for her property, but has no voice in the use of those contributions to society. She is arrested for breaking laws which were made without consulting her. She is tried before judges and juries who cannot understand or appreciate a woman's weakness or temptations, and is often driven into further crime, and at last buried in the holes of a "potter's field," because of the unwise decisions of her male judges. She is often at the head of a family, owing to the death of her husband, and though intrusted with a man's cares and responsibilities, she has none of man's political power. In fine, she is under the continued oppression of many foolish and injurious laws, which man wilfully or ignorantly made, and which he wilfully or carelessly refuses to abolish; to none of which has she ever been asked to give her consent, although a hundred and fifty thousand of her sex in the United States must live and die under those laws single and unprotected.

––––––––––

Not, however, to one law, not to one class, not to one people, do I ask the reader's entire attention; but rather to all those measures which will do justly by all those men and all those women, wherever they may be found, who can show an undisputed title to an honorable rank in

NATURE'S ARISTOCRACY.

SOURCE

Collins, Jennie. "Woman's Suffrage." In *Nature's Aristocracy: Or, Battles and Wounds in Time of Peace. A Plea for the Oppressed*, edited by Russell H. Conwell, 298–322. Boston: Lee and Shepard, 1871.

NOTES

1. From Alexander Pope's satirical "An Essay on Criticism" (1711).
2. See the Margaret Fuller section later in this volume.
3. [Author's footnote.] Meeting of the Woman's Club, Boston.

Anna Julia Cooper

1858–1964

ANNA JULIA COOPER was born into bondage in Raleigh, North Carolina, to an enslaved Black mother and her white slaveholder. She obtained her master's degree in mathematics and taught the subject, becoming principal of the M Street High School in Washington, DC, and helping African American students gain admission to prestigious colleges. She was a lifelong champion of education for African Americans and women. Her first book, *A Voice From the South by a Black Woman of the South* (1892), has become a classic African American feminist text. In the 1890s Cooper became a popular public speaker and helped found the Colored Women's League and branches of the YMCA and YWCA for African Americans. At age 67, she earned her PhD from the Sorbonne in Paris, having written her dissertation on slavery.

Womanhood: A Vital Element in the Regeneration and Progress of a Race (1892)

The two sources from which, perhaps, modern civilization has derived its noble and ennobling ideal of woman are Christianity and the Feudal System.

In Oriental countries woman has been uniformly devoted to a life of ignorance, infamy, and complete stagnation. The Chinese shoe of to-day does not more entirely dwarf, cramp, and destroy her physical powers, than have the customs, laws, and social instincts, which from remotest ages have governed our Sister of the East, enervated and blighted her mental and moral life.

Mahomet makes no account of woman whatever in his polity. The Koran, which, unlike our Bible, was a product and not a growth, tried to address itself to the needs of Arabian civilization as Mahomet with his circumscribed powers saw them. The Arab was a nomad. Home to him meant his present camping place. That deity who, according to our western ideals, makes and sanctifies the home, was to him a transient bauble to be toyed with so long as it gave pleasure and then to be thrown aside for a new one. As a personality, an individual soul, capable of eternal growth and unlimited development, and destined to mould and shape the civilization of the future to an incalculable extent, Mahomet did not know woman. There was no hereafter, no paradise for her. The heaven of the Mussulman is peopled and made gladsome not by the departed wife, or sister, or mother, but by *houri*[1]—a figment of Mahomet's brain, partaking of the ethereal qualities of angels, yet imbued with all the vices and inanity of Oriental women. The harem here, and—"dust to dust" hereafter, this was the hope, the inspiration, the *summum bonum* of the Eastern woman's life! With what result on the life of the nation, the "Unspeakable Turk," the "sick man" of modern Europe can to-day exemplify.

Says a certain writer: "The private life of the Turk is vilest of the vile, unprogressive, unambitious, and inconceivably low." And yet Turkey is not without her great men. She has produced most brilliant minds; men skilled in all the intricacies of diplomacy and statesmanship; men whose intellects could grapple with the deep problems of empire and manipulate the subtle agencies which check-mate kings. But these minds were not the normal outgrowth of a healthy trunk. They seemed rather ephemeral excrescencies which shoot far out with all the vigor and promise, apparently, of strong branches; but soon alas fall into decay and ugliness because there is no soundness in the root, no life-giving sap, permeating, strengthening and perpetuating the whole. There is a worm at the core! The homelife is impure! and when we look for fruit, like apples of Sodom, it crumbles within our grasp into dust and ashes.

It is pleasing to turn from this effete and immobile civilization to a society still fresh and vigorous, whose seed is in itself, and whose very name is synonymous with all that is progressive, elevating and inspiring, viz., the European bud and the American flower of modern civilization.

And here let me say parenthetically that our satisfaction in American institutions rests not on the fruition we now enjoy, but springs rather from the possibilities and promise that are inherent in the system, though as yet, perhaps, far in the future.

"Happiness," says Madame de Stael, "consists not in perfections attained, but in a sense of progress, the result of our own endeavor under conspiring circumstances *toward* a goal which continually advances and broadens and deepens till it is swallowed up in the Infinite." Such conditions in embryo are all that we claim for the land of the West. We have not yet reached our ideal in American civilization. The pessimists even declare that we are not marching in that direction. But there can be no doubt that here in America is the arena in which the next triumph of civilization is to be won; and here too we find promise abundant and possibilities infinite.

Now let us see on what basis this hope for our country primarily and fundamentally rests. Can any one doubt that it is chiefly on the homelife and on the influence of good women in those homes? Says Macaulay: "You may judge a nation's rank in the scale of civilization from the way they treat their women." And Emerson, "I have thought that a sufficient measure of civilization is the influence of good women." Now this high regard for woman, this germ of a prolific idea which in our own day is bearing such rich and varied fruit, was ingrafted into European civilization, we have said, from two sources, the Christian Church and the Feudal System. For although the Feudal System can in no sense be said to have originated the idea, yet there can be no doubt that the habits of life and modes of thought to which Feudalism gave rise, materially fostered and developed it; for they gave us chivalry, than which no institution has more sensibly magnified and elevated woman's position in society.

Tacitus dwells on the tender regard for woman entertained by these rugged barbarians before they left their northern homes to overrun Europe. Old Norse legends too, and primitive poems, all breathe the same spirit of love of home and veneration for the pure and noble influence there presiding—the wife, the sister, the mother.

And when later on we see the settled life of the Middle Ages "oozing out," as M. Guizot expresses it, from the plundering and pillaging life of barbarism and crystallizing into the Feudal System, the tiger of the field is brought once more within the charmed circle of the goddesses of his castle, and his imagination weaves around them a halo whose reflection possibly has not yet altogether vanished.

It is true the spirit of Christianity had not yet put the seal of catholicity on this sentiment. Chivalry, according to Bascom, was but the toning down and softening of a rough and lawless period. It gave a roseate glow to a bitter winter's day. Those who looked out from castle windows revelled in its "amethyst tints." But God's poor, the weak, the unlovely, the commonplace were still freezing and starving none the less, in unpitied, unrelieved loneliness.

Respect for woman, the much lauded chivalry of the Middle Ages, meant what I fear it still means to some men in our own day—respect for the elect few among whom they expect to consort.

The idea of the radical amelioration of womankind, reverence for woman as woman regardless of rank, wealth, or culture, was to come from that rich and bounteous fountain from which flow all our liberal and universal ideas—the Gospel of Jesus Christ.

And yet the Christian Church at the time of which we have been speaking would seem to have been doing even less to protect and elevate woman than the little done by secular society. The Church as an organization committed a double offense against woman in the Middle Ages. Making of marriage a sacrament and at the same time insisting on the celibacy of the clergy and other religious orders, she gave an inferior if not an impure character to the marriage relation, especially fitted to reflect discredit on woman. Would this were all or the worst! but the Church by the licentiousness of its chosen servants invaded the household and established too often as vicious connections those relations which it forbade to assume openly and in good faith. "Thus," to use the words of our authority, "the religious corps became as numerous, as searching, and as unclean as the frogs of Egypt, which penetrated into all quarters, into the ovens and kneading troughs, leaving their filthy trail wherever they went." Says Chaucer with characteristic satire, speaking of the Friars:

"Women may now go safely up and doun,
In every bush, and under every tree,
Ther is non other incubus but he,
And he ne will don hem no dishonour."[2]

Henry, Bishop of Liege, could unblushingly boast the birth of twenty-two children in fourteen years.[3]

It may help us under some of the perplexities which beset our way in "the one Catholic and Apostolic Church" to-day, to recall some of the corruptions and incongruities against which the Bride of Christ has had to struggle in her past history and in spite of which she has kept, through many vicissitudes, the faith once delivered to the saints. Individuals, organizations, whole sections of the Church militant may outrage the Christ whom they profess, may ruthlessly trample under foot both the spirit and the letter of his precepts, yet not till we hear the voices audibly saying "Come let us depart hence," shall we cease to believe and cling to the promise, "*I am with you to the end of the world.*"[4]

"Yet saints their watch are keeping,
The cry goes up 'How long!'
And soon the night of weeping
Shall be the morn of song."[5]

However much then the facts of any particular period of history may seem to deny it, I for one do not doubt that the source of the vitalizing principle of woman's development and amelioration is the Christian Church, so far as that church is coincident with Christianity.

Christ gave ideals not formulæ. The Gospel is a germ requiring millennia for its growth and ripening. It needs and at the same time helps to form around itself a soil enriched in civilization, and perfected in culture and insight without which the embryo can neither be unfolded or comprehended. With all the strides our civilization has made from the first to the nineteenth century, we can boast not an idea, not a principle of action, not a progressive social force but was already mutely foreshadowed, or directly enjoined in that simple tale of a meek and lowly life. The quiet face of the Nazarene is ever seen a little way ahead, never too far to come down to and touch the life of the lowest in days the darkest, yet ever leading onward, still onward, the tottering childish feet of our strangely boastful civilization.

By laying down for woman the same code of morality, the same standard of purity, as for man; by refusing to countenance the shameless and equally guilty monsters who were gloating over her fall,—graciously stooping in all the majesty of his own spotlessness to wipe away the filth and grime of her guilty past and bid her go in peace and sin no more; and again in the moments of his own careworn and footsore dejection, turning trustfully and lovingly, away from the heartless snubbing and sneers, away from the cruel malignity of mobs and prelates in the dusty marts of Jerusalem to the ready sympathy, loving appreciation and unfaltering friendship of that quiet home at Bethany; and even at the last, by his dying bequest to the disciple whom he loved, signifying the protection and tender regard to be extended to that sorrowing mother and ever afterward to the sex she represented;—throughout his life and in his death he has given to men a rule and guide for the estimation of woman as an equal, as a helper, as a friend, and as a sacred charge to be sheltered and cared for with a brother's love and sympathy, lessons which nineteen centuries' gigantic strides in knowledge, arts, and sciences, in social and ethical principles have not been able to probe to their depth or to exhaust in practice.

It seems not too much to say then of the vitalizing, regenerating, and progressive influence of womanhood on the civilization of today, that, while it was foreshadowed among Germanic nations in the far away dawn of their history as a narrow, sickly and stunted growth, it yet owes its catholicity and power, the deepening of its roots and broadening of its branches to Christianity.

The union of these two forces, the Barbaric and the Christian, was not long delayed after the Fall of the Empire. The Church, which fell with Rome, finding herself in danger of being swallowed up by barbarism, with characteristic vigor and fertility of resources, addressed herself immediately to the task of conquering her conquerers. The means chosen does credit to her power of penetration and adaptability, as well as to her profound, unerring, all-compassing diplomacy; and makes us even now wonder if aught human can successfully and ultimately withstand her far-seeing designs and brilliant policy, or gainsay her well-earned claim to the word *Catholic.*

She saw the barbarian, little more developed than a wild beast. She forbore to antagonize and mystify his warlike nature by a full blaze of the heartsearching and humanizing tenets of her great Head. She said little of the rule "If thy brother smite thee on one cheek, turn to him the other also;" but thought it sufficient for the needs of those times, to establish the so-called "Truce of God" under which men were bound to abstain from butchering one another for three days of each week and on Church festivals. In other words, she respected their individuality: non-resistance pure and simple being for them an utter impossibility, she contented herself with less radical measures calculated to lead up finally to the full measure of the benevolence of Christ.

Next she took advantage of the barbarian's sensuous love of gaudy display and put all her magnificent garments on. She could not capture him by physical force, she would dazzle him by gorgeous spectacles. It is said that Romanism gained more in pomp and ritual during this trying period of the Dark Ages than throughout all her former history.

The result was she carried her point. Once more Rome laid her ambitious hand on the temporal power, and allied with Charlemagne, aspired to rule the world through a civilization dominated by Christianity and permeated by the traditions and instincts of those sturdy barbarians.

Here was the confluence of the two streams we have been tracing, which, united now, stretch before us as a broad majestic river. In regard to woman it was the meeting of two noble and ennobling forces, two kindred ideas the resultant of which, we doubt not, is destined to be a potent force in the betterment of the world.

Now after our appeal to history comparing nations destitute of this force and so destitute also of the principle of progress, with other nations among whom the influence of woman is prominent coupled with a brisk, progressive, satisfying civilization,—if in addition we find this strong presumptive evidence corroborated by reason and experience, we may conclude that these two equally varying concomitants are linked as cause and effect; in other words, that the position of woman in society determines the vital elements of its regeneration and progress.

Now that this is so on *a priori* grounds all must admit. And this not because woman is better or stronger or wiser than man, but from the nature of the case, because it is she who must first form the man by directing the earliest impulses of his character.

Byron and Wordsworth were both geniuses and would have stamped themselves on the thought of their age under any circumstances; and yet we find the one a savor of life unto life, the other of death unto death. "Byron, like a rocket, shot his way upward with scorn and repulsion, flamed out in wild, explosive, brilliant excesses and disappeared in darkness made all the more palpable."[6]

Wordsworth lent of his gifts to reinforce that "power in the Universe which makes for righteousness"[7] by taking the harp handed him from Heaven and using it to swell the strains of angelic choirs. Two locomotives equally mighty stand facing opposite tracks; the one to rush headlong to destruction with all its precious freight, the other to toil grandly and gloriously up the steep embattlements to Heaven and to God. Who—who can say what a world of consequences hung on the first placing and starting of these enormous forces!

Woman, Mother,—your responsibility is one that might make angels tremble and fear to take hold! To trifle with it, to ignore or misuse it, is to treat lightly the most sacred and solemn trust ever confided by God to human kind. The training of children is a task on which an infinity of weal or woe depends. Who does not covet it? Yet who does not stand awe-struck before its momentous issues! It is a matter of small moment, it seems to me, whether that lovely girl in whose accomplishments you take such pride and delight, can enter the gay and crowded salon with the ease and elegance of this or that French or English gentlewoman, compared with the decision as to whether her individuality is going to reinforce the good or the evil elements of the world. The lace and the diamonds, the dance and the theater, gain a new significance when scanned in their bearings on such issues. Their influence on the individual personality, and through her on the society and civilization which she vitalizes and inspires—all this and more must be weighed in the balance before the jury can return a just and intelligent verdict as to the innocence or banefulness of these apparently simple amusements.

Now the fact of woman's influence on society being granted, what are its practical bearings on the work which brought together this conference of colored clergy and laymen in Washington? "We come not here to talk." Life is too busy, too pregnant with meaning and far reaching consequences to allow you to come this far for mere intellectual entertainment.

The vital agency of womanhood in the regeneration and progress of a race, as a general question, is conceded almost before it is fairly stated. I confess one of the difficulties for me in the subject assigned lay in its obviousness. The plea is taken away by the opposite attorney's granting the whole question.

"Woman's influence on social progress"—who in Christendom doubts or questions it? One may as well be called on to prove that, the sun is the source of light and heat and energy to this many-sided little world.

Nor, on the other hand, could it have been intended that I should apply the position when taken and proven, to the needs and responsibilities of the women of our race in the South. For is it not written, "Cursed is he that cometh after the king?" and has not the King already preceded me in "The Black Woman of the South"?[8]

They have had both Moses and the Prophets in Dr. Crummell and if they hear not him, neither would they be persuaded though one came up from the South.

I would beg, however, with the Doctor's permission, to add my plea for the *Colored Girls* of the South:—that large, bright, promising fatally beautiful class that stand shivering like a delicate plantlet before the fury of tempestuous elements, so full of promise and possibilities, yet so sure of destruction; often without a father to whom they dare apply the loving term, often without a stronger brother to espouse their cause and defend their honor with his life's blood; in the midst of pitfalls and snares, waylaid by the lower classes of white men, with no shelter, no protection nearer than the great blue vault above, which half conceals and half reveals the one Care-Taker they know so little of. Oh, save them, help them, shield, train, develop, teach, inspire them! Snatch them, in God's name, as brands from the burning! There is material in them well worth your while, the hope in germ of a staunch, helpful, regenerating womanhood on which, primarily, rests the foundation stones of our future as a race.

It is absurd to quote statistics showing the Negro's bank account and rent rolls, to point to the hundreds of newspapers edited by colored men and lists of lawyers, doctors, professors, D D's, LL D's, etc., etc., etc., while the source from which the life-blood of the race is to flow is subject to taint and corruption in the enemy's camp.

True progress is never made by spasms. Real progress is growth. It must begin in the seed. Then, "first the blade, then the ear, after that the full corn in the ear."[9] There is something to encourage and inspire us in the advancement of individuals since their emancipation from slavery. It at least proves that there is nothing irretrievably wrong in the shape of the black man's skull, and that under given circumstances his development, downward or upward, will be similar to that of other average human beings.

But there is no time to be wasted in mere felicitation. That the Negro has his niche in the infinite purposes of the Eternal, no one who has studied the history of the last fifty years in America will deny. That much depends on his own right comprehension of his responsibility and rising to the demands of the hour, it will be good for him to see; and how best to use his present so that the structure of the future shall be stronger and higher and brighter and nobler and holier than that of the past, is a question to be decided each day by every one of us.

The race is just twenty-one years removed from the conception and experience of a chattel, just at the age of ruddy manhood. It is well enough to pause a moment for retrospection, introspection, and prospection. We look back, not to become inflated with conceit because of the depths from which we have arisen, but that we may learn wisdom from experience. We look within that we may gather together once more our forces, and, by improved and more practical methods, address ourselves to the tasks before us. We look forward with hope and trust that the same God whose guiding hand led our fathers through and out of the gall and bitterness of oppression, will still lead and direct their children, to the honor of His name, and for their ultimate salvation.

But this survey of the failures or achievements of the past, the difficulties and embarrassments of the present, and the mingled hopes and fears for the future, must not degenerate into mere dreaming nor consume the time which belongs to the practical and effective handling of the crucial questions of the hour; and there can be no issue more vital and momentous than this of the womanhood of the race.

Here is the vulnerable point, not in the heel, but at the heart of the young

Achilles; and here must the defenses be strengthened and the watch re-doubled. We are the heirs of a past which was not our fathers' moulding. "Every man the arbiter of his own destiny" was not true for the American Negro of the past: and it is no fault of his that he finds himself to-day the inheritor of a manhood and womanhood impoverished and debased by two centuries and more of compression and degradation.

But weaknesses and malformations, which to-day are attributable to a vicious schoolmaster and a pernicious system, will a century hence be rightly regarded as proofs of innate corruptness and radical incurability.

Now the fundamental agency under God in the regeneration, the re-training of the race, as well as the ground work and starting point of its progress upward, must be the *black woman*.

With all the wrongs and neglects of her past, with all the weakness, the debasement, the moral thralldom of her present, the black woman of to-day stands mute and wondering at the Herculean task devolving around her. But the cycles wait for her. No other hand can move the lever. She must be loosed from her bands and set to work.

Our meager and superficial results from past efforts prove their futility; and every attempt to elevate the Negro, whether undertaken by himself or through the philanthropy of others, cannot but prove abortive unless so directed as to utilize the indispensable agency of an elevated and trained womanhood.

A race cannot be purified from without. Preachers and teachers are helps, and stimulants and conditions as necessary as the gracious rain and sunshine are to plant growth. But what are rain and dew and sun-shine and cloud if there be no life in the plant germ? We must go to the root and see that it is sound and healthy and vigorous; and not deceive ourselves with waxen flowers and painted leaves of mock chlorophyll.

We too often mistake individuals' honor for race development and so are ready to substitute pretty accomplishments for sound sense and ear-nest purpose.

A stream cannot rise higher than its source. The atmosphere of homes is no rarer and purer and sweeter than are the mothers in those homes. A race is but a total of families. The nation is the aggregate of its homes. As the whole is sum of all its parts, so the character of the parts will de-termine the characteristics of the whole. These are all axioms and so evident that it seems gratuitous to remark it; and yet, unless I am greatly mistaken, most of the unsatisfaction from our past results arises from just such a radical and palpable error, as much almost on our own part as on that of our benevolent white friends.

The Negro is constitutionally hopeful and proverbially irrepressible; and naturally stands in danger of being dazzled by the shimmer and tinsel of superficials. We often mistake foliage for fruit and overestimate or wrongly estimate brilliant results.

The late Martin R. Delany,[10] who was an unadulterated black man, used to say when honors of state fell upon him, that when he entered the council of kings the black race entered with him; meaning, I suppose, that there was no discounting his race identity and attributing his achievements to some admixture of Saxon blood. But our present record of eminent men, when placed beside the actual status of the race in America to-day, proves that no man can represent the race. Whatever the attainments of the individual may be, unless his home has moved on *pari passu*,[11] he can never be regarded as identical with or representative of the whole.

Not by pointing to sun-bathed mountain tops do we prove that Phœbus warms the valleys. We must point to homes, average homes, homes of the rank and file of horny handed toiling men and women of the South (where the masses are) lighted and cheered by the good, the beautiful, and the true,—then and not till then will the whole plateau be lifted into the sunlight.

Only the BLACK WOMAN can say "when and where I enter, in the quiet, undisputed dignity of my womanhood, without violence and without suing or special patronage, then and there the whole *Negro race enters with me*." Is it not evident then that as individual workers for this race we must address ourselves with no half-hearted zeal to this feature of our mission. The need is felt and must be recognized by all. There is a call for workers, for missionaries, for men and women with the double consecration of a fundamental love of humanity and a desire for its melioration through the Gospel; but superadded to this we demand an intelligent and sympathetic comprehension of the interests and special needs of the Negro.

I see not why there should not be an organized effort for the protection and elevation of our girls such as the White Cross League in England. English women are strengthened and protected by more than twelve centuries of Christian influences, freedom and civilization; English girls are dispirited and crushed down by no such all-levelling prejudice as that supercilious caste spirit in America which cynically assumes "A Negro woman cannot be a lady." English womanhood is beset by no such snares and traps as betray the unprotected, untrained colored girl of the South, whose only crime and dire destruction often is her unconscious and marvelous beauty. Surely then if English indignation is aroused and English manhood thrilled under the leadership of a Bishop of the English church to build up bulwarks around their wronged sisters, Negro sentiment cannot remain callous and Negro effort nerveless in view of the imminent peril of the mothers of the next generation. *"I am my Sister's keeper!"*[12] should be the hearty response of every man and woman of the race, and this conviction should purify and exalt the narrow, selfish and petty personal aims of life into a noble and sacred purpose.

We need men who can let their interest and gallantry extend outside the circle of their æsthetic appreciation; men who can be a father, a brother, a friend to every weak, struggling unshielded girl. We need women who are so sure of their own social footing that they need not fear leaning to lend a hand to a fallen or falling sister. We need men and women who do not exhaust their genius splitting hairs on aristocratic distinctions and thanking God they are not as others; but earnest, unselfish souls, who can go into the highways and byways, lifting up and leading, advising and encouraging with the truly catholic benevolence of the Gospel of Christ.

As Church workers we must confess our path of duty is less obvious; or rather our ability to adapt our machinery to our conception of the peculiar exigencies of this work as taught by experience and our own consciousness of the needs of the Negro, is as yet not demonstrable. Flexibility and aggressiveness are not such strong characteristics of the Church today as in the Dark Ages.

As a Mission field for the Church the Southern Negro is in some aspects most promising; in others, perplexing. Aliens neither in language and customs, nor in associations and sympathies, naturally of deeply rooted religious instincts and taking most readily and kindly to the worship and teachings of the Church, surely the task of proselytizing the American Negro is infinitely less formidable than that which confronted the Church in the Barbarians of Europe. Besides, this people already look to the Church as the hope of their race. Thinking colored men almost uniformly admit that the Protestant Episcopal Church with its quiet, chaste dignity and decorous solemnity, its instructive and elevating ritual, its bright chanting and joyous hymning, is eminently fitted to correct the peculiar faults of worship—the rank exuberance and often ludicrous demonstrativeness of their people. Yet, strange to say, the Church, claiming to be missionary and Catholic, urging that schism is sin and denominationalism inexcusable, has made in all these years almost no inroads upon this semi-civilized religionism.

Harvests from this over ripe field of home missions have been gathered in by Methodists, Baptists, and not least by Congregationalists, who were unknown to the Freedmen before their emancipation.

Our clergy numbers less than two dozen[13] priests of Negro blood and we have hardly more than one self-supporting colored congregation in the entire Southland. While the organization known as the A.M.E. Church has 14,063 ministers, itinerant and local, 4,069 self-supporting churches, 4,2754,275 Sunday-schools, with property valued at $7,772,284, raising yearly for church purposes $1,427,000.

Stranger and more significant than all, the leading men of this race (I do not mean demagogues and politicians, but men of intellect, heart, and race devotion, men to whom the elevation of their people means more than personal ambition and sordid gain—and the men of that stamp have not all died yet) the Christian workers for the race, of younger and more cultured growth, are noticeably drifting into sectarian churches, many of them declaring all the time that they acknowledge the historic claims of the Church, believe her apostolicity, and would experience greater personal comfort, spiritual and intellectual, in her revered communion. It is a fact which any one may verify for himself, that representative colored men, professing that in their heart of hearts they are Episcopalians, are actually working in Methodist and Baptist pulpits; while the ranks of the Episcopal clergy are left to be filled largely by men who certainly suggest the propriety of a "*perpetual* Diaconate"[14] if they cannot be said to have created the necessity for it.

Now where is the trouble? Something must be wrong. What is it?

A certain Southern Bishop of our Church reviewing the situation, whether in Godly anxiety or in "Gothic antipathy" I know not, deprecates the fact that the colored people do not seem *drawn* to the Episcopal Church, and comes to the sage conclusion that the Church is not adapted to the rude untutored minds of the Freedmen, and that they may be left to go to the Methodists and Baptists whither their racial proclivities undeniably tend. How the good Bishop can agree that all-foreseeing Wisdom, and Catholic Love would have framed his Church as typified in his seamless garment and unbroken body, and yet not leave it broad enough and deep enough and loving enough to seek and save and hold seven millions of God's poor, I cannot see.

But the doctors while discussing their scientifically conclusive diagnosis of the disease, will perhaps not think it presumptuous in the patient if he dares to suggest where at least the pain is. If this be allowed, *a Black woman of the South* would beg to point out two possible oversights in this southern work which may indicate in part both a cause and a remedy for some failure. The first is *not calculating for the Black man's personality*; not having respect, if I may so express it, to his manhood or deferring at all to his conceptions of the needs of his people. When colored persons have been employed it was too often as machines or as manikins. There has been no disposition, generally, to get the black man's ideal or to let his individuality work by its own gravity, as it were. A conference of earnest Christian men have met at regular intervals for some years past to discuss the best methods of promoting the welfare and development of colored people in this country. Yet, strange as it may seem, they have never invited a colored man or even intimated that one would be welcome to take part in their deliberations. Their remedial contrivances are purely theoretical or empirical, therefore, and the whole machinery devoid of soul.

The second important oversight in my judgment is closely allied to this and probably grows out of it, and that is not developing Negro womanhood as an essential fundamental for the elevation of the race, and utilizing this agency in extending the work of the Church.

Of the first I have possibly already presumed to say too much since it does not strictly come within the province of my subject. However, Macaulay somewhere criticises the Church of England as not knowing how to use fanatics, and declares that had Ignatius Loyola been in the Anglican instead of the Roman communion, the Jesuits would have been schismatics instead of Catholics; and if the religious awakenings of the Wesleys had been in Rome, she would have shaven their heads, tied ropes around their waists, and sent them out under her own banner and blessing. Whether this be true or not, there is certainly a vast amount of force potential for Negro evangelization rendered latent, or worse, antagonistic by the halting, uncertain, I had almost said, *trimming* policy of the Church in the South. This may sound both presumptuous and ungrateful. It is mortifying, I know, to benevolent wisdom, after having spent itself in the execution of well conned theories for the ideal development of a particular work, to hear perhaps the weakest and humblest element of that work: asking "what doest thou?"

Yet so it will be in life. The "thus far and no farther" pattern cannot be fitted to any growth in God's kingdom. The universal law of development is "onward and upward." It is God-given and inviolable. From the unfolding of the germ in the acorn to reach the sturdy oak, to the growth of a human soul into the full knowledge and likeness of its Creator, the breadth and scope of the movement in each and all are too grand, too mysterious, too like God himself, to be encompassed and locked down in human molds.

After all the Southern slave owners were right: either the very alphabet of intellectual growth must be forbidden and the Negro dealt with absolutely as a chattel having neither rights nor sensibilities; or else the clamps and irons of mental and moral, as well as civil compression must be riven asunder and the truly enfranchised soul led to the entrance of that boundless vista through which it is to toil upwards to its beckoning God as the buried seed germ, to meet the sun.

A perpetual colored diaconate, carefully and kindly superintended by the white clergy; congregations of shiny faced peasants with their clean white aprons and sunbonnets catechised at regular intervals and taught to recite the creed, the Lord's prayer and the ten commandments—duty towards God and duty towards neighbor, surely such well tended sheep ought to be grateful to their shepherds and content in that station of life to which it pleased God to call them. True, like the old professor lecturing to his solitary student, we make no provision here for irregularities. "Questions must be kept till after class," or dispensed with altogether. That some do ask questions and insist on answers, in class too, must be both impertinent and annoying. Let not our spiritual pastors and masters however be grieved at such self-assertion as merely signifies we have a destiny to fulfill and as men and women we must *be about our Father's business.*

It is a mistake to suppose that the Negro is prejudiced against a white ministry. Naturally there is not a more kindly and implicit follower of a white man's guidance than the average colored peasant. What would to others be an ordinary act of friendly or pastoral interest he would be more inclined to regard gratefully as a condescension. And he never forgets such kindness. Could the Negro be brought near to his white priest or bishop, he is not suspicious. He is not only willing but often longs to unburden his soul to this intelligent guide. There are no reservations when he is convinced that you are his friend. It is a saddening satire on American history and manners that it takes something to convince him.

That our people are not "drawn" to a Church whose chief dignitaries they see only in the chancel, and whom they reverence as they would a painting or an angel, whose life never comes down to and touches theirs with the inspiration of an objective reality, may be "perplexing" truly (American caste and American Christianity both being facts) but it need not be surprising. There must be something of human nature in it, the same as that which brought about that "the Word was made flesh and dwelt among us"[15] that He might "draw" us towards God.

Men are not "drawn" by abstractions. Only sympathy and love can draw, and until our Church in America realizes this and provides a clergy that can come in touch with our life and have a fellow feeling for our woes, without being imbedded and frozen up in their "Gothic antipathies," the good bishops are likely to continue "perplexed" by the sparsity of colored Episcopalians.

A colored priest of my acquaintance recently related to me, with tears in his eyes, how his reverend Father in God, the Bishop who had ordained him, had met him on the cars on his way to the diocesan convention and warned him, not unkindly, not to take a seat in the body of the convention with the white clergy. To avoid disturbance of their godly placidity he would of course please sit back and somewhat apart. I do not imagine that that clergyman had very much heart for the Christly (!) deliberations of that convention.

To return, however, it is not on this broader view of Church work, which I mentioned as a primary cause of its halting progress with the colored people, that I am to speak. My proper theme is the second oversight of which in my judgment our Christian propagandists have been guilty: or, the necessity of church training, protecting and uplifting our colored womanhood as indispensable to the evangelization of the race.

Apelles did not disdain even that criticism of his lofty art which came from an uncouth cobbler; and may I not hope that the writer's oneness with her subject both in feeling and in being may palliate undue obtrusiveness of opinions here. That the race cannot be effectually lifted up till its women are truly elevated we take as proven. It is not for us to dwell on the needs, the neglects, and the ways of succor, pertaining to the black woman of the South. The ground has been ably discussed and an admirable and practical plan proposed by the oldest Negro priest in America, advising and urging that special organizations such as Church Sisterhoods and industrial schools be devised to meet her pressing needs in the Southland. That some such movements are vital to the life of this people and the extension of the Church among them, is not hard to see. Yet the pamphlet fell still-born from the press. So far as I am informed the Church has made no motion towards carrying out Dr. Crummell's suggestion.

The denomination which comes next our own in opposing the proverbial emotionalism of Negro worship in the South, and which in consequence like ours receives the cold shoulder from the old heads, resting as we do under the charge of not "having religion" and not believing in conversion—the Congregationalists—have quietly gone to work on the young, have established industrial and training schools, and now almost every community in the South is yearly enriched by a fresh infusion of vigorous young hearts, cultivated heads, and helpful hands that have been trained at Fisk, at Hampton, in Atlanta University, and in Tuskegee, Alabama.

These young people are missionaries actual or virtual both here and in Africa. They have learned to love the methods and doctrines of the Church which trained and educated them; and so Congregationalism surely and steadily progresses.

Need I compare these well known facts with results shown by the Church in the same field and during the same or even a longer time.

The institution of the Church in the South to which she mainly looks for the training of her colored clergy and for the help of the "Black Woman" and "Colored Girl" of the South, has graduated since the year 1868, when the school was founded, *five young women*;[16] and while yearly numerous young men have been kept and trained for the ministry by the charities of the Church, the number of indigent females who have here been supported, sheltered and trained, is phenomenally small. Indeed, to my mind, the attitude of the Church toward this feature of her work, is as if the solution of the problem of Negro missions depended solely on sending a quota of deacons and priests into the field, girls being a sort of *tertium quid* whose development may be promoted if they can pay their way and fall in with the plans mapped out for the training of the other sex.

Now I would ask in all earnestness, does not this force potential deserve by education and stimulus to be made dynamic? Is it not a solemn duty incumbent on all colored churchmen to make it so? Will not the aid of the Church be given to prepare our girls in head, heart, and hand for the duties and responsibilities that await the intelligent wife, the Christian mother, the earnest, virtuous, helpful woman, at once both the lever and the fulcrum for uplifting the race.

As Negroes and churchmen we cannot be indifferent to these questions. They touch us most vitally on both sides. We believe in the Holy Catholic Church. We believe that however gigantic and apparently remote the consummation, the Church will go on conquering and to conquer till the kingdoms of this world, not excepting the black man and the black woman of the South, shall have become the kingdoms of the Lord and of his Christ.

That past work in this direction has been unsatisfactory we must admit. That without a change of policy results in the future will be as meagre, we greatly fear. Our life as a race is at stake. The dearest interests of our hearts are in the scales. We must either break away from dear old landmarks and plunge out in any line and every line that enables us to meet the pressing need of our people, or we must ask the Church to allow and help us, untrammelled by the prejudices and theories of individuals, to work aggressively under her direction as we alone can, with God's help, for the salvation of our people.

The time is ripe for action. Self-seeking and ambition must be laid on the altar. The battle is one of sacrifice and hardship, but our duty is plain. We have been recipients of missionary bounty in some sort for twenty-one years. Not even the senseless vegetable is content to be a mere reservoir. Receiving without giving is an anomaly in nature. Nature's cells are all little workshops for manufacturing sunbeams, the product to be *given out* to earth's inhabitants in warmth, energy, thought, action. Inanimate creation always pays back an equivalent.

Now, *How much owest thou my Lord?* Will his account be overdrawn if he call for singleness of purpose and self-sacrificing labor for your brethren? Having passed through your drill school, will you refuse a general's commission even if it entail responsibility, risk and anxiety, with possibly some adverse criticism? Is it too much to ask you to step forward and direct the work for your race along those lines which you know to be of first and vital importance?

Will you allow these words of Ralph Waldo Emerson? "In ordinary," says he, "we have a snappish criticism which watches and contradicts the opposite party. We want the will which advances and dictates [acts]. Nature has made up her mind that what cannot defend itself, shall not be defended. Complaining never so loud and with never so much reason, is of no use. What cannot stand must fall; *and the measure of our sincerity and therefore of the respect of men is the amount of health and wealth we will hazard in the defense of our right.*"[17]

SOURCE

Cooper, Anna Julia. "Womanhood: A Vital Element in the Regeneration and Progress of a Race." In *A Voice from the South*, 9–47. Xenia, Ohio: Aldine, 1892.

NOTES

Chapter opening photo: Anna Julia Cooper, ca. 1901–3. Library of Congress, Prints & Photographs Division, C. M. Bell Studio Collection, LC-B5-50626.

1. In traditional Muslim theology, a *houri* is a virginal man or (in this case) woman, provided for the faithful in Paradise.
2. From the "Wife of Bath's Tale" in Geoffrey Chaucer's *Canterbury Tales* (ca. 1387–1400).
3. [Author's footnote.] Bascom.
4. "Let us depart hence" are words that the Roman historian Josephus (37–100 CE) reports were heard on the night before the destruction of Jerusalem (see his *Bellum Judaicum* 6:05.3). "I am with you to the end of the world" are Christ's final words in Matthew 28:20.
5. From English priest Samuel John Stone's 1866 hymn "The Church's One Foundation."
6. [Author's footnote.] Bascom's Eng. Lit, p. 253. [This is a reference to John Bascom, *Philosophy of English Literature: A Course of Lectures Delivered at the Lowell Institute* (New York: Putnam's, 1892).]
7. Source of quotation unknown, though in the nineteenth century it was commonly attributed to English poet Matthew Arnold (1822–1888).

8. [Author's footnote.] Pamphlet published by Dr. Alex. Crummell.

9. From Mark 4:28.

10. Martin Robinson Delany (1812–1885) was an African American physician, soldier, abolitionist, journalist, early Black nationalist, and Pan-Africanist.

11. Side by side; on equal footing (Latin).

12. An echo of Genesis 4:9: "And the Lord said unto Cain, 'Where is Abel thy brother?' And he said, 'I know not: Am I my brother's keeper?'"

13. [Author's footnote.] The published report of '91 shows 26 priests for the entire country, including one not engaged in work and one a professor in a non-sectarian school, since made Dean of an Episcopal Annex to Howard University known as King Hall.

14. A permanent deaconship.

15. From John 1:14.

16. [Author's footnote.] Five have been graduated since '86, two in '91, two in '92.

17. A slight misquotation from "Courage," chap. 10 of American transcendentalist Ralph Waldo Emerson's *Society and Solitude* (1870).

Lucy Delaney

ca. 1830–ca. 1890s

LUCY DELANEY was born into slavery in St. Louis, Missouri. Her mother, a free woman who was kidnapped and sold into slavery, was eventually able to prove to the courts that she had been born free and thereby freed her daughter Lucy at the age of fourteen. Lucy published her narrative of these events and her life, *From the Darkness Cometh the Light, or, Struggles for Freedom*, afterward, sometime in the 1890s. It is the only known first-person account of a freedom suit and one of the few slave narratives published after Emancipation. Delaney's and her mother's case files were discovered in the late 1990s.

From *From the Darkness Cometh the Light, or, Struggles for Freedom* (1891)

CHAPTER III.

Mrs. Cox was always very severe and exacting with my mother, and one occasion, when something did not suit her, she turned on mother like a fury, and declared, "I am just tired out with the 'white airs' you put on, and if you don't behave differently, I will make Mr. Cox sell you down the river at once."

Although mother turned grey with fear, she presented a bold front and retorted that "she didn't care, she was tired of that place, and didn't like to live there, nohow." This so infuriated Mr. Cox that he cried, "How dare a negro say what she liked or what she did not like; and he would show her what he should do."

So, on the day following, he took my mother to an auction-room on Main Street and sold her to the highest bidder, for five hundred and fifty dollars. Oh! God! the pity of it! "In the home of the brave and the land of the free," in the sight of the stars and stripes—that symbol of freedom—sold away from her child, to satisfy the anger of a peevish mistress!

My mother returned to the house to get her few belongings, and straining me to her breast, begged me to be a good girl, that she was going to run away, and would buy me as soon as she could. With all the inborn faith of a child, I believed it most fondly, and when I heard that she had actually made her escape, three weeks after, my heart gave an exultant throb and cried, "God is good!"

A large reward was offered, the bloodhounds (curse them and curse their masters) were set loose on her trail. In the day time she hid in caves and the surrounding woods, and in the night time, guided by the wondrous North Star, that blessed lodestone of a slave people, my mother finally reached Chicago, where she was arrested by the negro-catchers. At this time the Fugitive Slave Law was in full operation, and it was against the law of the whole country to aid and protect an escaped slave; not even a drink of water, for the love of the Master, might be given, and those who dared to do it (and there were many such brave hearts, thank God!) placed their lives in danger.

The presence of bloodhounds and "nigger-catchers" in their midst, created great excitement and scandalized the community. Feeling ran high and hundreds of people gathered together and declared that mother should not be returned to slavery; but fearing that Mr. Cox would wreak his vengeance upon me, my mother finally gave herself up to her captors, and returned to St. Louis. And so the mothers of Israel have been ever slain through their deepest affections!

After my mother's return, she decided to sue for her freedom, and for that purpose employed a good lawyer. She had ample testimony to prove that she was kidnapped, and it was so fully verified that the jury decided that she was a free woman, and papers were made out accordingly.

In the meanwhile, Miss Martha Berry had married Mr. Mitchell and taken me to live with her. I had never been taught to work, as playing with the babies had been my sole occupation; therefore, when Mrs. Mitchell commanded me to do the weekly washing and ironing, I had no more idea how it was to be done than Mrs. Mitchell herself. But I made the effort to do what she required, and my failure would have been amusing had it not been so appalling. In those days filtering was unknown and the many ways of clearing water were to me an unsolved riddle. I never had to do it, so it never concerned me how the clothes were ever washed clean.

As the Mississippi water was even muddier than now, the results of my washing can be better imagined than described. After soaking and boiling the clothes in its earthy depths, for a couple of days, in vain attempt to get them clean, and rinsing through several waters, I found the clothes were getting darker and darker, until they nearly approximated my own color. In my despair, I frantically rushed to my mother and sobbed out my troubles on her kindly breast. So in the morning, before the white people had arisen, a friend of my mother came to the house and washed out the clothes. During all this time, Mrs. Mitchell was scolding vigorously, saying over and over again, "Lucy, you do not want to work, you are a lazy, good-for-nothing nigger!" I was angry at being called a nigger, and replied, "You don't know nothing, yourself, about it, and you expect a poor ignorant girl to know more than you do yourself; if you had any feeling you would get somebody to teach me, and then I'd do well enough."

She then gave me a wrapper to do up, and told me if I ruined that as I did the other clothes, she would whip me severely. I answered, "You have no business to whip me. I don't belong to you."

My mother had so often told me that she was a free woman and that I should not die a slave, I always had a feeling of independence, which would invariably crop out in these encounters with my mistress; and when I thus spoke, saucily, I must confess, she opened her eyes in angry amazement and cried:

"You do belong to me, for my papa left you to me in his will, when you were a baby, and you ought to be ashamed of yourself to talk so to one that you have been raised with; now, you take that wrapper, and if you don't do it up properly, I will bring you up with a round turn."

Without further comment, I took the wrapper, which was too handsome to trust to an inexperienced hand, like Mrs. Mitchell very well knew I was, and washed it, with the same direful results as chronicled before. But I could not help it, as heaven is my witness. I was entirely and hopelessly ignorant! But of course my mistress would not believe it, and declared over and over again, that I did it on purpose to provoke her and show my defiance of her wishes. In vain did I disclaim any such intentions. She was bound to carry out her threat of whipping me.

I rebelled against such government, and would not permit her to strike me; she used shovel, tongs and broomstick in vain, as I disarmed her as fast as she picked up each weapon. Infuriated at her failure, my opposition and determination not to be whipped, Mrs. Mitchell declared she would report me to Mr. Mitchell and have him punish me.

When her husband returned home, she immediately entered a list of complaints against me as long as the moral law, including my failure to wash her clothes properly, and her inability to break my head for it; the last indictment seemed to be the heaviest she could bring against me. I was in the shadow of the doorway as the woman raved, while Mr. Mitchell listened patiently until the end of his wife's grievances reached an appeal to him to whip me with the strength that a man alone could possess.

Then he declared, "Martha, this thing of cutting up and slashing servants is something I know nothing about, and positively will not do. I don't believe in slavery, anyhow; it is a curse on this land, and I wish we were well rid of it."

"Mr. Mitchell, I will not have that saucy baggage around this house, for if she finds you won't whip her, there will be no living with her, so you shall just sell her, and I insist upon it."

"Well, Martha," he answered, "I found the girl with you when we were married, and as you claim her as yours, I shall not interpose any objections to the disposal of what you choose to call your property, in any manner you see fit, and I will make arrangements for selling her at once."

I distinctly overheard all that was said, and was just as determined not to be sold as I was not to be whipped. My mother's lawyer had told her to caution me never to go out of the city, if, at any time, the white people wanted me to go, so I was quite settled as to my course, in case Mr. Mitchell undertook to sell me.

Several days after this conversation took place, Mrs. Mitchell, with her baby and nurse, Lucy Wash, made a visit to her grandmother's, leaving orders that I should be sold before her return; so I was not surprised to be ordered by Mr. Mitchell to pack up my clothes and get ready to go down the river, for I was to be sold that morning, and leave, on the steamboat Alex. Scott, at 3 o'clock in the afternoon.

"Can't I go see my mother, first?" I asked.

"No," he replied, not very gently, "there is no time for that, you can see her when you come back. So hurry up and get ready, and let us have no more words about it!"

How I did hate him! To hear him talk as if I were going to take a pleasure trip, when he knew that if he sold me South, as he intended, I would never see my dear mother again.

However, I hastily ran up stairs and packed my trunk, but my mother's injunction, "never to go out of the city," was ever present in my mind.

Mr. Mitchell was Superintendent of Indian Affairs, his office being in the dwelling house, and I could hear him giving orders to his clerk, as I ran lightly down the stairs, out of the front door to the street, and with fleet foot, I skimmed the road which led to my mother's door, and, reaching it, stood trembling in every limb with terror and fatigue.

I could not gain admittance, as my mother was away to work and the door was locked. A white woman, living next door, and who was always friendly to mother, told me that she would not return until night. I clasped my hands in despair and cried, "Oh! the white people have sold me, and I had to run away to keep from being sent down the river."

This white lady, whose name I am sorry I cannot remember, sympathized with me, as she knew my mother's story and had written many letters for her, so she offered me the key of her house, which, fortunately, fitted my mother's door, and I was soon inside, cowering with fear in the darkness, magnifying every noise and every passing wind, until my imagination had almost converted the little cottage into a boat, and I was steaming down South, away from my mother, as fast as I could go.

Late at night mother returned, and was told all that had happened, and after getting supper she took me to a friend's house for concealment, until the next day.

As soon as Mr. Mitchell had discovered my unlooked-for departure, he was furious, for he did not think I had sense enough to run away; he accused the coachman of helping me off, and, despite the poor man's denials, hurried him away to the calaboose and put him under the lash, in order to force a confession. Finding this course unavailing, he offered a reward to the negro catchers, on the same evening, but their efforts were equally fruitless.

SOURCE

Delaney, Lucy. *From the Darkness Cometh the Light, or, Struggles for Freedom.* St. Louis, MO: J. T. Smith, 1891, 20–32.

Emily Dickinson

1830–1886

EMILY DICKINSON was part of a prominent white family from Amherst, Massachusetts. Largely unknown in her lifetime, she is now considered one of the greatest American poets of all time. Although often characterized as "reclusive" and narrow in experience because the majority of her life was spent on the grounds of her family's property, Dickinson's poetry and letters reveal a complex and passionate inner life. She exploded poetic conventions with her elliptical, experimental style and wrote about major historical events, such as the U.S. Civil War, as well as the vicissitudes of everyday life. Because she never married and had few overtly romantic relationships, Dickinson is often assumed to have been a functionally sexless adult, but the poems in volume 1, as well as her late-life letters to love interest Judge Otis Lord, suggest otherwise.

Letters to Judge Otis Lord (ca. 1878)

[ca. 1878]

Dont you know you are happiest while I withhold and not confer - dont you know that "No" is the wildest word we consign to Language?

You do, for you know all things – [*cut away*] to lie so near your longing - to touch it as I passed, for I am but a restive sleeper and often should journey from your Arms through the happy night, but you will lift me back, wont you, for only there I ask to be - I say, if I felt the longing nearer - than in our dear past, perhaps I could not resist to bless it, but must, because it would be right

The "Stile" is God's – My Sweet One – for your great sake – not mine – I will not let you cross – but its all your's, and when it is right I will lift the Bars, and lay you in the Moss – You showed me the word.

I hope it has no different guise when my fingers make it. It is Anguish I long conceal from you to let you leave me, hungry, but you ask the divine Crust and that would doom the Bread.

The unfrequented Flower

Embellish thee – ^{deserving be1} [*cut away*]

I was reading a little Book – because it broke my Heart I want it to break your's – Will you think that fair? I often have read it, but not before since loving you – I find that makes a difference – it makes a difference with all. Even the whistle of a Boy passing late at Night, or the Low of a Bird – [*cut away*] Satan" – but then what I have not heard is the sweet majority – the Bible says very roguishly, that the "wayfaring Man, though a Fool – need not err therein"; need the "wayfaring" Woman? Ask your throbbing Scripture.

It may surprise you I speak of God – I know him but a little, but Cupid taught Jehovah to many an untutored Mind – Witchcraft is wiser than we -

[ca. 1880]

~~I never heard you call anything beautiful before. It remained with me curiously –~~ There is a fashion in delight as other things.

Still ^{stern} as the Profile of a Tree against a winter sky ^{sunset sky – evening -}

~~I kissed the little blank – you made it on the second page you may have forgotten -~~ I will not wash my arm – the one you gave the scarf to – it is brown as an Almond – 'twill take your touch away.

~~I try to think when I wake in the night what the chapter would be for the chapter would be in the night would'nt it – but I cannot decide -~~

It is strange that I miss you at night so much when I was never with you – but the punctual love invokes you soon as my eyes are shut – and I wake warm with the want sleep had almost filled – I dreamed last week that you had died – and one had carved a statue of you and I was asked to unvail it – and I said what I had not done in Life I would not in death when your loved eyes could not forgive – ~~The length of the hour was beautiful. The length of the heavenly hour how sweetly you counted it. The numerals of Eden do not oppress the student long~~ for Eden ebbs away to diviner Edens. ~~Therefore Love is so speechless – Seems to withold Darling~~

I never seemed toward you

Lest I had been too franky was often my fear -

How could I long to give who never saw your natures Face –

This has been a beautiful Day – dear – given solely to you – carried in my thin hand to your distant hope ~~offer~~ offered softly and added – The haste of early summer is gone and a foreboding leisure is stealing over ~~natures~~ bustling things -

But why did you distrust your little Simon Peter yesterday – you said you did'nt but she knew you did – What did Nestor say you begun to tell me – To rest ^{cling} with you swept all day -

I sometimes ~~have~~ almost feared Language was done between us – ~~if you grew~~ too dear, except for breath, then words flowed softly in like ~~some~~ a shining secret, the Lode of which the miner dreams

I wonder we ever leave the Improbable – it is so fair a Home, and perhaps we dont -

What is half so improbable [*remainder is missing*]

SOURCE

Dickinson, Emily. Letters to Judge Otis Lord. Reprinted with permission from Harvard University Press, from *The Letters of Emily Dickinson*, edited by Thomas H. Johnson, associate editor, Theodora Ward, Cambridge, Mass.: The Belknap Press of Harvard University Press, Copyright © 1958 by the President and Fellows of Harvard College. Copyright © renewed 1986 by the President and Fellows of Harvard College. Copyright © 1914, 1924, 1932, 1942 by Martha Dickinson Bianchi. Copyright © 1952 by Alfred Leete Hampson. Copyright © 1960 by Mary L. Hampson.

NOTE

1. Superscripted text represents Dickinson's smaller lettering, which generally indicates insertions or additions on her part.

Sarah Mapps Douglass

1806–1882

SARAH MAPPS DOUGLASS, pseud. Zillah, grew up in a distinguished African American abolitionist family in Philadelphia. Along with her mother, she helped found the racially integrated Philadelphia Female Anti-Slavery Society in 1833. Douglass wrote about the racism she experienced within the Quaker community, despite its abolitionist politics. She also helped lead the Female Literary Association and founded her own school for African American girls in 1833, before moving on to teach at the Institute for Colored Youth. From 1853 to 1877, Douglass studied anatomy and female health and hygiene and obtained basic medical training. She lectured and taught night classes for African American women on these subjects and worked to incorporate them into standard curriculum.

To a Friend (1832)

You ask me if I do not despair on account of the Bill now before our Legislature?[1] I am cast down, but not in despair. I am aware that it will be our lot to suffer much persecution, and I have endeavored, for the last year, to fortify my mind against approaching trials, by reading what others have suffered. In perusing Sewell's History of the people called the Quakers, I was particularly struck with the account of Barbara Blaugdon, a young and timid woman, who, by the help of the Almighty, was enabled to endure persecution, not only with patience but with joy. On one occasion, being severely whipped, even until the blood streamed down her back, she sang the praises of her God aloud, rejoicing that she was counted worthy to suffer for his name; which increased the anger of the executioner, and made him say, "Do ye sing? I'll make you cry by and by." But Barbara was strengthened by an invisible power, and afterwards declared if she had been whipped to death, she should not have been dismayed. Earnestly have I prayed, my friend, that a double portion of her humility and fortitude may be ours. In despair! no, no—God is on our side. With the eye of faith, I pierce the veil of futurity, and I see our advocate, after having honorably borne the burden and heat of the day, sitting down peaceably by his "ain fire-side." Time has scattered a few blossoms on his head, but left his manly brow without a wrinkle. Hundreds of liberated slaves are pressing round him, eager to testify their gratitude.

See yonder mother, with her infant! She approaches him, and kneels at his feet, raises her eyes to heaven, and would speak her gratitude; but tears and sobs impede her utterance. O, her tears are far more eloquent than words.

I see black and white mingle together in social intercourse, without a shadow of disgust appearing on the countenance of either; no wailing is heard, no clanking chains; but the voice of peace and love and joy is wafted to my ear on every breeze.

And what has wrought this mighty change? Religion, my sister; the religion of the meek and lowly Jesus; and such are its effects wherever it appears. Could I not thus look forward, I should indeed despair.[2]

ZILLAH.

Philadelphia, April 1st, 1832.

A Mother's Love (1832)

"All other passions change
With changing circumstances; rise or fall,
Dependent on their object; claim returns;

Live on reciprocation and expire
Unfed by hope. A mother's fondness reigns
Without a rival, and without an end."[3]

And dost thou, poor slave, feel this holy passion? Dost thy heart swell with anguish, when thy helpless infant is torn from thy arms, and carried thou knowest not whither? when thou hast no hope left that thou shalt ever see his innocent face again? Yes, I know thou dost feel all this.

I well remember conversing with a liberated slave, who told me of the many hardships she had to encounter while in a state of captivity. At one time, after having been reaping all the morning, she returned at noon to a spring near her master's house to carry water to some hired laborers. At this spring her babe was tied; she had not been allowed to come near it since sunrise, the time at which it was placed there; her heart yearned with pity and affection for her boy, and while she kneeled at the spring and dipped the water with one hand, she drew her babe to her aching bosom with the other. She would have fed it from this fountain, troubled and almost dried with grief; but, alas! this consolation was denied her. Her cruel mistress observed her from the window where she was sitting, and immediately ran to her, and seizing a large stick beat her cruelly upon her neck and bosom, bidding her begone to her work. Poor creature! rage against her mistress almost emboldened her to return the blow; she cared not for herself, but when she reflected that her child would probably be the sufferer, maternal tenderness triumphed over every other feeling, and she again tied her child, and returned to the labors of the field.

American Mothers! can you doubt that the slave feels as tenderly for her offspring as you do for yours? Do your hearts feel no throb of pity for her woes? Will you not raise your voices, and plead for her emancipation—her immediate emancipation?

At another time, when assisting her mistress to get dinner, she dropped the skin of a potato into what she was preparing. The angry woman snatched the knife from her hand, and struck her with it upon the bosom! My countenance expressed so much horror at this account, that I believe the poor woman thought I doubted her veracity. Baring her aged bosom, "Look," said she, "my child, here is the scar"—and I looked and wept that woman should have so far forgot her gentle nature. Soon after this, she was sold to another person, and at his death freed. Her old mistress, after a series of misfortunes, was reduced almost to beggary, and bent her weary footsteps to the same city: and would you believe it, reader? She sent for the woman she had so cruelly wronged, to come and assist her. Her friends persuaded her not to go; but she, noble creature! woman-like, weeping that a lady should be so reduced, obeyed the call, and waited upon her as faithfully as if she had been her dearest friend.

Calumniators of my despised race, read this and blush.   ZILLAH.[4]

Philadelphia, July 8th, 1832

SOURCES

Zillah [Sarah Mapps Douglass]. "To a Friend." *Liberator* 2, no. 26 (June 30, 1832), 103. ProQuest Historical Newspapers.

———. "A Mother's Love." *Liberator* 2, no. 30 (July 28, 1832), 118. ProQuest Historical Newspapers.

NOTES

Chapter opening art: Illustration in Sarah Mapps Douglass, "To a Friend," *The Liberator,* June 30, 1832. Image source: GRANGER.

1. [Source editor's note.] This Bill is "to prohibit the migration of negroes and mulattoes into the Commonwealth." It has been postponed to the next Legislature—we trust, for the honor of Pennsylvania, postponed forever.

2. This essay is preceded in the *Liberator* not only by the seal of the Philadelphia Female Anti-Slavery Society but also by the following editorial note:

> During his recent sojourn in Philadelphia, (rendered inexpressibly delightful by the kindness of friends,) the Editor of the Liberator had the privilege of visiting and addressing a society of colored ladies, called the 'FEMALE LITERARY ASSOCIATION.' It was one of the most interesting spectacles he had ever witnessed. If the traducers of the colored race could be acquainted with the moral worth, just refinement, and large intelligence of this association, their mouths would hereafter be dumb. The members assemble together every Tuesday evening, for the purpose of mutual improvement in moral and literary pursuits. Nearly all of them write, almost weekly, original pieces, which are put anonymously into a box, and afterwards criticised by a committee. Having been permitted to bring with him several of these pieces, he ventures to

commence their publication, not only for their merit, but in order to induce the colored ladies of other places to go and do likewise. This society is at present composed of about twenty members, but is increasing, and full of intellectual promise.

3. From the play *Moses in the Bulrushes* (1782) by English playwright and poet Hannah More (1745–1833).
4. Originally published under the byline "By a young lady of color."

Sarah Jane Woodson Early

1825–1907

SARAH JANE WOODSON EARLY, an African American educator, author, and feminist, was born free in Chillicothe, Ohio. Her father helped found the all–African American community of Berlin Crossroads, and her childhood home was a station on the Underground Railroad. A graduate of Oberlin College, she was a teacher and school principal for thirty years. In 1866 she became the first African American woman professor when she joined the faculty of Wilberforce University to teach English and Latin. She is known for her addresses, such as the following selection, which encourages African American youth to pursue education and become involved in politics. In 1894 she published a biography of her husband, depicting his escape from slavery and work in the A.M.E. Church.

Address to the Youth (1866)

That we are beings who occupy a place among intelligent existences, and are endowed with minds capable of endless duration, and unlimited improvement, is a fact which should engage the attention, and enlist the energies of every individual.

The faculties of the mind, though scarcely perceptible in the first stages of human existence, may, by means of proper culture, become so expanded and developed as to form one of the noblest structures of God's creation.

The cultivation of the mind, then, is the first object to which the youthful attention should be directed. By cultivation is implied the education and training of each faculty, so as not only to be able to acquire a mere physical subsistence, but to apply the means which will invigorate and strengthen; to enlighten and refine each part, that it may perform its function in such a manner as to elevate the being to that degree of perfection, which will enable him to occupy a position among the higher orders of creation, which the Great Author designed him to enjoy.

It is a fact worthy of notice, that things which are most valuable are placed the farthest from the reach of common agencies. The Creator, in wisdom, has seen fit to place the bright gems, and richest treasures of earth, the deepest beneath the soil; so, in like manner, has he concealed the richest treasures that the mind possess beneath the grosser senses, to be drawn forth only by the most patient, and persevering energy. It is natural that human beings should acquire possessions; and that they should desire those especially which are the most eminent among mortals; yet few of real value ever came into our hands by means of accident.

No man was ever a skilled architect, or physician, or mechanic by chance. The excellencies of the mental powers are not the gifts of genius, or the intuitions of nature; but the precious boon is obtained, or, the shining goal reached, only by those whose care has been the most unceasing, and whose zeal has been the most untiring.

Wealth and honor are not the offspring of ease and luxury, but they are the legitimate reward of constant toil and perseverance. Neither is mental opulence, or intellectual competency enjoyed by the imbecile and indolent.

No one ever slaked his thirst for knowledge from a fountain which gushed spontaneously; but he who would taste the delicious stream must dig deep and toil hard, ere he can enjoy a draught of the pellucid waters.

The knowledge of arts and sciences, which are the most profound and intricate in themselves, and which most deeply concern us, is not granted on easier terms than these. Not even the lowest organs of the body, not a muscle or a sinew can perform its action without having undergone a lengthened and elaborate process of instruction. The hand, the ear, the eye, must each be trained and taught. And though we may be unconscious of the education, it has as really been received, as that was by which we learned to read and write.

If, then, the most corporeal sense demands an appropriate education, without which they would prove rather incumbrances than messengers with which we keep up our communications with the external world, shall we suppose that the noblest capacities of man's spirit are alone independent of all training and culture? That the baser senses only are capable of refinement and expansion? That in the whole territory of human nature, this is the only field that promises to reward the tillage with no fruit?

But this question more deeply concerns the youth of the present than of any other age. An age in which intellectual acquirements are more widely diffused than any other preceding it. Let not, then, the youth of the present age, who are the subjects of oppression and outrage, suppose that they are not called upon to solve the questions which so much interest every individual. What are our relations to God and to the universe? What is required of us in the present age? and what are we doing to facilitate the prospects of our people in the future? It is true, that we experience daily many discouragements, and the path of intellectual prosperity seems obstructed with innumerable difficulties, yet the fact is none the less obvious, that we are called upon to act as great a part as any other people, in the great work of human refinement and moral elevation. Yes, we, as a people, have severe conflicts, both with regard to our individual and national rights. We inherit from our fathers nought but subjugation and dishonor. No history records the deeds of our great and good, no tongue ever heralded the praise of our brave and noble. No banner was ever inscribed with the insignia of our national existence; yet our history, humiliating as it may be, is not without a precedent.

Others have endured trials similar to ours, in their struggles for national existence. Yet, by a succession of events, they passed unscathed to the highest point of national glory. God's chosen people were overwhelmed in Egyptian darkness, only that the light of Jehovah's truth might be revealed amid the thunderings of Sinai.

If you take a retrospect of the past, you perceive that in the darkest periods, when truth and virtue appeared to sleep, when science had dropped her telescope and philosophy its torch, when the world would have seemed to be standing still, the inscrutable wisdom of Divine Providence was preparing new agents, and evolving new principles, to aid in the work of individual and social improvement.

It would appear as if the world, like the year, had its seasons; and that the seed disseminated in spring time, must first die before it can vegetate and produce the rich harvests of autumn. The developments of one period seem obscured for a season, by the unfolding of the great mysterious curtain, by which to disclose the glories of the next. History has marked to us such periods, and we are disheartened by the necessary and successive seasons of darkness, because the revolution is so great, or, our own position so humble, that we cannot look beyond the shade that surrounds us, and behold the distant but gradual approach of a better day. Though for a season darkness has covered the land, and gross darkness the people, and the energies of our people have been stultified by the accumulated prejudices of generations, which have been heaped upon us, yet there is reason to be encouraged, for

"From the darkest night of sorrow,
   From the deadliest field of strife
Dawns a clearer, brighter morrow,
   Springs a truer, nobler life."[1]

Yes, the sombre clouds of ignorance and superstition which so long enshrouded us and seemed ready to close upon us, as the funeral pall of our national existence, is being dispersed before the light of eternal truth. The sign of promise, the great precursor of a brighter day, has already enlightened the long night of our oppression, and the broad sun of our liberty begins to illuminate our political horizon. The mighty empire of despotism and oppression is trembling to its foundation, it must soon crumble and fall; but will we submit to sink and be buried beneath its ruins? Will we alone be quiescent and passive, while all around us is agitation and progress?

Do the revolutions which surround us awaken in our souls no desire to partake of the onward movement? The world moves right on, and he who moves not with it, must be crushed beneath its revolving wheels. You stand on the eve of a brighter day than has ever enlightened your pathway. The obstacles which have so long barred you from the portals of knowledge, are fast being removed, and the temple of science from which you have hitherto been ousted with tenacious jealousy, will soon disclose to you the glory of his inner sanctuary. Wisdom, with a friendly hand, beckons you to enter and revel in her courts. Suffer not the evanescent pleasures of sensual gratifications to allure you from the pursuit of the great object which lies before you. Will you not arouse from the long slumber of inactivity which pervades you, and prepare for the events which the revolutions of the affairs of men are fast bringing upon you? Who shall answer for you, when you are called upon to take your position among the nations of the earth, if you are found wanting in mental capacity and intellectual energy?

If the high privileges you now enjoy pass by you unimproved, and you are found incapable to fill positions of trust and honor in coming life, great will be your condemnation.

Apply your minds, then, early and vigorously to those studies which will not only endow you with the power and privilege to walk abroad, interested spectators of all that is magnificent and beautiful, above and around you, but to commune with that which is illustrious in the records of the past, and noble and divine in the development of the future.

Would you be eminent among your fellow-mortals, and have your name inscribed on the pages of history, as a living representative of truth, morality and virtue? Would you, by deeds of heroism and noble achievements, vie with the proud sons of honor, and share with them the immortal wreath which the hand of time has placed upon their brow? Would you ascend the hill of science, and there contend with their votaries for the laurels plucked from its fair summit? Would you penetrate the secret labyrinths of the universe, and gather from their hoarded mysteries that knowledge which will bless generations to come? Then apply your minds to study, profound, intricate study. Let your time, your money, your interest all be spent in the pursuit of this one great object, the improvement of your mind. It is only from the deepest furrows that the richest harvests are gathered. The breathings of genius are not produced "ad libitum." The lyres of the soul bring no sound to the touch of unpracticed hands. So the creative powers of the mind are never developed till drawn forth by the deep, harrowing process of education. Oh, there are wells of inspiration in every human heart, from which angels might draw, and leave them unexhausted. Fathom the depths of your nature, draw from its profound resources those principles which will ennoble and strengthen your intellectual powers. Educate the youth of the present, and our nation will produce a constellation of glowing minds, whose light will brighten the path of generations to come. Hitherto there has scarcely been a mind among us, which has sent forth a spark into the vast region of science. The arts have received but little attention, and literature has found no place among us. Yet, by the efforts which may be put forth by the present generation, the arts, science and literature may be as widely diffused among us, and we may become as eminent, in point of intellectual attainments as any people who have had an existence.

We call upon you to accept the means which God has placed in your power. The great and the good, and the noble, who have preceded you, and have bequeathed to you the hoarded treasures of their richly cultivated minds, call upon you. The voice of millions, who are perishing without a ray of intellectual light, call upon you. Everything above and around you combine to stimulate you to the work of removing darkness and error, and establishing truth and virtue. And may God speed the work, till science, philosophy and religion, the great elevators of fallen humanity, shall have completed the work of moral refinement, and we in the enjoyment of all our rights, both political and civil, will stand at the summit of national glory.

SOURCE

Early, Sarah Jane Woodson. "Address to the Youth." In *The Semi-Centenary and the Retrospection of the African Meth. Episcopal Church in the United States of America*, edited by Daniel A. Payne, 134–39. Baltimore: Sherwood, 1866. https://hdl.handle.net/2027/emu.010002588604?urlappend=%3Bseq=142. Written for the *Christian Recorder*; read before the Colored Teachers' Association of Ohio in 1863.

NOTE

1. From J. Hagen, "All Is Action, All Is Motion," *Union Magazine* (New York), July 1848, 11.

Zilpha Elaw

ca. 1790–1873

ZILPHA ELAW was born near Philadelphia to free African American parents. She joined the A.M.E. Church at a young age after having a religious vision. In 1817 she attended a revival camp and fell into a trance, giving her first public speech. She opened a school for African American children in Burlington, New Jersey, but ultimately felt called upon to become a minister. Elaw traveled throughout the United States giving sermons, including to enslaved people in the South, and then in England until the end of her life. Her *Memoirs of the Life, Religious Experience, and Ministerial Travels and Labours of Mrs. Zilpha Elaw, an American Female of Colour* (1846) is one of the earliest examples of the genre written by an African American woman.

From *Memoirs of the Life, Religious Experience, and Ministerial Travels and Labours of Mrs. Zilpha Elaw, an American Female of Colour; Together with Some Account of the Great Religious Revivals in America* (1846)

I left Hartford for Boston, in the state of Massachusets, in company with a lady, who was from the latter city: and the Lord went before me and cleared up the way; for, in the city of Boston, many doors were opened for my reception; and the Lord wrought wonderfully among the people. Many of the brethren were going to a camp meeting at Cape Codd, about sixty miles from Boston, and invited me to go with them, which I did with great pleasure, and we had very pleasant weather. Many thousands attended at that meeting, and the Lord manifested forth his glory and his grace. Hundreds came to that camp-meeting, to make sport and derision of the saints, and of their worship, who returned home themselves rejoicing in God their Saviour. A band of young gentlemen, connected with the highest families in the town of Lynn, chartered a large vessel, brought their tent, provisions, and every other necessary for a week's sojourn on the camp ground, with the wicked intention not only of greatly annoying us, but of dispersing the camp meeting altogether: the manner in which they approached the encampment rendered it but too evident what kind of persons they were, and for what purpose they came. When these wanton young gentlemen arrived upon the ground, they went from tent to tent, and appeared to be greatly struck with astonishment at the novel appearance of the scene; for the Lord had set the hearts and consciences of the people in motion; some of them were weeping with godly penitence; others were rejoicing in the salvation of Christ, manifested to their souls; in the public services, the ministers were as a flaming torch, and their words as a two edged sword; and the powerful discourses they preached from the platform, made a wonderful impression on these giddy young men, and their conduct became greatly altered. On the Thursday, between twelve and two o'clock, matters were so changed that they prepared their tent for religious service, and sent for me to come and preach to them; I went accordingly, and commenced the meeting, and some of our ablest preachers followed soon after and assisted me, and the Lord owned and blessed our message, and many of these young gentlemen became deeply affected, and cried to God for mercy. The ministers evinced the greatest attention and tender care of them; but they more particularly desired to hear, "the woman:" and the next day I was sent for to preach to them again; after which, we all attended the prayer meeting at the preachers' stand; and many of them found mercy with God. When the camp meeting broke up, all of them with the exception of four, together with many others both white and coloured, manifested the triumphs of redeeming grace, and evinced a saving conversion to God; and the happy result of that meeting was, that, in a short space of time, in the town of Lynn alone, upwards of two hundred persons were added to the Methodist Episcopal Church.

The brethren residing at the Cape having strongly solicited me to tarry for a time with them, I consented, and instead of returning with the brethren to Boston, went home with the Cape friends, and travelled with the itinerating preachers on the different circuits of the Cape district, and with great success; for the glorious camp meeting we had just before attended, had laid the foundation for an extensive and continuous revival: the fields were indeed white, already to harvest; and we went to reap them, and receive the rich wages of souls for our hire.

SOURCE

Elaw, Zilpha. *Memoirs of the Life, Religious Experience, and Ministerial Travels and Labours of Mrs. Zilpha Elaw, an American Female of Colour; Together with Some Account of the Great Religious Revivals in America*, 94–96. London: published by the author, 1846.

Julia A. J. Foote

1823–1901

JULIA A. J. FOOTE was a Black evangelist and author, born to formerly enslaved parents in Schenectady, New York. She converted to Methodism at age fifteen and through a series of religious experiences came to the realization that she was called to preach. Facing opposition and censure from the church and her husband, Foote fought for women to be able to become ministers and speak in their congregations. She traveled the United States and Canada for decades as an itinerant minister and documented her experiences in *A Brand Plucked from the Fire* (1879). Foote became the first woman deacon in the A.M.E. Church in 1894 and the second to be ordained as an elder in 1899.

From *A Brand Plucked from the Fire: An Autobiographical Sketch* (1879)

CHAPTER XVII:
My Call to Preach the Gospel

For months I had been moved upon to exhort and pray with the people, in my visits from house to house; and in meetings my whole soul seemed drawn out for the salvation of souls. The love of Christ in me was not limited. Some of my mistaken friends said I was too forward, but a desire to work for the Master, and to promote the glory of his kingdom in the salvation of souls, was food to my poor soul.

When called of God, on a particular occasion, to a definite work, I said, "No, Lord, not me." Day by day I was more impressed that God would have me work in his vineyard. I thought it could not be that I was called to preach—I, so weak and ignorant. Still, I knew all things were possible with God, even to confounding the wise by the foolish things of this earth. Yet in me there was a shrinking. I took all my doubts and fears to the Lord in prayer, when, what seemed to be an angel, made his appearance. In his hand was a scroll, on which were these words: "Thee have I chosen to preach my Gospel without delay." The moment my eyes saw it, it appeared to be printed on my heart. The angel was gone in an instant, and I, in agony, cried out, "Lord, I cannot do it!" It was eleven o'clock in the morning, yet everything grew dark as night. The darkness was so great that I feared to stir.

At last "Mam" Riley entered. As she did so, the room grew lighter, and I arose from my knees. My heart was so heavy I scarce could speak. Dear "Mam" Riley saw my distress, and soon left me.

From that day my appetite failed me and sleep fled from my eyes. I seemed as one tormented. I prayed, but felt no better. I belonged to a band of sisters whom I loved dearly, and to them I partially opened my mind. One of them seemed to understand my case at once, and advised me to do as God had bid me, or I would never be happy here or hereafter. But it seemed too hard—I could not give up and obey.

One night, as I lay weeping and beseeching the dear Lord to remove this burden from me, there appeared the same angel that came to me before, and on his breast were these words: "You are lost unless you obey

God's righteous commands." I saw the writing, and that was enough. I covered my head and awoke my husband, who had returned a few days before. He asked me why I trembled so, but I had not power to answer him. I remained in that condition until morning, when I tried to arise and go about my usual duties, but was too ill. Then my husband called a physician, who prescribed medicine, but it did me no good.

I had always been opposed to the preaching of women, and had spoken against it, though, I acknowledge, without foundation. This rose before me like a mountain, and when I thought of the difficulties they had to encounter, both from professors and non-professors, I shrank back and cried, "Lord, I cannot go!"

The trouble my heavenly Father has had to keep me out of the fire that is never quenched, he alone knoweth. My husband and friends said I would die or go crazy if something favorable did not take place soon. I expected to die and be lost, knowing I had been enlightened and had tasted the heavenly gift. I read again and again the sixth chapter of Hebrews.

CHAPTER XVIII:
Heavenly Visitations Again

Nearly two months from the time I first saw the angel, I said that I would do anything or go anywhere for God, if it were made plain to me. He took me at my word, and sent the angel again with this message: "You have I chosen to go in my name and warn the people of their sins." I bowed my head and said, "I will go, Lord."

That moment I felt a joy and peace I had not known for months. But strange as it may appear, it is not the less true, that, ere one hour had passed, I began to reason thus: "I am elected to preach the Gospel without the requisite qualifications, and, besides, my parents and friends will forsake me and turn against me; and I regret that I made a promise." At that instant all the joy and peace I had felt left me, and I thought I was standing on the brink of hell, and heard the devil say: "Let her go! let her go! I will catch her." Reader, can you imagine how I felt? If you were ever snatched from the mouth of hell, you can, in part, realize my feelings.

I continued in this state for some time, when, on a Sabbath evening—ah! that memorable Sabbath evening—while engaged in fervent prayer, the same supernatural presence came to me once more and took me by the hand. At that moment I became lost to everything of this world. The angel led me to a place where there was a large tree, the branches of which seemed to extend either way beyond sight. Beneath it sat, as I thought, God the Father, the Son, and the Holy Spirit, besides many others, whom I thought were angels. I was led before them: they looked me over from head to foot, but said nothing. Finally, the Father said to me: "Before these people make your choice, whether you will obey me or go from this place to eternal misery and pain." I answered not a word. He then took me by the hand to lead me, as I thought, to hell, when I cried out, "I will obey thee, Lord!" He then pointed my hand in different directions, and asked if I would go there. I replied, "Yes, Lord." He then led me, all the others following, till we came to a place where there was a great quantity of water, which looked like silver, where we made a halt. My hand was given to Christ, who led me into the water and stripped me of my clothing, which at once vanished from sight. Christ then appeared to wash me, the water feeling quite warm.

During this operation, all the others stood on the bank, looking on in profound silence. When the washing was ended, the sweetest music I had ever heard greeted my ears. We walked to the shore, where an angel stood with a clean, white robe, which the Father at once put on me. In an instant I appeared to be changed into an angel. The whole company looked at me with delight, and began to make a noise which I called shouting. We all marched back with music. When we reached the tree to which the angel first led me, it hung full of fruit, which I had not seen before. The Holy Ghost plucked some and gave me, and the rest helped themselves. We sat down and ate of the fruit, which had a taste like nothing I had ever tasted before. When we had finished, we all arose and gave another shout. Then God the Father said to me: "You are now prepared, and must go where I have commanded you." I replied, "If I go, they will not believe me." Christ then appeared to write something with a golden pen and golden ink, upon golden paper. Then he rolled it up, and said to me: "Put this in your bosom, and, wherever you go, show it, and they will know that I have sent you to proclaim salvation to all." He then put it into my bosom, and they all went with me to a bright, shining gate, singing and shouting. Here they embraced me, and I found myself once more on earth.

When I came to myself, I found that several friends had been with me all night, and my husband had called a physician, but he had not been able to do anything for me. He ordered those around me to keep very quiet, or to go home. He returned in the morning, when I told him, in part, my story. He seemed amazed, but made no answer, and left me.

Several friends were in, daring the day. While talking to them, I would, without thinking, put my hand into my bosom, to show them my letter of authority. But I soon found, as my friends told me, it was in my heart, and was to be shown in my life, instead of in my hand. Among others, my minister, Jehial C. Beman, came to see me. He looked very coldly upon me and said: "I guess you will find out your mistake before you are many months older." He was a scholar, and a fine speaker; and the sneering, indifferent way in which he addressed me, said most plainly: "You don't know anything." I replied: "My gifts are very small, I know, but I can no longer be shaken by what you or any one else may think or say."

CHAPTER XIX:
Public Effort—Excommunication

From this time the opposition to my lifework commenced, instigated by the minister, Mr. Beman. Many in the church were anxious to have me preach in the hall, where our meetings were held at that time, and were not a little astonished at the minister's cool treatment of me. At length two of the trustees got some of the elder sisters to call on the minister and ask him to let me preach. His answer was: "No; she can't preach her holiness stuff here, and I am astonished that you should ask it of me." The sisters said he seemed to be in quite a rage, although he said he was not angry.

There being no meeting of the society on Monday evening, a brother in the church opened his house to me, that I might preach, which displeased Mr. Beman very much. He appointed a committee to wait upon the brother and sister who had opened their doors to me, to tell them they must not allow any more meetings of that kind, and that they must abide by the rules of the church, making them believe they would be excommunicated if they disobeyed him. I happened to be present at this interview, and the committee remonstrated with me for the course I had taken. I told them my business was with the Lord, and wherever I found a door opened I intended to go in and work for my Master.

There was another meeting appointed at the same place, which I, of course, attended; after which the meetings were stopped for that time, though I held many more there after these people had withdrawn from Mr. Beman's church.

I then held meetings in my own house; whereat the minister told the members that if they attended them he would deal with them, for they were breaking the rules of the church. When he found that I continued the meetings, and that the Lord was blessing my feeble efforts, he sent a committee of two to ask me if I considered myself a member of his church. I told them I did, and should continue to do so until I had done something worthy of dismemberment.

At this, Mr. Beman sent another committee with a note, asking me to meet him with the committee, which I did. He asked me a number of questions, nearly all of which I have forgotten. One, however, I do remember: he asked if I was willing to comply with the rules of the discipline. To this I answered: "Not if the discipline prohibits me from doing what God has bidden me to do; I fear God more than man." Similar questions were asked and answered in the same manner. The committee said what they wished to say, and then told me I could go home. When I reached the door, I turned and said: "I now shake off the dust of my feet as a witness against you. See to it that this meeting does not rise in judgment against you."

The next evening, one of the committee came to me and told me that I was no longer a member of the church, because I had violated the rules of the discipline by preaching.

When this action became known, the people wondered how any one could be excommunicated for trying to do good. I did not say much, and my friends simply said I had done nothing but hold meetings. Others, anxious to know the particulars, asked the minister what the trouble was. He told them he had given me the privilege of speaking or preaching as long as I chose, but that he could not give me the right to use the pulpit, and that I was not satisfied with any other place. Also, that I had appointed meeting on the evening of his meetings, which was a thing no member had a right to do. For these reasons he said he had turned me out of the church.

Now, if the people who repeated this to me told the truth—and I have no doubt but they did—Mr. Beman told an actual falsehood. I had never asked for his pulpit, but had told him and others, repeatedly, that I did not care where I stood—any corner of the hall would do. To which Mr. Beman had answered: "You cannot have any place in the hall." Then I said: "I'll preach in a private house." He answered me: "No, not in this place; I am stationed over all Boston." He was determined I should not preach in the city of Boston. To cover up his deceptive, unrighteous course toward me, he told the above falsehoods.

From his statements, many erroneous stories concerning me gained credence with a large number of people. At that time, I thought it my duty as well as privilege to address a letter to the Conference, which I took to them in person, stating all the facts. At the same time I told them it was not in the power of Mr. Beman, or any one else, to truthfully bring anything against my moral or religious character—that my only offence was in trying to preach the Gospel of Christ—and that I cherished no ill feelings toward Mr. Beman or any one else, but that I desired the Conference to give the case an impartial hearing, and then give me a written statement expressive of their opinion. I also said I considered myself a member of the Conference, and should do so until they said I was not, and gave me their reasons, that I might let the world know what my offence had been.

My letter was slightingly noticed, and then thrown under the table. Why should they notice it? It was only the grievance of a woman, and there was no justice meted out to women in those days. Even ministers of Christ did not feel that women had any rights which they were bound to respect.

SOURCE

Foote, Julia A. J. *A Brand Plucked from the Fire: An Autobiographical Sketch*, 65–76. Cleveland: W. F. Schneider, 1879.

NOTE

Chapter opening photo: Julia A. J. Foote. Frontispiece from Foote's *A Brand Plucked from the Fire: An Autobiographical Sketch* (Cleveland: W. F. Schneider, 1879).

Margaret Fuller

1810–1850

MARGARET FULLER OSSOLI was an American journalist, transcendentalist, abolitionist, and women's rights advocate, whose *Woman in the Nineteenth Century* is widely considered the central First-Wave feminist text in American literature. From 1840 to 1842 she edited *The Dial*, the premier journal of American transcendentalism. Her essay "The Great Lawsuit," published in *The Dial* in 1843, would appear in greatly expanded form as *Woman in the Nineteenth Century* in 1845. Even the usually caustic Edgar Allan Poe admitted it was "a book which few women in the country could have written, and no woman in the country would have published, with the exception of Miss Fuller," given its independent and "unmitigated radicalism." In 1850, Fuller, along with her husband and young son, died in a shipwreck off Fire Island, New York.

From *Woman in the Nineteenth Century* (1845)

It may well be an Anti-Slavery party that pleads for woman, if we consider merely that she does not hold property on equal terms with men; so that, if a husband dies without making a will, the wife, instead of taking at once his place as head of the family, inherits only a part of his fortune, often brought him by herself, as if she were a child, or ward only, not an equal partner.

We will not speak of the innumerable instances in which profligate and idle men live upon the earnings of industrious wives; or if the wives leave them, and take with them the children, to perform the double duty of mother and father, follow from place to place, and threaten to rob them of the children, if deprived of the rights of a husband, as they call them, planting themselves in their poor lodgings, frightening them into paying tribute by taking from them the children, running into debt at the expense of these otherwise so overtasked helots. Such instances count up by scores within my own memory. I have seen the husband who had stained himself by a long course of low vice, till his wife was wearied from her heroic forgiveness, by finding that his treachery made it useless, and that if she would provide bread for herself and her children, she must be separate from his ill fame. I have known this man come to instal himself in the chamber of a woman who loathed him and say she should never take food without his company. I have known these men steal their children whom they knew they had no means to maintain, take them into dissolute company, expose them to bodily danger, to frighten the poor woman, to whom, it seems, the fact that she alone had borne the pangs of their birth, and nourished their infancy, does not give an equal right to them. I do believe that this mode of kidnapping, and it is frequent enough in all classes of society, will be by the next age viewed as it is by Heaven now, and that the man who avails himself of the shelter of men's laws to steal from a mother her own children, or arrogate any superior right in them, save that of superior virtue, will bear the stigma he deserves, in common with him who steals grown men from their mother land, their hopes, and their homes.

I said, we will not speak of this now, yet I have spoken, for the subject makes me feel too much. I could give instances that would startle the most vulgar and callous, but I will not, for the public opinion of their own sex is already against such men, and where cases of extreme tyranny are made known, there is private action in the wife's favor. But she ought not to need this, nor, I think, can she long. Men must soon see that, on their own ground, that woman is the weaker party, she ought to have legal protection, which would make such oppression impossible. But I would not deal with "atrocious instances" except in the way of illustration, neither demand from men a partial redress in some one matter, but go to the root of the whole. If principles could be established, particulars would adjust themselves aright. Ascertain the true destiny of woman, give her legitimate hopes, and a standard within herself; marriage and all other relations would by degrees be harmonized with these.

But to return to the historical progress of this matter. Knowing that there exists in the minds of men a tone of feeling towards women as towards slaves, such as is expressed in the common phrase, "Tell that to women and children," that the infinite soul can only work through them

in already ascertained limits; that the gift of reason, man's highest pre-
rogative, is allotted to them in much lower degree; that they must be kept
from mischief and melancholy by being constantly engaged in active
labor, which is to be furnished and directed by those better able to think,
&c. &c.; we need not multiply instances, for who can review the experience of last week without recalling words which imply, whether in jest or
earnest, these views or views like these; knowing this, can we wonder that
many reformers think that measures are not likely to be taken in behalf
of women, unless their wishes could be publicly represented by women?

That can never be necessary, cry the other side. All men are privately
influenced by women; each has his wife, sister, or female friends, and is
too much biased by these relations to fail of representing their interests,
and, if this is not enough, let them propose and enforce their wishes with
the pen. The beauty of home would be destroyed, the delicacy of the sex
be violated, the dignity of halls of legislation degraded by an attempt to
introduce them there. Such duties are inconsistent with those of a mother;
and then we have ludicrous pictures of ladies in hysterics at the polls, and
senate chambers filled with cradles.

But if, in reply, we admit as truth that woman seems destined by nature
rather for the inner circle, we must add that the arrangements of civilized
life have not been, as yet, such as to secure it to her. Her circle, if the duller,
is not the quieter. If kept from "excitement," she is not from drudgery.
Not only the Indian squaw carries the burdens of the camp, but the fa-
vorites of Louis the Fourteenth accompany him in his journeys, and the
washerwoman stands at her tub and carries home her work at all seasons,
and in all states of health. Those who think the physical circumstances
of woman would make a part in the affairs of national government un-
suitable, are by no means those who think it impossible for the negresses
to endure field work, even during pregnancy, or the sempstresses to go
through their killing labors.

As to the use of the pen, there was quite as much opposition to woman's
possessing herself of that help to free agency, as there is now to her seizing
on the rostrum or the desk; and she is likely to draw, from a permission
to plead her cause that way, opposite inferences to what might be wished
by those who now grant it.

As to the possibility of her filling with grace and dignity, any such position, we should think those who had seen the great actresses, and heard

the Quaker preachers of modern times, would not doubt, that woman can express publicly the fulness of thought and creation, without losing any of the peculiar beauty of her sex. What can pollute and tarnish is to act thus from any motive except that something needs to be said or done. Woman could take part in the processions, the songs, the dances of old religion; no one fancied their delicacy was impaired by appearing in public for such a cause.

As to her home, she is not likely to leave it more than she now does for balls, theatres, meetings for promoting missions, revival meetings, and others to which she flies, in hope of an animation for her existence, commensurate with what she sees enjoyed by men. Governors of ladies' fairs are no less engrossed by such a change, than the Governor of the state by his; presidents of Washingtonian societies no less away from home than presidents of conventions. If men look straitly to it, they will find that, unless their lives are domestic, those of the women will not be. A house is no home unless it contain food and fire for the mind as well as for the body. The female Greek, of our day, is as much in the street as the male to cry, What news? We doubt not it was the same in Athens of old. The women, shut out from the market place, made up for it at the religious festivals. For human beings are not so constituted that they can live without expansion. If they do not get it in one way, they must another, or perish.

As to men's representing women fairly at present, while we hear from men who owe to their wives not only all that is comfortable or graceful, but all that is wise in the arrangement of their lives, the frequent remark, "You cannot reason with a woman," when from those of delicacy, nobleness, and poetic culture, the contemptuous phrase "women and children," and that in no light sally of the hour, but in works intended to give a permanent statement of the best experiences, when not one man, in the million, shall I say? no, not in the hundred million, can rise above the belief that woman was made *for man*, when such traits as these are daily forced upon the attention, can we feel that man will always do justice to the interests of woman? Can we think that he takes a sufficiently discerning and religious view of her office and destiny, *ever* to do her justice, except when prompted by sentiment, accidentally or transiently, that is, for the sentiment will vary according to the relations in which he is placed. The lover, the poet, the artist, are likely to view her nobly. The father and the philosopher have some chance of liberality; the man of the world, the legislator for expediency, none.

Under these circumstances, without attaching importance, in themselves, to the changes demanded by the champions of woman, we hail them as signs of the times. We would have every arbitrary barrier thrown down. We would have every path laid open to woman as freely as to man. Were this done and a slight temporary fermentation allowed to subside, we should see crystallizations more pure and of more various beauty. We believe the divine energy would pervade nature to a degree unknown in the history of former ages, and that no discordant collision, but a ravishing harmony of the spheres would ensue.

Yet, then and only then, will mankind be ripe for this, when inward and outward freedom for woman as much as for man shall be acknowledged as a right, not yielded as a concession. As the friend of the negro assumes that one man cannot by right, hold another in bondage, so should the friend of woman assume that man cannot, by right, lay even well-meant restrictions on woman. If the negro be a soul, if the woman be a soul, appareled in flesh, to one Master only are they accountable. There is but one law for souls, and if there is to be an interpreter of it, he must come not as man, or son of man, but as son of God.

Were thought and feeling once so far elevated that man should esteem himself the brother and friend, but nowise the lord and tutor of woman, were he really bound with her in equal worship, arrangements as to function and employment would be of no consequence.

[. . .]

There are two aspects of woman's nature, represented by the ancients as Muse and Minerva. It is the former to which the writer in the Pathfinder looks. It is the latter which Wordsworth has in mind, when he says—

> "With a placid brow,
> Which woman ne'er should forfeit, keep thy vow.["][1]

The especial genius of woman I believe to be electrical in movement, intuitive in function, spiritual in tendency. She excels not so easily in classification, or re-creation, as in an instinctive seizure of causes, and a simple breathing out of what she receives that has the singleness of life, rather than the selecting and energizing of art.

More native is it to her to be the living model of the artist than to set apart from herself any one form in objective reality; more native to inspire and receive the poem, than to create it. In so far as soul is in her completely developed, all soul is the same; but as far as it is modified in her as woman, it flows, it breathes, it sings, rather than deposits soil, or finishes work, and that which is especially feminine flushes, in blossom, the face of earth, and pervades, like air and water, all this seeming solid globe, daily renewing and purifying its life. Such may be the especially feminine element, spoken of as Femality. But it is no more the order of nature that it should be incarnated pure in any form, than that the masculine energy should exist unmingled with it in any form.

Male and female represent the two sides of the great radical dualism. But, in fact, they are perpetually passing into one another. Fluid hardens to solid, solid rushes to fluid. There is no wholly masculine man, no purely feminine woman.

History jeers at the attempts of physiologists to bind great original laws by the forms which flow from them. They make a rule; they say from observation, what can and cannot be. In vain! Nature provides exceptions to every rule. She sends women to battle, and sets Hercules spinning; she enables women to bear immense burdens, cold, and frost; she enables the man, who feels maternal love, to nourish his infant like a mother. Of late she plays still gayer pranks. Not only she deprives organizations, but organs, of a necessary end. She enables people to read with the top of the head, and see with the pit of the stomach. Presently she will make a female Newton, and a male Syren.

Man partakes of the feminine in the Apollo, woman of the masculine as Minerva.

What I mean by the Muse is the unimpeded clearness of the intuitive powers which a perfectly truthful adherence to every admonition of the higher instincts would bring to a finely organized human being. It may appear as prophecy or as poesy. It enabled Cassandra to foresee the results of actions passing round her; the Seeress to behold the true character of the person through the mask of his customary life. (Sometimes she saw a feminine form behind the man, sometimes the reverse.) It enabled the daughter of Linnæus to see the soul of the flower exhaling from the flower.[2] It gave a man, but a poet man, the power of which he thus speaks: "Often in my contemplation of nature, radiant intimations, and as it were sheaves of light appear before me as to the facts of cosmogony in which my mind has, perhaps, taken especial part." He wisely adds, "but it is necessary with earnestness to verify the knowledge we gain by these flashes of light."[3] And none should forget this. Sight must be verified by life before it can deserve the honors of piety and genius. Yet sight comes first, and of this sight of the world of causes, this approximation to the region of primitive motions, women I hold to be especially capable. Even without equal freedom with the other sex, they have already shown themselves so, and should these faculties have free play, I believe they will open new, deeper and purer sources of joyous inspiration than have as yet refreshed the earth.

Let us be wise and not impede the soul. Let her work as she will. Let us have one creative energy, one incessant revelation. Let it take what form it will, and let us not bind it by the past to man or woman, black or white. Jove sprang from Rhea, Pallas from Jove. So let it be.

[. . .]

SOURCE

Fuller, S. Margaret. *Woman in the Nineteenth Century*, 20–27, 102–5. New York: Greeley & McElrath, 1845.

NOTES

1. From "Liberty," by English Romantic poet William Wordsworth (1770–1850).
2. [Author's footnote.] The daughter of Linnaeus states, that, while looking steadfastly at the red lily, she saw its spirit hovering above it, as a red flame. It is true, this, like many fair spirit-stories, may be explained away as an optical illusion, but its poetic beauty and meaning would, even then, make it valuable, as an illustration of the spiritual fact.
3. Source of quotation unknown.

Charlotte Perkins Gilman

1860–1935

CHARLOTTE PERKINS GILMAN—a feminist, political theorist, and social activist who called for women to gain economic independence— is probably best known today for her story "The Yellow Wall-Paper" (1892), inspired by her own experience with postpartum depression. The author of a great deal of poetry and fiction as well as essays, Gilman published much of her work in *The Forerunner*, a magazine focused on women's issues and social reform, which she established, edited, and for seven years wrote single-handedly. Though radically progressive, some of Gilman's views, particularly her eugenicist theories, are problematic by contemporary standards. She was nevertheless widely considered one of the leading minds of the early twentieth-century women's move- ment. After being diagnosed with inoperable breast cancer, she died by suicide in 1935. Gilman had previously written in favor of the right to die (see the final essay in this section).

Maternity Benefits and Reformers (1916)

One of the saddest obstacles in the way of legitimate social progress is seen when some of the noblest workers in one line oppose a movement of advance in others.

The American Association for Labor Legislation, through its commit- tee on Social Insurance, has prepared the tentative draft of an act on Health Insurance, carefully drawn, and largely in accordance with the best measures now advocated and used in so many other countries, as England, Germany, Hungary, Italy, France, Switzerland and Russia.

In this act there was recognition of the great need of maternity benefits, and Section 15 provides as follows: "Maternity Benefits shall consist of:

All necessary medical, surgical and obstetrical aid, materials and appliances, which shall be given insured women and the wives of insured men;

A weekly maternity benefit, payable to insured women, equal to the regular sick benefit, of the insured, for a period of eight weeks, of which at least six shall be subsequent to delivery, on condition that the beneficiary abstain from gainful employment during period of payment."

In the remarks preparatory to the act, we are told that in our country we have a standing sick list of three million persons at any one time; that each of our thirty million wage earners loses on an average about nine days a year from sickness, with a total wage loss of $500,000,000, and a cost for medical treatment of $180,000,000. This is a total cost of $680,000,000, well over half a billion, coming out of the class which can least afford to lose it, as well as the interruption of industry that affects us all; and it is found that in some 75 per cent. of applications for aid, made to the New York Charity Organization Society, sickness was responsible for the distress. Few reasonable persons will object to the general plan of health insurance; why should anyone object to it for women? And if they do not object to it for other forms of temporary disability in women, why should the maternity benefit be objected to? It would seem as if there could be but three possible reasons; a desire to prevent maternity, to penalize maternity, or to prevent mothers from undertaking gainful occupations.

As the really good and in many ways wise people who are so valiantly opposing the maternity benefit cannot be suspected of the first two, it appears that their one desire is to prevent mothers from working; that is, from working at anything for which they are paid.

A more pitiful misconception of the best lines of social advance by those apparently well qualified to judge has seldom been offered. It is on a par with the opposition to "teacher mothers"—which frankly admits its object to be to prevent mothers from holding their positions as teachers.

All this foolish and wasted effort ignores one of the largest and most vitally important movements of the day—the specialization of women. Women are irresistibly pushing forward into all manner of "gainful occupations," first unprovided for spinsters and widows who "had to work"; then the growing multitude of young girls who worked to help their families and for their own freedom; then married women, to meet family wants and to preserve their own integrity; then, more and more, mothers.

This is the most important feature of the whole movement. Young girls are not women. Spinsters and widows are more or less unfortunate exceptions. The term "woman" should connote wifehood and motherhood. Until "mothers" earn their livings "women" will not.

The first steps of working motherhood, usually enforced by extreme poverty, bring the woman and the child in contact with some of our worst conditions; and we, in our dull social conscience, seeing evil fall upon mother and baby, seek only to push them back where they came from—instead of striving to make conditions fit for them.

What we must recognize is this:

Women; wives and mothers; are becoming a permanent half of the world workers. In their interest we shall inevitably change the brutal and foolish hardships now surrounding labor into such decent and healthful conditions as shall be no injury to any one. That children should be forced to work for their livings is an unnatural outrage, wholly injurious. That adult women should do it, is in no way harmful, if the hours and conditions of labor are suitable; and they never will be made suitable until overwhelming numbers of working women compel them.

Now since maternity is not "a preventable illness"—unless we wish the race to die out, but merely a temporary disability in which the woman discontinues one form of social service to practice another; there is even more reason for providing for it than for the "occupational diseases," which can largely be prevented; or the general diseases which attack us indiscriminately.

The efforts of any army to nurse back to health its fighting units, and to keep them in health—until they are killed!—should be paralleled by the efforts of a peaceful state to preserve the health of its workers, and to nurse them when disabled.

The theory that women must at all costs be kept in the home grows feebler daily. They will not stay there—they have definitely come out. By coming out, by bringing the mothers of the world into industry, we shall at last make the conditions of our workers what they ought to be. When these conditions are right, in hours of labor, in surroundings, in payment, then we shall have less sickness, and less need of health insurance; but with things as they are now, such insurance is wise and right, and most assuredly so for mothers.

What Is Feminism? (1916)

What indeed?

Here is a question as big as the better half of the world, and as small as the tightest little hard-boiled prejudice of the meanest mummified relic of an ancestral mind, an inherited mind, a mind that never takes a step of its own volition, but merely goes through the motions in which it was brought up, or sits, immovable, as it was carefully instructed to sit.

Feminism, really, is the social awakening of the women of all the world. It is that great movement, partly conscious and more largely unconscious, which is changing the centre of gravity in human life. We have had, all these ages, a man-made world, a world in which women were loved as a sex, valued as mothers, and exploited as servants. Outside of being loved, being valued, being exploited, they had no existence. Talk of "the submerged tenth"—they have been the submerged half. "Feminism" is their emergence.

Women are coming out, coming up, coming forward, by millions and millions.

What is the nature of this movement?

It is as manifold as modern life, and as simple as any other process of nature. Women are going through, in a century or so, swiftly, and in large measure voluntarily, the same steps of social progress which men have been struggling through in hundreds of thousands of years.

From *The Living of Charlotte Perkins Gilman* (1935)

In January, 1932, I discovered that I had cancer of the breast. My only distress was for Houghton. I had not the least objection to dying. But I did not propose to die of this, so I promptly bought sufficient chloroform as a substitute. Human life consists in mutual service. No grief, pain, misfortune or "broken heart" is excuse for cutting off one's life while any power of service remains. But when all usefulness is over, when one is assured of unavoidable and imminent death, it is the simplest of human rights to choose a quick and easy death in place of a slow and horrible one.

Public opinion is changing on this subject. The time is approaching when we shall consider it abhorrent to our civilization to allow a human being to die in prolonged agony which we should mercifully end in any other creature. Believing this open choice to be of social service in promoting wiser views on this question, I have preferred chloroform to cancer.

Going to my doctor for definite assurance, he solemnly agreed with my diagnosis and thought the case inoperable.

"Well," said I cheerfully, "how long does it take?" He estimated a year and a half. "How long shall I be able to type?" I asked. "I must finish my Ethics." He thought I might be quite comfortable for six months. It is now three and a half years and this obliging malady has given me no pain yet.

Then came what was pain—telling Houghton. He wanted an expert opinion, and we got it. No mistake. Then, since I utterly refused a late operation, he urged me to try X-ray treatment, which I did with good effects. He suffered a thousand times more than I did—but not for long. On the fourth of May, 1934, he suddenly died, from cerebral hemorrhage.

Whatever I felt of loss and pain was outweighed by gratitude for an instant, painless death for him, and that he did not have to see me wither and die—and he be left alone.

I flew to Pasadena, California, in the fall of 1934, to be near my daughter and grandchildren. Grace Channing, my lifelong friend, has come out to be with me. We two have a little house next door but one to my Katharine, who is a heavenly nurse and companion. Dorothy and Walter, her children, are a delight. Mr. Chamberlin, my son-in-law, has made the place into a garden wherein I spend happy afternoons under an orange-tree— the delicious fragrance drifting over me, the white petals lightly falling— in May! Now it is small green oranges occasionally thumping.

One thing I have had to complain of—shingles. *Shingles*—for six weeks. A cancer that doesn't show and doesn't hurt, I can readily put up with; it is easy enough to be sick as long as you feel well—but *shingles*!

People are heavenly good to me. Dear friends write to me, with outrageous praises. I am most unconcernedly willing to die when I get ready. I have no faintest belief in personal immortality—no interest in nor desire for it.

My life is in Humanity—and that goes on. My contentment is in God— and That goes on. The Social Consciousness, fully accepted, automatically eliminates both selfishness and pride. The one predominant duty is to find one's work and do it, and I have striven mightily at that.

The religion, the philosophy, set up so early, have seen me through.

The Right to Die (1935)

I

Should an incurable invalid, suffering constant pain and begging for a quicker, easier death, be granted that mercy?

Should a hopeless idiot, lunatic, or helpless paretic be laboriously kept alive?

Should certain grades of criminals be painlessly removed—or cruelly condemned to the cumulative evil of imprisonment?

Is suicide sometimes quite justifiable?

We have changed our minds more than once on these matters and are in process of changing them again. On the above questions, asked a hundred or even fifty years ago, there would have been scant discussion. Humans were mainly agreed that certain criminals deserved death, that suicide was a sin, and that agonized invalids and healthy idiots were to be cherished carefully.

The influence of the Christian religion has done much to establish a sort of dogma of the "sanctity of human life," but the ancient religions of India went further, holding all life sacred, to such an extent that the pious Jain sweeps the path before him lest he step on a worm.

What is the "sanctity of human life"? Why is it sacred? How is it sacred? When is it sacred?

Is it sacred where we lavishly reproduce it, without thought or purpose? While it is going on? Or only when it is about to end?

Our mental attics are full of old ideas and emotions, which we preserve sentimentally but never examine. The advance of the world's thought is promoted by those whose vigorous minds seize upon inert doctrines and passive convictions and shake them into life or into tatters. This theory that suicide is a sin is being so shaken today.

Why has not a man the right to take his own life? Shaw, the inveterate shaker of old ideas, says that his own life is the only one a man has a right to take.

Against this apparently natural right stand two assumptions, one that it is cowardly, the other that it is a sin. The brave man is supposed to endure long, hopeless agony to the bitter end, as an exhibition of courage; the moral man similarly to bear incurable suffering, because to shorten his torment would be wrong.

How much more reasonable is the spirit of the sturdy old country doctor who was found dead in his bed, with a revolver by his side and the brief note, "There's no damn cancer going to get ahead of me!"

Why it should please God to have a harmless victim suffer prolonged agony was never made clear; but those who so thought also assumed that whatever happened was God's will, that He was afflicting us for some wise purpose of His own and did not like to be thwarted, balked in his plan of punishment so to speak. Astonishing calumnies have been believed of God.

There is a pleasant tale of an ingenious person, captive of savages and obliged to watch the horrors of his comrades' dreadful deaths. When his turn came, he told the credulous natives that he knew of an herb which, when rubbed upon the skin, rendered it impervious to any weapon and which he would show them if they would spare him.

So they accompanied him here and there in the forest, till he picked a certain rare plant, which he rubbed well on the side of his neck. Then he laid his head on a log and told them to strike as hard as they liked. Down came the ax, and off went a grinning ghost, enjoying their discomfiture— at least it is pleasant to think so. At any rate he was not tortured. But he had lied, to be sure, and practically committed suicide. Was it sin?

Suicide was a gentleman's exit in ancient Rome, as it is yet in the Orient. It must have been too popular in the misery of the Dark Ages, for a discerning church soon decided that it was extremely wrong. It was a difficult offense to penalize, the offender having escaped, so they punished the corpse, burying it with a stake through the body, at a crossroads, that, instead of enjoying seclusion and consecrated ground, it might be trampled over by all who passed.

II

A very special damnation having been provided for such rebellious souls, suicide fell into disrepute. It is now becoming popular again, not merely as a justifiable escape from an unbearable position but as a hopeful experiment for discouraged youth. And no more pathetic instance of the blind groping of such religionless young people could be asked. They no longer believe in the kind of God worshiped by their ancestors, not in "His canon 'gainst self-slaughter."[1] They quite repudiate the earlier moral sense and have not yet succeeded in evolving any satisfactory substitute.

It might be advanced, as consolation in these too-frequent tragedies, that minds so word-befuddled would not in all probability have been of much service to the world had they survived; but such harsh criticism fails to estimate the capacity for suffering which belongs to youth.

As with most moral questions, the confusion lies in our outdated sense of individuality, our failure to recognize social responsibility. Youth is, of course, naturally egotistical, and in home, school, church, and ordinary contact little is done to develop social consciousness.

That an individual's life, growth, and happiness are dependent on interrelation with other people and that each of us owes to others the best service of a lifetime is not accepted by those who back out of life because it hurts. Such premature and ill-based suicide is timid, feeble, foolish, and, in respect to social responsibility, dishonorable. It is desertion, not in the face of the enemy but before imagined enemies.

On the other hand, military law forbids the attempt to hold an indefensible position. There are times when surrender is quite justifiable. If men or women are beyond usefulness, feel that they are of no service or comfort to any one but a heavy burden and expense, and, above all, if they suffer hopelessly, they have a right to leave.

But, while we are beginning to open the door for a man to take his own life with good reason, we are trying to close it upon the right of society to take the life of a criminal. The opponents of capital punishment rest their arguments largely on the alleged sanctity of human life and further on the fact that the severe and cruel penalties of earlier times did not prevent crime.

This sudden application of sanctity to man at the point of death, a life neglected and corrupted from babyhood, is unconvincing. It is true that severe punishment does not prevent crime, but neither does light punishment or no punishment at all. Can we prevent crime after it has been committed? The prevention must begin with birth, must ensure the best conditions for growth and education, for rightly chosen employment, for rest and recreation.

But, unfortunately, criminals sometimes appear from families of the enlightened and well-to-do, cases of atavism, primitive characters breaking out into the modern world most mischievously. And, furthermore, society is open to many kinds of perversion and disease.

Since we have criminals, engaged in transmitting and increasing evil, what are we to do with them? The most tenderly sentimental would hardly suggest leaving them at large.

To remove such a diseased character as this is not an act of "punishment"; it is social surgery, the prompt excision of the affected part. Those who call death cruel and urge imprisonment instead do not realize the greater cruelty and cumulative danger of confinement.

Much of vice and crime is distinctly infectious. "Evil communications corrupt good manners," and no antitoxin has been found to prevent that corruption. We may call our prisons isolation hospitals if we like, but if the prisoner is really isolated he goes mad—no punishment is so cruel as solitary confinement. Not being isolated, the prisoners infect and reinfect one another. The cumulative influence of these carefully maintained collections of diseased characters affects not only the prisoners but those who restrain them. It is held by some that the care of the helpless develops noble qualities in those who tend them. These theorists have failed to study the effect of such activity on warders, keepers, guards, and those who wait on and serve utter idiots and maniacs.

III

The elimination of diseased parts from our body politic should not be discussed as punishment but as an operation on the social body. One does not either "forgive" or "punish" an inflamed appendix but one does cut it out.

The same position may be taken in regard to the incurable idiot or maniac. If, to the best of our present knowledge, such cases are hopeless, why should we isolate and preserve the affected parts? Why should we not painlessly remove them? Affection, gratitude for previous services may be urged, but this attitude is based on the assumption that it is some pleasure or advantage to the ruined minds to live thus ignominiously.

Here is a case of a fine woman who has lived a good and fruitful life. She is affected with a progressive mental disorder, and for fifteen years two daughters are sacrificed to the unfruitful service of increasing idiocy, their lives crippled, wrecked.

But she is their mother, she has loved and served them, we protest. Yes, and what would any mother feel, if she could know it, to realize that she who loved them was now the means of slowly ruining her children?

In another instance we see a man once strong and intellectual, eminent in scholarship, honorable in service to society, now a paretic.[2] Slowly he fails in physical and mental power, reaching the condition of a gross baby, a huge, brainless baby lying like a log in an unclean bed, while nurse and doctor wait for him—for it—to die. What is sacred in that dreadful ignominy? When intelligent consciousness is gone forever, the man is gone, and the body should be decently removed.

The record of a previously noble life is precisely what makes it sheer insult to allow death in pitiful degradation. We may not wish to "die with our boots on" but we may well prefer to die with our brains on.

In New York, some years ago, an elderly woman was suffering from a complication of diseases; recovery was impossible; she knew that she must die; and her constant and terrible pain was such that she begged piteously for release. She was attended by a devoted daughter and by a trained nurse, a sturdy Nova Scotian, rigidly religious.

The patient died somewhat sooner than was expected by the physician. The nurse testified that she had seen the daughter put something in her mother's drinking glass. Careful inquiry ascertained that there was no inheritance to offer a "motive" for murder and that this mother and daughter had been attached and congenial friends, wholly devoted to each other. The inquest ignored the nurse's testimony, and no charge, fortunately, was brought against the daughter.

More recently, in England, a man whose beloved little girl was in constant suffering from an incurable disease, after long daily and nightly care and tender nursing, relieved the child's agony with a quick death. The judge, in charging the jury, pointed out how long and lovingly the poor father had nursed his child and urged upon them that, if he had allowed a dog in his possession to so linger in pain, he would have been liable to punishment for cruelty. The prisoner, and rightly, was not convicted.

IV

Practical Germany has discussed a law allowing physicians to administer euthanasia in certain cases. It was not passed, the two principal objections being the chance of a safe variety of murder and the effect of the patient's loss of confidence in his physician. That confidence is a valuable asset in the cure of disease. If a sick man felt that, if his doctor decided he could not recover, anesthesia would be promptly administered, it would certainly add fear to his other difficulties and jeopardize his chance of life.

No such power should be left to any individual, physician or other, though it might be advanced that no doctor would voluntarily shorten his "case." Too many mistakes in diagnosis have been made, too many patients have been given up to die and rebelliously recovered, to permit of any one man governing such a decision.

But suitable legal methods may be devised by a civilized society. When the sufferer begs for release or when the mind is gone and the body going, as in a case where intestinal cancer is accompanied by senile dementia and when the attending physician gives his opinion that there is no hope, then an application to the Board of Health should be made.

That Board should promptly appoint a consulting committee, varying from case to case, to avoid possible collusion and including a lawyer as well as doctors for inquiry should be made in regard to possible motives for the sufferer's death, among members of the family, and in regard to their attitude toward the patient.

If this committee recommends euthanasia, the Board of Health should issue a permit, and merciful sleep end hopeless misery. What rational objection can anyone make to such procedure?

There is the suggestion that sometimes doctors are all mistaken, and recovery is made after life has been despaired of. That is of course true.

There might be a small percentage of error, even with careful consulting assistance. This error is present in all matters involving the human equation. It is too small to weigh equally with the mass of misery to be relieved. And it does not apply at all to those still able to decide for themselves.

Our love, our care, our vivid sympathy with human life should be applied most strongly at the other end. With eugenics and euthenics, care and education from infancy, better living conditions for everyone, all that can be done to safeguard and improve human life we should do as a matter of course.

But the dragging weight of the grossly unfit and dangerous could be lightened, with great advantage to the normal and progressive. The millions spent in restraining and maintaining social detritus should be available for the safeguarding and improving of better lives.

Instead of being hardened by such measures of release, we shall develop a refinement of tenderness which will shrink with horror at the thought of the suffering and waste we now calmly endure. Death is not an evil when it comes in the course of nature, and when it is administered legitimately it is far less than the evil of unnecessary anguish.

SOURCES

Gilman, Charlotte Perkins. *The Living of Charlotte Perkins Gilman: An Autobiography,* 333–35. New York: D. Appleton-Century, 1935. Reprinted with the permission of the Literary Estate of Charlotte Perkins Gilman.

———. "Maternity Benefits and Reformers." *Forerunner* 7, no. 3 (March 1916): 65–66.

———. "The Right to Die." *Forum and Century* 94, no. 5 (November 1935): 297–300. Reprinted with the permission of the Literary Estate of Charlotte Perkins Gilman.

———. "What Is Feminism?" *Boston Sunday Herald Magazine,* September 3, 1916, 7.

NOTES

1. From Shakespeare's *Hamlet,* act I, scene 2.
2. That is, a paralytic.

Emma Goldman

1869–1940

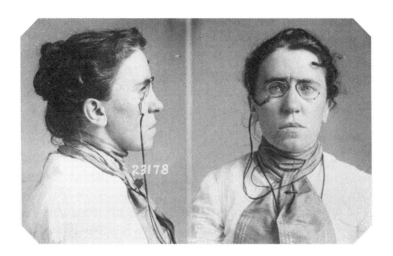

EMMA GOLDMAN was an anarchist and feminist activist who emigrated to the United States from the Russian Empire (now Lithuania) in 1885. Disillusioned by her experiences working in clothing factories, she traveled around the country advocating for women's rights, birth control, free love, free speech, radical education, and the right for workers to organize. Goldman edited and contributed to *Mother Earth*, an anarchist publication, from 1906 until it was shut down in 1917 under the Espionage Act. The first selection from her work was published in *Mother Earth* in 1909. She also wrote several books, including *Anarchism and Other Essays* (1910), from which the second selection is excerpted, and *Living My Life* (1931). Goldman was arrested several times for revolutionary activities, including making "incendiary speeches," "inciting riots," lecturing on birth control, and criticizing mandatory military conscription during World War I. She received a two-year prison sentence for the last offense, and in 1919, Goldman was deported from the United States under the newly passed Anti-Anarchist Act.

A New Declaration of Independence (1909)

When, in the course of human development, existing institutions prove inadequate to the needs of man, when they serve merely to enslave, rob, and oppress mankind, the people have the eternal right to rebel against, and overthrow, these institutions.

The mere fact that these forces—inimical to life, liberty, and the pursuit of happiness—are legalized by statute laws, sanctified by divine rights, and enforced by political power, in no way justifies their continued existence.

We hold these truths to be self-evident: that all human beings, irrespective of race, color, or sex, are born with the equal right to share at the table of life; that to secure this right, there must be established among men economic, social, and political freedom; we hold further that government exists but to maintain special privilege and property rights; that it coerces man into submission and therefore robs him of dignity, self-respect, and life.

The history of the American kings of capital and authority is the history of repeated crimes, injustice, oppression, outrage, and abuse, all aiming at the suppression of individual liberties and the exploitation of the people. A vast country, rich enough to supply all her children with all possible comforts, and insure well-being to all, is in the hands of a few, while the nameless millions are at the mercy of ruthless wealth gatherers, unscrupulous lawmakers, and corrupt politicians. Sturdy sons of America are forced to tramp the country in a fruitless search for bread, and many of her daughters are driven into the street, while thousands of tender children are daily sacrificed on the altar of Mammon. The reign of these kings is holding mankind in slavery, perpetuating poverty and disease, maintaining crime and corruption; it is fettering the spirit of liberty, throttling the voice of justice, and degrading and oppressing humanity. It is engaged in continual war and slaughter, devastating the country and destroying the best and finest qualities of man; it nurtures superstition and ignorance, sows prejudice and strife, and turns the human family into a camp of Ishmaelites.

We, therefore, the liberty-loving men and women, realizing the great injustice and brutality of this state of affairs, earnestly and boldly do hereby declare, That each and every individual is and ought to be free to own himself and to enjoy the full fruit of his labor; that man is absolved from all allegiance to the kings of authority and capital; that he has, by the very fact of his being, free access to the land and all means of production, and entire liberty of disposing of the fruits of his efforts; that each and every individual has the unquestionable and unabridgeable right of free and voluntary association with other equally sovereign individuals for economic, political, social, and all other purposes, and that to achieve this end man must emancipate himself from the sacredness of property, the respect for man-made law, the fear of the Church, the cowardice of public opinion, the stupid arrogance of national, racial, religious, and sex superiority, and from the narrow puritanical conception of human life. And for the support of this Declaration, and with a firm reliance on the harmonious blending of man's social and individual tendencies, the lovers of liberty joyfully consecrate their uncompromising devotion, their energy and intelligence, their solidarity and their lives.

This "Declaration" was written at the request of a certain newspaper, which subsequently refused to publish it, though the article was already in composition.

Minorities versus Majorities (1910)

If I were to give a summary of the tendency of our times, I would say, Quantity. The multitude, the mass spirit, dominates everywhere, destroying quality. Our entire life—production, politics, and education—rests on quantity, on numbers. The worker who once took pride in the thoroughness and quality of his work, has been replaced by brainless, incompetent automatons, who turn out enormous quantities of things, valueless to themselves, and generally injurious to the rest of mankind. Thus quantity, instead of adding to life's comforts and peace, has merely increased man's burden.

In politics, naught but quantity counts. In proportion to its increase, however, principles, ideals, justice, and uprightness are completely swamped by the array of numbers. In the struggle for supremacy the various political parties outdo each other in trickery, deceit, cunning, and shady machinations, confident that the one who succeeds is sure to be hailed by the majority as the victor. That is the only god,—Success. As to what expense, what terrible cost to character, is of no moment. We have not far to go in search of proof to verify this sad fact.

Never before did the corruption, the complete rottenness of our government stand so thoroughly exposed; never before were the American people brought face to face with the Judas nature of that political body, which has claimed for years to be absolutely beyond reproach, as the mainstay of our institutions, the true protector of the rights and liberties of the people.

Yet when the crimes of that party became so brazen that even the blind could see them, it needed but to muster up its minions, and its supremacy was assured. Thus the very victims, duped, betrayed, outraged a hundred times, decided, not against, but in favor of the victor. Bewildered, the few asked how could the majority betray the traditions of American liberty? Where was its judgment, its reasoning capacity? That is just it, the majority cannot reason; it has no judgment. Lacking utterly in originality and moral courage, the majority has always placed its destiny in the hands of others. Incapable of standing responsibilities, it has followed its leaders even unto destruction. Dr. Stockman was right: "The most dangerous enemies of truth and justice in our midst are the compact majorities, the damned compact majority."[1] Without ambition or initiative, the compact mass hates nothing so much as innovation. It has always opposed, condemned, and hounded the innovator, the pioneer of a new truth.

The oft repeated slogan of our time is, among all politicians, the Socialists included, that ours is an era of individualism, of the minority. Only those who do not probe beneath the surface might be led to entertain this view. Have not the few accumulated the wealth of the world? Are they not the masters, the absolute kings of the situation? Their success, however, is due not to individualism, but to the inertia, the cravenness, the utter submission of the mass. The latter wants but to be dominated, to be led, to be coerced. As to individualism, at no time in human history did it have less chance of expression, less opportunity to assert itself in a normal, healthy manner.

The individual educator imbued with honesty of purpose, the artist or writer of original ideas, the independent scientist or explorer, the noncompromising pioneers of social changes are daily pushed to the wall by men whose learning and creative ability have become decrepit with age.

Educators of Ferrer's[2] type are nowhere tolerated, while the dietitians of predigested food, à la Professors Eliot and Butler, are the successful perpetuators of an age of nonentities, of automatons. In the literary and dramatic world, the Humphrey Wards and Clyde Fitches are the idols of the mass, while but few know or appreciate the beauty and genius of an Emerson, Thoreau, Whitman; an Ibsen, a Hauptmann, a Butler Yeats, or a Stephen Phillips. They are like solitary stars, far beyond the horizon of the multitude.

Publishers, theatrical managers, and critics ask not for the quality inherent in creative art, but will it meet with a good sale, will it suit the palate of the people? Alas, this palate is like a dumping ground; it relishes anything that needs no mental mastication. As a result, the mediocre, the ordinary, the commonplace represents the chief literary output.

Need I say that in art we are confronted with the same sad facts? One has but to inspect our parks and thoroughfares to realize the hideousness and vulgarity of the art manufacture. Certainly, none but a majority taste would tolerate such an outrage on art. False in conception and barbarous in execution, the statuary that infests American cities has as much relation to true art, as a totem to a Michael Angelo. Yet that is the only art that succeeds. The true artistic genius, who will not cater to accepted notions, who exercises originality, and strives to be true to life, leads an obscure and wretched existence. His work may some day become the fad of the mob, but not until his heart's blood had been exhausted; not until the pathfinder has ceased to be, and a throng of an idealless and visionless mob has done to death the heritage of the master.

It is said that the artist of today cannot create because Prometheus-like he is bound to the rock of economic necessity. This, however, is true of art in all ages. Michael Angelo was dependent on his patron saint, no less than the sculptor or painter of today, except that the art connoisseurs of those days were far away from the madding crowd. They felt honored to be permitted to worship at the shrine of the master.

The art protector of our time knows but one criterion, one value,—the dollar. He is not concerned about the quality of any great work, but in the quantity of dollars his purchase implies. Thus the financier in Mirbeau's *Les Affaires sont les Affaires* points to some blurred arrangement in colors, saying: "See how great it is; it cost 50,000 francs." Just like our own parvenus. The fabulous figures paid for their great art discoveries must make up for the poverty of their taste.

The most unpardonable sin in society is independence of thought. That this should be so terribly apparent in a country whose symbol is democracy, is very significant of the tremendous power of the majority.

Wendell Phillips[3] said fifty years ago: "In our country of absolute, democratic equality, public opinion is not only omnipotent, it is omnipresent. There is no refuge from its tyranny, there is no hiding from its reach, and the result is that if you take the old Greek lantern and go about to seek among a hundred, you will not find a single American who has not, or who does not fancy at least he has, something to gain or lose in his ambition, his social life, or business, from the good opinion and the votes of those around him. And the consequence is that instead of being a mass of individuals, each one fearlessly blurting out his own conviction, as a nation compared to other nations we are a mass of cowards. More than any other people we are afraid of each other." Evidently we have not advanced very far from the condition that confronted Wendell Phillips.

Today, as then, public opinion is the omnipresent tyrant; today, as then, the majority represents a mass of cowards, willing to accept him who mirrors its own soul and mind poverty. That accounts for the unprecedented rise of a man like Roosevelt. He embodies the very worst element of mob psychology. A politician, he knows that the majority cares little for ideals or integrity. What it craves is display. It matters not whether that be a dog show, a prize fight, the lynching of a "nigger," the rounding up of some petty offender, the marriage exposition of an heiress, or the acrobatic stunts of an ex-president. The more hideous the mental contortions, the greater the delight and bravos of the mass. Thus, poor in ideals and vulgar of soul, Roosevelt continues to be the man of the hour.

On the other hand, men towering high above such political pygmies, men of refinement, of culture, of ability, are jeered into silence as mollycoddles. It is absurd to claim that ours is the era of individualism. Ours is merely a more poignant repetition of the phenomenon of all history: every effort for progress, for enlightenment, for science, for religious, political, and economic liberty, emanates from the minority, and not from the mass. Today, as ever, the few are misunderstood, hounded, imprisoned, tortured, and killed.

The principle of brotherhood expounded by the agitator of Nazareth preserved the germ of life, of truth and justice, so long as it was the beacon light of the few. The moment the majority seized upon it, that great principle became a shibboleth and harbinger of blood and fire, spreading suffering and disaster. The attack on the omnipotence of Rome, led by the colossal figures of Huss, Calvin, and Luther, was like a sunrise amid the darkness of the night. But so soon as Luther and Calvin turned politicians and began catering to the small potentates, the nobility, and the mob spirit, they jeopardized the great possibilities of the Reformation. They won success and the majority, but that majority proved no less cruel and bloodthirsty in the persecution of thought and reason than was the Catholic monster. Woe to the heretics, to the minority, who would not bow to its dicta. After infinite zeal, endurance, and sacrifice, the human mind is at last free from the religious phantom; the minority has gone on in pursuit of new conquests, and the majority is lagging behind, handicapped by truth grown false with age.

Politically the human race would still be in the most absolute slavery, were it not for the John Balls, the Wat Tylers, the Tells,[4] the innumerable individual giants who fought inch by inch against the power of kings and tyrants. But for individual pioneers the world would have never been shaken to its very roots by that tremendous wave, the French Revolution. Great events are usually preceded by apparently small things. Thus the eloquence and fire of Camille Desmoulins was like the trumpet before Jericho, razing to the ground that emblem of torture, of abuse, of horror, the Bastille.

Always, at every period, the few were the banner bearers of a great idea, of liberating effort. Not so the mass, the leaden weight of which does not let it move. The truth of this is borne out in Russia with greater force than elsewhere. Thousands of lives have already been consumed by that bloody régime, yet the monster on the throne is not appeased. How is such a thing possible when ideas, culture, literature, when the deepest and finest emotions groan under the iron yoke? The majority, that compact, immobile, drowsy mass, the Russian peasant, after a century of struggle, of sacrifice, of untold misery, still believes that the rope which strangles "the man with the white hands"[5] brings luck.

In the American struggle for liberty, the majority was no less of a stumbling block. Until this very day the ideas of Jefferson, of Patrick Henry, of Thomas Paine, are denied and sold by their posterity. The mass wants none of them. The greatness and courage worshipped in Lincoln have been forgotten in the men who created the background for the panorama of that time. The true patron saints of the black men were represented in that handful of fighters in Boston, Lloyd Garrison, Wendell Phillips, Thoreau, Margaret Fuller, and Theodore Parker, whose great courage and sturdiness culminated in that somber giant John Brown. Their untiring zeal, their eloquence and perseverance undermined the stronghold of the Southern lords. Lincoln and his minions followed only when abolition had become a practical issue, recognized as such by all.

About fifty years ago, a meteor-like idea made its appearance on the social horizon of the world, an idea so far-reaching, so revolutionary, so all-embracing as to spread terror in the hearts of tyrants everywhere. On the other hand, that idea was a harbinger of joy, of cheer, of hope to the millions. The pioneers knew the difficulties in their way, they knew the opposition, the persecution, the hardships that would meet them, but proud and unafraid they started on their march onward, ever onward. Now that idea has become a popular slogan. Almost everyone is a Socialist today: the rich man, as well as his poor victim; the upholders of law and authority, as well as their unfortunate culprits; the freethinker, as well as the perpetuator of religious falsehoods; the fashionable lady, as well as the shirtwaist girl. Why not? Now that the truth of fifty years ago has become a lie, now that it has been clipped of all its youthful imagination, and been robbed of its vigor, its strength, its revolutionary ideal—why not? Now that it is no longer a beautiful vision, but a "practical, workable scheme," resting on the will of the majority, why not? Political cunning ever sings the praise of the mass: the poor majority, the outraged, the abused, the giant majority, if only it would follow us.

Who has not heard this litany before? Who does not know this never-varying refrain of all politicians? That the mass bleeds, that it is being robbed and exploited, I know as well as our vote-baiters. But I insist that not the handful of parasites, but the mass itself is responsible for this horrible state of affairs. It clings to its masters, loves the whip, and is the first to cry Crucify! the moment a protesting voice is raised against the sacredness of capitalistic authority or any other decayed institution. Yet how long would authority and private property exist, if not for the willingness of the mass to become soldiers, policemen, jailers, and hangmen. The Socialist demagogues know that as well as I, but they maintain the myth of the virtues of the majority, because their very scheme of life means the perpetuation of power. And how could the latter be acquired without numbers? Yes, authority, coercion, and dependence rest on the mass, but never freedom or the free unfoldment of the individual, never the birth of a free society.

Not because I do not feel with the oppressed, the disinherited of the earth; not because I do not know the shame, the horror, the indignity of the lives the people lead, do I repudiate the majority as a creative force for good. Oh, no, no! But because I know so well that as a compact mass it has never stood for justice or equality. It has suppressed the human voice, subdued the human spirit, chained the human body. As a mass its aim has always been to make life uniform, gray, and monotonous as the desert. As a mass it will always be the annihilator of individuality, of free initiative, of originality. I therefore believe with Emerson that "the masses are crude, lame, pernicious in their demands and influence, and need not to be flattered, but to be schooled. I wish not to concede anything to them, but to drill, divide, and break them up, and draw individuals out of them. Masses! The calamity are the masses. I do not wish any mass at all, but honest men only, lovely, sweet, accomplished women only."[6]

In other words, the living, vital truth of social and economic well-being will become a reality only through the zeal, courage, the non-compromising determination of intelligent minorities, and not through the mass.

Marriage and Love (1910)

The popular notion about marriage and love is that they are synonymous, that they spring from the same motives, and cover the same human needs. Like most popular notions this also rests not on actual facts, but on superstition.

Marriage and love have nothing in common; they are as far apart as the poles; are, in fact, antagonistic to each other. No doubt some marriages have been the result of love. Not, however, because love could assert itself only in marriage; much rather is it because few people can completely outgrow a convention. There are today large numbers of men and women to whom marriage is naught but a farce, but who submit to it for the sake of public opinion. At any rate, while it is true that some marriages are based on love, and while it is equally true that in some cases love continues in married life, I maintain that it does so regardless of marriage, and not because of it.

On the other hand, it is utterly false that love results from marriage. On rare occasions one does hear of a miraculous case of a married couple falling in love after marriage, but on close examination it will be found that it is a mere adjustment to the inevitable. Certainly the growing-used to each other is far away from the spontaneity, the intensity, and beauty of love, without which the intimacy of marriage must prove degrading to both the woman and the man.

Marriage is primarily an economic arrangement, an insurance pact. It differs from the ordinary life insurance agreement only in that it is more binding, more exacting. Its returns are insignificantly small compared with the investments. In taking out an insurance policy one pays for it in dollars and cents, always at liberty to discontinue payments. If, however, woman's premium is a husband, she pays for it with her name, her privacy, her self-respect, her very life, "until death doth part." Moreover, the marriage insurance condemns her to life-long dependency, to parasitism, to complete uselessness, individual as well as social. Man, too, pays his toll, but as his sphere is wider, marriage does not limit him as much as woman. He feels his chains more in an economic sense.

Thus Dante's motto over Inferno applies with equal force to marriage: "Ye who enter here leave all hope behind."

That marriage is a failure none but the very stupid will deny. One has but to glance over the statistics of divorce to realize how bitter a failure marriage really is. Nor will the stereotyped Philistine argument that the laxity of divorce laws and the growing looseness of woman account for the fact that: first, every twelfth marriage ends in divorce; second, that since 1870 divorces have increased from 28 to 73 for every hundred thousand population; third, that adultery, since 1867, as ground for divorce, has increased 270.8 per cent.; fourth, that desertion increased 369.8 per cent.

Added to these startling figures is a vast amount of material, dramatic and literary, further elucidating this subject. Robert Herrick, in *Together*; Pinero, in *Mid-Channel*; Eugene Walter, in *Paid in Full*, and scores of other writers are discussing the barrenness, the monotony, the sordidness, the inadequacy of marriage as a factor for harmony and understanding.

The thoughtful social student will not content himself with the popular superficial excuse for this phenomenon. He will have to dig down deeper into the very life of the sexes to know why marriage proves so disastrous.

Edward Carpenter[7] says that behind every marriage stands the life-long environment of the two sexes; an environment so different from each other that man and woman must remain strangers. Separated by an insurmountable wall of superstition, custom, and habit, marriage has not the potentiality of developing knowledge of, and respect for, each other, without which every union is doomed to failure.

Henrik Ibsen, the hater of all social shams, was probably the first to realize this great truth. Nora leaves her husband, not—as the stupid critic would have it—because she is tired of her responsibilities or feels the need of woman's rights, but because she has come to know that for eight years she had lived with a stranger and borne him children. Can there be any thing more humiliating, more degrading than a life-long proximity between two strangers? No need for the woman to know anything of the man, save his income. As to the knowledge of the woman—what is there to know except that she has a pleasing appearance? We have not yet outgrown the theologic myth that woman has no soul, that she is a mere appendix to man, made out of his rib just for the convenience of the gentleman who was so strong that he was afraid of his own shadow.

Perchance the poor quality of the material whence woman comes is responsible for her inferiority. At any rate, woman has no soul—what is there to know about her? Besides, the less soul a woman has the greater her asset as a wife, the more readily will she absorb herself in her husband. It is this slavish acquiescence to man's superiority that has kept the marriage institution seemingly intact for so long a period. Now that woman is coming into her own, now that she is actually growing aware of herself as a being outside of the master's grace, the sacred institution of marriage is gradually being undermined, and no amount of sentimental lamentation can stay it.

From infancy, almost, the average girl is told that marriage is her ultimate goal; therefore her training and education must be directed towards that end. Like the mute beast fattened for slaughter, she is prepared for that. Yet, strange to say, she is allowed to know much less about her function as wife and mother than the ordinary artisan of his trade. It is indecent and filthy for a respectable girl to know anything of the marital relation. Oh, for the inconsistency of respectability, that needs the marriage vow to turn something which is filthy into the purest and most sacred arrangement that none dare question or criticize. Yet that is exactly the attitude of the average upholder of marriage. The prospective wife and mother is kept in complete ignorance of her only asset in the competitive field—sex. Thus she enters into life-long relations with a man only to find herself shocked, repelled, outraged beyond measure by the most natural and healthy instinct, sex. It is safe to say that a large percentage of the unhappiness, misery, distress, and physical suffering of matrimony is due to the criminal ignorance in sex matters that is being extolled as a great virtue. Nor is it at all an exaggeration when I say that more than one home has been broken up because of this deplorable fact.

If, however, woman is free and big enough to learn the mystery of sex without the sanction of State or Church, she will stand condemned as utterly unfit to become the wife of a "good" man, his goodness consisting of an empty head and plenty of money. Can there be anything more outrageous than the idea that a healthy, grown woman, full of life and passion, must deny nature's demand, must subdue her most intense craving, undermine her health and break her spirit, must stunt her vision, abstain from the depth and glory of sex experience until a "good" man comes along to take her unto himself as a wife? That is precisely what marriage means. How can such an arrangement end except in failure? This is one, though not the least important, factor of marriage, which differentiates it from love.

Ours is a practical age. The time when Romeo and Juliet risked the wrath of their fathers for love, when Gretchen exposed herself to the gossip of her neighbors for love, is no more. If, on rare occasions young people allow themselves the luxury of romance, they are taken in care by the elders, drilled and pounded until they become "sensible."

The moral lesson instilled in the girl is not whether the man has aroused her love, but rather is it, "How much?" The important and only God of practical American life: Can the man make a living? Can he support a wife? That is the only thing that justifies marriage. Gradually this saturates every thought of the girl; her dreams are not of moonlight and kisses, of laughter and tears; she dreams of shopping tours and bargain counters. This soul-poverty and sordidness are the elements inherent in the marriage institution. The State and the Church approve of no other ideal, simply because it is the one that necessitates the State and Church control of men and women.

Doubtless there are people who continue to consider love above dollars and cents. Particularly is this true of that class whom economic necessity has forced to become self-supporting. The tremendous change in woman's position, wrought by that mighty factor, is indeed phenomenal when we reflect that it is but a short time since she has entered the industrial arena. Six million women wage workers; six million women, who have the equal right with men to be exploited, to be robbed, to go on strike; aye, to starve even. Anything more, my lord? Yes, six million wage workers in every walk of life, from the highest brain work to the most difficult menial labor in the mines and on the railroad tracks; yes, even detectives and policemen. Surely the emancipation is complete.

Yet with all that, but a very small number of the vast army of women wage workers look upon work as a permanent issue, in the same light as does man. No matter how decrepit the latter, he has been taught to be independent, self-supporting. Oh, I know that no one is really independent in our economic treadmill; still, the poorest specimen of a man hates to be a parasite; to be known as such, at any rate.

The woman considers her position as worker transitory, to be thrown aside for the first bidder. That is why it is infinitely harder to organize women than men. "Why should I join a union? I am going to get married, to have a home." Has she not been taught from infancy to look upon that as her ultimate calling? She learns soon enough that the home, though not so large a prison as the factory, has more solid doors and bars. It has a keeper so faithful that naught can escape him. The most tragic part, however, is that the home no longer frees her from wage slavery; it only increases her task.

According to the latest statistics submitted before a Committee "on labor and wages, and congestion of population," ten per cent. of the wage workers in New York City alone are married, yet they must continue to work at the most poorly paid labor in the world. Add to this horrible aspect the drudgery of house work, and what remains of the protection and glory of the home? As a matter of fact, even the middle class girl in marriage can not speak of her home, since it is the man who creates her sphere. It is not important whether the husband is a brute or a darling.

What I wish to prove is that marriage guarantees woman a home only by the grace of her husband. There she moves about in *his* home, year after year until her aspect of life and human affairs becomes as flat, narrow, and drab as her surroundings. Small wonder if she becomes a nag, petty, quarrelsome, gossipy, unbearable, thus driving the man from the house. She could not go, if she wanted to; there is no place to go. Besides, a short period of married life, of complete surrender of all faculties, absolutely incapacitates the average woman for the outside world. She becomes reckless in appearance, clumsy in her movements, dependent in her decisions, cowardly in her judgment, a weight and a bore, which most men grow to hate and despise. Wonderfully inspiring atmosphere for the bearing of life, is it not?

But the child, how is it to be protected, if not for marriage? After all, is not that the most important consideration? The sham, the hypocrisy of it! Marriage protecting the child, yet thousands of children destitute and homeless. Marriage protecting the child, yet orphan asylums and reformatories overcrowded, the Society for the Prevention of Cruelty to Children keeping busy in rescuing the little victims from "loving" parents, to place them under more loving care, the Gerry Society. Oh, the mockery of it!

Marriage may have the power to "bring the horse to water," but has it ever made him drink? The law will place the father under arrest, and put him in convict's clothes; but has that ever stilled the hunger of the child? If the parent has no work, or if he hides his identity, what does marriage do then? It invokes the law to bring the man to "justice," to put him safely behind closed doors; his labor, however, goes not to the child, but to the State. The child receives but a blighted memory of its father's stripes.

As to the protection of the woman,—therein lies the curse of marriage. Not that it really protects her, but the very idea is so revolting, such an outrage and insult on life, so degrading to human dignity, as to forever condemn this parasitic institution.

It is like that other paternal arrangement—capitalism. It robs man of his birthright, stunts his growth, poisons his body, keeps him in ignorance, in poverty and dependence, and then institutes charities that thrive on the last vestige of man's self-respect.

The institution of marriage makes a parasite of woman, an absolute dependent. It incapacitates her for life's struggle, annihilates her social consciousness, paralyzes her imagination, and then imposes its gracious protection, which is in reality a snare, a travesty on human character.

If motherhood is the highest fulfillment of woman's nature, what other protection does it need save love and freedom? Marriage but defiles, outrages, and corrupts her fulfillment. Does it not say to woman, Only when you follow me shall you bring forth life? Does it not condemn her to the block, does it not degrade and shame her if she refuses to buy her right to motherhood by selling herself? Does not marriage only sanction motherhood, even though conceived in hatred, in compulsion? Yet, if motherhood be of free choice, of love, of ecstasy, of defiant passion, does it not place a crown of thorns upon an innocent head and carve in letters of blood the hideous epithet, Bastard? Were marriage to contain all the virtues claimed for it, its crimes against motherhood would exclude it forever from the realm of love.

Love, the strongest and deepest element in all life, the harbinger of hope, of joy, of ecstasy; love, the defier of all laws, of all conventions; love, the freest, the most powerful moulder of human destiny; how can such an all-compelling force be synonymous with that poor little State and Church-begotten weed, marriage?

Free love? As if love is anything but free! Man has bought brains, but all the millions in the world have failed to buy love. Man has subdued bodies, but all the power on earth has been unable to subdue love. Man has conquered whole nations, but all his armies could not conquer love. Man has chained and fettered the spirit, but he has been utterly helpless before love. High on a throne, with all the splendor and pomp his gold can command, man is yet poor and desolate, if love passes him by. And if it stays, the poorest hovel is radiant with warmth, with life and color. Thus love has the magic power to make of a beggar a king. Yes, love is free; it can dwell in no other atmosphere. In freedom it gives itself unreservedly, abundantly, completely. All the laws on the statutes, all the courts in the universe, cannot tear it from the soil, once love has taken root. If, however, the soil is sterile, how can marriage make it bear fruit? It is like the last desperate struggle of fleeting life against death.

Love needs no protection; it is its own protection. So long as love begets life no child is deserted, or hungry, or famished for the want of affection. I know this to be true. I know women who became mothers in freedom by the men they loved. Few children in wedlock enjoy the care, the protection, the devotion free motherhood is capable of bestowing.

The defenders of authority dread the advent of a free motherhood, lest it will rob them of their prey. Who would fight wars? Who would create wealth? Who would make the policeman, the jailer, if woman were to refuse the indiscriminate breeding of children? The race, the race! shouts the king, the president, the capitalist, the priest. The race must be preserved, though woman be degraded to a mere machine,—and the marriage institution is our only safety valve against the pernicious sex-awakening of woman. But in vain these frantic efforts to maintain a state of bondage. In vain, too, the edicts of the Church, the mad attacks of rulers, in vain even the arm of the law. Woman no longer wants to be a party to the production of a race of sickly, feeble, decrepit, wretched human beings, who have neither the strength nor moral courage to throw off the yoke of poverty and slavery. Instead she desires fewer and better children, begotten and reared in love and through free choice; not by compulsion, as marriage imposes. Our pseudo-moralists have yet to learn the deep sense of responsibility toward the child, that love in freedom has awakened in the breast of woman. Rather would she forego forever the glory of motherhood than bring forth life in an atmosphere that breathes only destruction and death. And if she does become a mother, it is to give to the child the deepest and best her being can yield. To grow with the child is her motto; she knows that in that manner alone can she help build true manhood and womanhood.

Ibsen must have had a vision of a free mother, when, with a master stroke, he portrayed Mrs. Alving. She was the ideal mother because she had outgrown marriage and all its horrors, because she had broken her chains, and set her spirit free to soar until it returned a personality, regenerated and strong. Alas, it was too late to rescue her life's joy, her Oswald; but not too late to realize that love in freedom is the only condition of a beautiful life. Those who, like Mrs. Alving, have paid with blood and tears for their spiritual awakening, repudiate marriage as an imposition, a shallow, empty mockery. They know, whether love last but one brief span of time or for eternity, it is the only creative, inspiring, elevating basis for a new race, a new world.

In our present pygmy state love is indeed a stranger to most people. Misunderstood and shunned, it rarely takes root; or if it does, it soon withers and dies. Its delicate fiber can not endure the stress and strain of the daily grind. Its soul is too complex to adjust itself to the slimy woof of our social fabric. It weeps and moans and suffers with those who have need of it, yet lack the capacity to rise to love's summit.

Some day, some day men and women will rise, they will reach the mountain peak, they will meet big and strong and free, ready to receive, to partake, and to bask in the golden rays of love. What fancy, what imagination, what poetic genius can foresee even approximately the potentialities of such a force in the life of men and women. If the world is ever to give birth to true companionship and oneness, not marriage, but love will be the parent.

SOURCES

Goldman, Emma. "Marriage and Love." In *Anarchism and Other Essays*, 233–45. New York: Mother Earth, 1910.

———. "Minorities versus Majorities." In *Anarchism and Other Essays*, 75–84. New York: Mother Earth, 1910.

———. "A New Declaration of Independence." *Mother Earth* 4, no. 5 (July 1909): 137–38.

NOTES

Chapter opening photo: Emma Goldman's mugshot, September 1901. She was arrested because authorities claimed that one of her lectures had inspired President William McKinley's assassin, Leon Czolgosz. She was interrogated and released. Library of Congress, Prints & Photographs Division, LC-B2-127-11.

1. Goldman quotes Dr. Thomas Stockmann in Norwegian playwright Henrik Ibsen's *An Enemy of the People* (1882), act IV.
2. Spanish anarchist, freethinker, and education reformer Francisco Ferrer i Guàrdia (1859–1909) founded the Escuela Moderna in Barcelona, which emphasized anarchism, secularism, rationalism, scientific observation, and self-reliance. In 1909, after being falsely charged with orchestrating Barcelona's "Tragic Week" (a violent clash between anarchists, republicans, socialists, and the Spanish army), Ferrer was summarily tried and executed.
3. Wendell Phillips (1811–1884) was a Bostonian attorney, orator, abolitionist, and advocate for Native Americans. The speech Goldman quotes is on Irish political reformer Daniel O'Connell, delivered at an O'Connell Celebration held in Boston on August 6, 1870.
4. European folk heroes and leaders of peasants' revolts.
5. [Author's footnote.] The intellectuals.

6. A slight misquotation of American transcendentalist Ralph Waldo Emerson (1803–1882) in "Considerations by the Way," an essay from his *The Conduct of Life* (1860).
7. Edward Carpenter (1844–1929) was an English philosopher, poet, anthologist, animal rights activist, gay rights activist, and friend of poets Walt Whitman and Rabindranath Tagore.

Charlotte Forten Grimké

1837–1914

CHARLOTTE FORTEN GRIMKÉ was born into a wealthy African American abolitionist family in Philadelphia. She was an influential activist, educator, and writer and is best known for the five volumes of posthumously published journals she wrote in 1854–64 and 1885–92. Forten Grimké was a member of the Salem Female Anti-Slavery Society and helped found the Colored Women's League in Washington, DC, and the National Association of Colored Women. She wrote poetry and essays throughout her life, including "Life on the Sea Islands," which is based on her experience teaching formerly enslaved children on the Union-occupied coastal sea islands of South Carolina during the Civil War.

From *The Journal of Charlotte L. Forten* (1854)

May 25, 1854. Did not intend to write this evening, but have just heard of something that is worth recording;—something which must ever rouse in the mind of every true friend of liberty and humanity, feelings of the deepest indignation and sorrow. Another fugitive from bondage has been arrested; a poor man, who for two short months has trod the soil and breathed the air of the "Old Bay State," was arrested like a criminal in the streets of her capital, and is now kept strictly guarded,[1]—a double police force is required, the military are in readiness; and all this done to prevent a man, whom God has created in his own image, from regaining that freedom with which, he, in common with every human being, is endowed. I can only hope and pray most earnestly that Boston will not again disgrace herself by sending him back to a bondage worse than death; or rather that she will redeem herself from the disgrace which his arrest alone has brought upon her. [. . .]

May 26, 1854. Had a conversation with Miss Shepard about slavery; she is, as I thought, thoroughly opposed to it, but does not agree with me in thinking that the churches and ministers are generally supporters of the infamous system; I believe it firmly. Mr. Barnes, one of the most prominent of the Philadelphia clergy, who does not profess to be an abolitionist, has declared his belief that "the American church is the bulwark of slavery." Words cannot express all that I feel; all that is felt by the friends of Freedom, when thinking of this great obstacle to the removal of slavery from our land. Alas! that it should be so.—I was much disappointed in not seeing the eclipse, which, it was expected would be the most entire that has taken place for years; but the weather was rainy, and the sky obscured by clouds; so after spending half the afternoon on the roof of the house in eager expectation, I saw nothing; heard since that the sun made his appearance for a minute or two, but I was not fortunate enough to catch even that momentary glimpse of him. [. . .]

May 27, 1854. [. . .] Returned home, read the Anti-Slavery papers, and then went down to the depot to meet father; he had arrived in Boston early in the morning, regretted very much that he had not reached there the evening before to attend the great meeting at Faneuil Hall. He says that the excitement in Boston is very great; the trial of the poor man takes place on Monday. We scarcely dare to think of what may be the result; there seems to be nothing too bad for these Northern tools of slavery to do.

May 30, 1854. Rose very early and was busy until nine o'clock; then, at Mrs. Putnam's urgent request, went to keep store for her while she went to Boston to attend the [New England] Anti-Slavery Convention. I was very anxious to go, and will certainly do so to-morrow; the arrest of the alleged fugitive will give additional interest to the meetings, I should think. His trial is still going on and I can scarcely think of anything else; read again today as most suitable to my feelings and to the times, "The Runaway Slave at Pilgrim's Point," by Elizabeth B. Browning; how powerfully it is written! how earnestly and touchingly does the writer portray the bitter anguish of the poor fugitive as she thinks over all the wrongs and sufferings that she has endured, and of the sin to which tyrants have driven her but which they alone must answer for! It seems as if no one could read this poem without having his sympathies roused to the utmost in behalf of the oppressed.—After a long conversation with my friends on their return, on this all-absorbing subject, we separated for the night, and I went to bed, weary and sad.

May 31, 1854. [. . .] Sarah[2] and I went to Boston in the morning. Everything was much quieter—outwardly than we expected, but still much real indignation and excitement prevail. We walked past the Court-House, which is now lawlessly converted into a prison, and filled with soldiers, some of whom were looking from the windows, with an air of insolent authority which made my blood boil, while I felt the strongest contempt for their cowardice and servility. We went to the meeting, but the best speakers were absent, engaged in the most arduous and untiring efforts in behalf of the poor fugitive; but though we missed the glowing eloquence of Phillips, Garrison, and Parker, still there were excellent speeches made, and our hearts responded to the exalted sentiments of Truth and Liberty which were uttered. The exciting intelligence which occasionally came in relation to the trial, added fresh zeal to the speakers, of whom Stephen Foster and his wife were the principal. The latter addressed, in the most eloquent language, the women present, entreating them to urge their husbands and brothers to action, and also to give their aid on all occasions in our just and holy cause.—I did not see father the whole day; he, of course, was deeply interested in the trial.—Dined at Mr. Garrison's;[3] his wife is one of the loveliest persons I have ever seen, worthy of such a husband. At the table, I watched earnestly the expression of that noble face, as he spoke beautifully in support of the non-resistant principles to which he has kept firm; he is indeed the very highest Christian spirit, to which I cannot hope to reach, however, for I believe in "resistance to tyrants," and would fight for liberty until death. We came home in the evening, and felt sick at heart as we passed through the streets of Boston on our way to the depot, seeing the military as they rode along, ready at any time to prove themselves the minions of the south.

June 1, 1854. [. . .] The trial is over at last; the commissioner's decision will be given to-morrow. We are all in the greatest suspense; what will that decision be? Alas! that any one should have the power to decide the right of a fellow being to himself! It is thought by many that he will be acquitted of the great crime of leaving a life of bondage, as the legal evidence is not thought sufficient to convict him. But it is only too probable that they will sacrifice him to propitiate the South, since so many at the North dared oppose the passage of the infamous [Kansas-]Nebraska Bill.—Miss Putnam was carried this evening. Mr. Frothingham performed the ceremony, and in his prayer alluded touchingly to the events of this week; he afterwards in conversation with the bridegroom, (Mr. Gilliard), spoke in the most feeling manner about this case;—his sympathies are all on the right side. The wedding was a pleasant one; the bride looked very lovely; and we enjoyed ourselves as much as possible in these exciting times. It is impossible to be happy now.

June 2, 1854. Our worst fears are realized; the decision was against poor Burns, and he has been sent back to a bondage worse, a thousand times worse than death. Even an attempt at rescue was utterly impossible; the prisoner was completely surrounded by soldiers with bayonets fixed, a cannon loaded, ready to be fired at the slightest sign. To-day Massachusetts has again been disgraced; again she has shewed her submission to the Slave Power; and Oh! with what deep sorrow do we think of what will doubtless be the fate of that poor man, when he is again consigned to the horrors of Slavery. With what scorn must that government be regarded, which cowardly assembles thousands of soldiers to satisfy the demands of slaveholders; to deprive of his freedom a man, created in God's own image, whose sole offense is the color of his skin! And if resistance is offered to this outrage, these soldiers are to shoot down American citizens without mercy; and this by the express orders of a government which proudly boasts of being the freest in the world; this on the very soil where the Revolution of 1776 began; in sight of the battle-field, where thousands of brave men fought and died in opposing British tyranny, which was nothing compared with the American oppression to-day. In looking over my diary, I perceive that I did not mention that there was on the Friday night after the man's arrest, an attempt made to rescue him, but although it failed, on account of there not being men enough engaged in it, all honor should be given to those who bravely made the attempt. I can write no more. A cloud seems hanging over me, over all our persecuted race, which nothing can dispel.

SOURCE

Forten, Charlotte L. *The Journal of Charlotte L. Forten*, edited by Ray Allen Billington, 34–37. New York: Dryden, 1953. Reproduced with permission from the Francis James Grimke Papers, Moorland-Spingarn Research Center, Howard University.

NOTES

1. The fugitive slave to whom Forten refers is Anthony Burns (1834–1862), whose arrest in Boston and return to slavery (under the racist Fugitive Slave Act of 1850) further galvanized Northern abolitionist sentiments. Two days after Burns's arrest, on May 26, 1854, a crowd of abolitionists attempted to forcibly free him during his trial, resulting in the death of a U.S. Marshal and a standoff between antislavery activists, police, and federal troops—but not in Burns's release. "Old Bay State" refers to Massachusetts.
2. A free Black woman born in Massachusetts, Sarah Parker Remond (1826–1894) was an abolitionist, orator, and member of the American Anti-Slavery Society.
3. William Lloyd Garrison (1805–1879) was an influential American journalist, abolitionist, suffragist, and founder-editor of the prominent Boston antislavery newspaper the *Liberator*, which he published between 1831 and 1865.

Frances E. W. Harper

1825–1911

FRANCES ELLEN WATKINS HARPER was born in Baltimore to two
free Black parents. She began her writing career by publishing poetry
in abolitionist periodicals, including Frederick Douglass's *North Star*.
Her activism began in 1854, when she was exiled from Maryland because of fugitive slave laws decreeing that even free Blacks like herself
could be arrested and sold into slavery. The success of her first public speech, "Education and the Elevation of the Colored Race," led to
a two-year speaking tour on behalf of the Maine Anti-Slavery Society.
Her lectures incorporated her poetry and prose and were revolutionary
in that they addressed racism, feminism, and classism as intersecting
issues. Harper formed alliances with feminist activists such as Susan B.
Anthony, spoke at the National Women's Rights Convention in 1866 (her
speech, "We Are All Bound Up Together," follows), and was elected vice
president of the National Association of Colored Women in 1897. Today
she is best known for her poem "Learning to Read" (1855) and her novel,
Iola Leroy, or Shadows Uplifted (1892).

We Are All Bound Up Together (1866)

I feel I am something of a novice upon this platform.[1] Born of a race whose
inheritance has been outrage and wrong, most of my life had been spent
in battling against those wrongs. But I did not feel as keenly as others,
that I had these rights, in common with other women, which are now
demanded. About two years ago, I stood within the shadows of my home.
A great sorrow had fallen upon my life. My husband had died suddenly,
leaving me a widow, with four children, one my own, and the others

stepchildren. I tried to keep my children together. But my husband died in debt; and before he had been in his grave three months, the administrator had swept the very milk crocks and wash tubs from my hands. I was a farmer's wife and made butter for the Columbus market; but what could I do, when they had swept all away? They left me one thing and that was a looking glass! Had I died instead of my husband, how different would have been the result! By this time he would have had another wife, it is likely; and no administrator would have gone into his house, broken up his home, and sold his bed, and taken away his means of support. I took my children in my arms, and went out to seek my living. While I was gone; a neighbor to whom I had once lent five dollars, went before a magistrate and swore that he believed I was a non-resident, and laid an attachment on my very bed. And I went back to Ohio with my orphan children in my arms, without a single feather bed in this wide world, that was not in the custody of the law. I say, then, that justice is not fulfilled so long as woman is unequal before the law.

We are all bound up together in one great bundle of humanity, and society cannot trample on the weakest and feeblest of its members without receiving the curse in its own soul. You tried that in the case of the negro. You pressed him down for two centuries; and in so doing you crippled the moral strength and paralyzed the spiritual energies of the white men of the country. When the hands of the black were fettered, white men were deprived of the liberty of speech and the freedom of the press. Society cannot afford to neglect the enlightenment of any class of its members. At the South, the legislation of the country was in behalf of the rich slaveholders, while the poor white man was neglected. What is the consequence to day? From that very class of neglected poor white men, comes the man who stands to-day, with his hand upon the helm of the nation. He fails to catch the watchword of the hour, and throws himself, the incarnation of meanness, across the pathway of the nation. My objection to Andrew Johnson is not that he has been a poor white man; my objection is that he keeps "poor whites" all the way through. (Applause.) That is the trouble with him.

This grand and glorious revolution which has commenced, will fail to reach its climax of success, until throughout the length and breadth of the American Republic, the nation shall be so color-blind, as to know no man by the color of his skin or the curl of his hair. It will then have no privileged class, trampling upon outraging the unprivileged classes, but will be then one great privileged nation, whose privilege will be to produce the loftiest manhood and womanhood that humanity can attain.

I do not believe that giving the woman the ballot is immediately going to cure all the ills of life. I do not believe that white women are dew-drops just exhaled from the skies. I think that like men they may be divided into three classes, the good, the bad, and the indifferent. The good would vote according to their convictions and principles; the bad, as dictated by prejudice or malice; and the indifferent will vote on the strongest side of the question, with the winning party.

You white women speak here of rights. I speak of wrongs. I, as a colored woman, have had in this country an education which has made me feel as if I were in the situation of Ishmael, my hand against every man, and every man's hand against me. Let me go to-morrow morning and take my seat in one of your street cars—I do not know that they will do it in New York, but they will in Philadelphia—and the conductor will put up his hand and stop the car rather than let me ride.

A Lady—They will not do that here.

Mrs. Harper—They do in Philadelphia. Going from Washington to Baltimore this Spring, they put me in the smoking car. (Loud Voices—"Shame.") Aye, in the capital of the nation, where the black man consecrated himself to the nation's defence, faithful when the white man was faithless, they put me in the smoking car! They did it once; but the next time they tried it, they failed; for I would not go in. I felt the fight in me; but I don't want to have to fight all the time. To-day I am puzzled where to make my home. I would like to make it in Philadelphia, near my own friends and relations. But if I want to ride in the streets of Philadelphia, they send me to ride on the platform with the driver. (Cries of "Shame.") Have women nothing to do with this? Not long since, a colored woman took her seat in an Eleventh Street car in Philadelphia, and the conductor stopped the car, and told the rest of the passengers to get out, and left the car with her in it alone, when they took it back to the station. One day I took my seat in a car, and the conductor came to me and told me to take another seat. I just screamed "murder." The man said if I was black I ought to behave myself. I knew that if he was white he was not behaving himself. Are there no wrongs to be righted?

In advocating the cause of the colored man, since the Dred Scott decision, I have sometimes said I thought the nation had touched bottom. But let me tell you there is a depth of infamy lower than that. It is when the nation, standing upon the threshold of a great peril, reached out its hands to a feebler race, and asked that race to help it, and when the peril was over, said, You are good enough for soldiers, but not good enough for citizens. When Judge Taney said that the men of my race had no rights which the white man was bound to respect, he had not seen the bones of the black man bleaching outside of Richmond. He had not seen the thinned ranks and the thickened graves of the Louisiana Second, a regiment which went into battle nine hundred strong, and came out with three hundred. He had not stood at Olustee and seen defeat and disaster crushing down the pride of our banner, until word was brought to Col. Hallowell, "The day is lost; go in and save it;" and black men stood in the gap, beat back the enemy, and saved your army. (Applause.)

We have a woman in our country who has received the name of "Moses," not by lying about it, but by acting out (applause)—a woman who has gone down into the Egypt of slavery and brought out hundreds of our people into liberty. The last time I saw that woman, her hands were swollen. That woman who had led one of Montgomery's most successful expeditions, who was brave enough and secretive enough to act as a scout for the American army, had her hands all swollen from a conflict with a brutal conductor, who undertook to eject her from her place. That woman, whose courage and bravery won a recognition from our army and from every black man in the land, is excluded from every thoroughfare of travel. Talk of giving women the ballot-box? Go on. It is a normal school, and the white women of this country need it. While there exists this brutal element in society which tramples upon the feeble and treads down the weak, I tell you that if there is any class of people who need to be lifted out of their airy nothings and selfishness, it is the white women of America. (Applause.)

Woman's Political Future (1894)

If before sin had cast its deepest shadows or sorrow had distilled its bitterest tears, it was true that it was not good for man to be alone, it is no less true, since the shadows have deepened and life's sorrows have increased, that the world has need of all the spiritual aid that woman can give for the social advancement and moral development of the human race. The tendency of the present age, with its restlessness, religious upheavals, failures, blunders, and crimes, is toward broader freedom, an increase of knowledge, the emancipation of thought, and a recognition of the brotherhood of man; in this movement woman, as the companion of man, must be a sharer. So close is the bond between man and woman that you can not raise one without lifting the other. The world can not move without woman's sharing in the movement, and to help give a right impetus to that movement is woman's highest privilege.

If the fifteenth century discovered America to the Old World, the nineteenth is discovering woman to herself. Little did Columbus imagine, when the New World broke upon his vision like a lovely gem in the coronet of the universe, the glorious possibilities of a land where the sun should be our engraver, the winged lightning our messenger, and steam our beast of burden. But as mind is more than matter, and the highest ideal always the true real, so to woman comes the opportunity to strive for richer and grander discoveries than ever gladdened the eye of the Genoese mariner.

Not the opportunity of discovering new worlds, but that of filling this old world with fairer and higher aims than the greed of gold and the lust of power, is hers. Through weary, wasting years men have destroyed, dashed in pieces, and overthrown, but to-day we stand on the threshold of woman's era, and woman's work is grandly constructive. In her hand are possibilities whose use or abuse must tell upon the political life of the nation, and send their influence for good or evil across the track of unborn ages.

As the saffron tints and crimson flushes of morn herald the coming day, so the social and political advancement which woman has already gained bears the promise of the rising of the full-orbed sun of emancipation. The result will be not to make home less happy, but society more holy; yet I do not think the mere extension of the ballot a panacea for all the ills of our national life. What we need to-day is not simply more voters, but better voters. To-day there are red-handed men in our republic, who walk unwhipped of justice, who richly deserve to exchange the ballot of the freeman for the wristlets of the felon; brutal and cowardly men, who torture, burn, and lynch their fellow-men, men whose defenselessness should be their best defense and their weakness an ensign of protection. More than the changing of institutions we need the development of a national conscience, and the upbuilding of national character. Men may boast of the aristocracy of blood, may glory in the aristocracy of talent, and be proud of the aristocracy of wealth, but there is one aristocracy which must ever outrank them all, and that is the aristocracy of character; and it is the women of a country who help to mold its character, and to influence if not determine its destiny; and in the political future of our nation woman will not have done what she could if she does not endeavor to have our republic stand foremost among the nations of the earth, wearing sobriety as a crown and righteousness as a garment and a girdle. In coming into her political estate woman will find a mass of illiteracy to be dispelled. If knowledge is power, ignorance is also power. The power that educates wickedness may manipulate and dash against the pillars of any state when they are undermined and honeycombed by injustice.

I envy neither the heart nor the head of any legislator who has been born to an inheritance of privileges, who has behind him ages of education, dominion, civilization, and Christianity, if he stands opposed to the passage of a national education bill, whose purpose is to secure education to the children of those who were born under the shadow of institutions which made it a crime to read.

To-day women hold in their hands influence and opportunity, and with these they have already opened doors which have been closed to others. By opening doors of labor woman has become a rival claimant for at least some of the wealth monopolized by her stronger brother. In the home she is the priestess, in society the queen, in literature she is a power, in legislative halls law-makers have responded to her appeals, and for her sake have humanized and liberalized their laws. The press has felt the impress of her hand. In the pews of the church she constitutes the majority; the pulpit has welcomed her, and in the school she has the blessed privilege of teaching children and youth. To her is apparently coming the added responsibility of political power; and what she now possesses should only be the means of preparing her to use the coming power for the glory of God and the good of mankind; for power without righteousness is one of the most dangerous forces in the world.

Political life in our country has plowed in muddy channels, and needs the infusion of clearer and cleaner waters. I am not sure that women are naturally so much better than men that they will clear the stream by the virtue of their womanhood; it is not through sex but through character that the best influence of women upon the life of the nation must be exerted.

I do not believe in unrestricted and universal suffrage for either men or women. I believe in moral and educational tests. I do not believe that the most ignorant and brutal man is better prepared to add value to the strength and durability of the government than the most cultured, upright, and intelligent woman. I do not think that willful ignorance should swamp earnest intelligence at the ballot-box, nor that educated wickedness, violence, and fraud should cancel the votes of honest men. The unsteady hands of a drunkard can not cast the ballot of a freeman. The hands of lynchers are too red with blood to determine the political character of the government for even four short years. The ballot in the hands of woman means power added to influence. How well she will use that power I can not foretell. Great evils stare us in the face that need to be throttled by the combined power of an upright manhood and an enlightened womanhood; and I know that no nation can gain its full measure of enlightenment and happiness if one-half of it is free and the other half is fettered. China compressed the feet of her women and thereby retarded the steps of her men. The elements of a nation's weakness must ever be found at the hearthstone.

More than the increase of wealth, the power of armies, and the strength of fleets is the need of good homes, of good fathers, and good mothers.

The life of a Roman citizen was in danger in ancient Palestine, and men had bound themselves with a vow that they would eat nothing until they had killed the Apostle Paul. Pagan Rome threw around that imperiled life a bulwark of living clay consisting of four hundred and seventy human hearts, and Paul was saved. Surely the life of the humblest American citizen should be as well protected in America as that of a Roman citizen was in heathen Rome. A wrong done to the weak should be an insult to the strong. Woman coming into her kingdom will find enthroned three great evils, for whose overthrow she should be as strong in a love of justice and humanity as the warrior is in his might. She will find intemperance sending its flood of shame, and death, and sorrow to the homes of men, a fretting leprosy in our politics, and a blighting curse in our social life; the social evil sending to our streets women whose laughter is sadder than their tears, who slide from the paths of sin and shame to the friendly shelter of the grave; and lawlessness enacting in our republic deeds over which angels might weep, if heaven knows sympathy.

How can any woman send petitions to Russia against the horrors of

Siberian prisons if, ages after the Inquisition has ceased to devise its tortures, she has not done all she could by influence, tongue, and pen to keep men from making bonfires of the bodies of real or supposed criminals?

O women of America! into your hands God has pressed one of the sublimest opportunities that ever came into the hands of the women of any race or people. It is yours to create a healthy public sentiment; to demand justice, simple justice, as the right of every race; to brand with everlasting infamy the lawless and brutal cowardice that lynches, burns, and tortures your own countrymen.

To grapple with the evils which threaten to undermine the strength of the nation and to lay magazines of powder under the cribs of future generations is no child's play.

Let the hearts of the women of the world respond to the song of the herald angels of peace on earth and good will to men. Let them throb as one heart unified by the grand and holy purpose of uplifting the human race, and humanity will breathe freer, and the world grow brighter. With such a purpose Eden would spring up in our path, and Paradise be around our way.

SOURCES

Harper, Frances Ellen Watkins. "We Are All Bound Up Together." In *Proceedings of the Eleventh Women's Rights Convention*, 45–48. New York: Robert J. Johnston, 1866.

———. "Woman's Political Future." In *The World's Congress of Representative Women: A Historical Resume for Popular Circulation of the World's Congress of Representative Women, Convened in Chicago on May 15, and adjourned on May 22, 1893, under the auspices of the Women's Branch of the World's Congress Auxiliary*, vol. 1, edited by May Wright Sewall, 433–37. Chicago: Rand, McNally and Company, 1894.

NOTE

1. Harper was one of a number of prominent speakers, including Susan B. Anthony, Elizabeth Cady Stanton, and Lucretia Mott, to address the convention.

Edmonia Goodelle Highgate

1844–1870

EDMONIA GOODELLE HIGHGATE was an African American educator, activist, and writer born in Syracuse, New York. She taught in several capacities, including educating newly freed people in the South. She cofounded the Louisiana Educational Relief Organization to raise funds for schools for Black children and gave lectures on abolition and education. In 1865 she began writing for the *Christian Recorder*, documenting conditions in the Reconstruction-era South, including an account of the New Orleans massacre of 1866, described in the first of the following selections. Highgate also contributed to the *American Missionary* and the *American Freedman*. She fell in love with a white man named John Henry Vosberg and died of a botched abortion at the age of twenty-six.

New Orleans Correspondence (1866)

Mr. Editor:—During a lull in the grand saturnalia of blood I write to you. Any reconstructionist who has fanatically believed Louisiana's loyalty, beyond doubt has had demonstration to the contrary which would convince the most incredulous. On Monday, the 30th ultimo, the friends of universal suffrage, including Michael Hahn, the ex-Governor, Dr. Dorstie, Revs. Jackson and Horton, also, one Mr. Judd, met in Convention, and endeavored to revive the Conventional measures of 1864.[1] They assembled in the Assembly Hall, Mechanics' Institute, only to be assailed by armed policemen, who shot into the crowd of colored men who gathered outside, killing and wounding white and colored as they chanced to be within the range of their shot. All of the mentioned persons were wounded, some of them mortally, beside over one hundred negroes, who were also, many of them taken to the Marine Hospital, and were humanely cared for by Dr. Harris, surgeon in charge, his faithful assistants, and the noble-hearted Madame Domortie.[2] Your correspondent did what she could of wound-dressing until near midnight. Some ten died, to say nothing of those who died in the workhouse, and were locked up in the several stations by the "policemen under orders," "all honorable men." One of the local preachers in St. James' Chapel was severely injured. There has been some equally unnecessary shooting of colored residents since the 30th, by our civil guard. For a day or two the city was under martial law, and we expected thorough justice from the Military Commission which was trying these rioters, but now civil power is supreme, and the revivers of the "'64 Convention" are considered "the disturbers of the public peace," and they are to be tried before a *civil* tribunal. That being the translation which our mayor gave Andy Johnson's telegram "to prevent the establishment of a new form of government here." He was literally obeyed, and so bloodshed and carnage have their sway, all save the bloodhounds, as they had six years ago! But we must have no better government, even though the proved loyalists desire it, and simply because the government would be "new." Dost thou forget, old Judas, that Freedom's and Justice's sway is as old as the heavens? Nor is New Orleans yet perfectly safe. The hunted non-recognized defenders of the Republic are yet threatened, and the creole fire in their veins burns—for what they syllable in a whisper—REVENGE—but it is as forcible as the serpent's hiss, and the portents are fearful. When unoffending people are treated like dogs while returning from their daily toil; even slaughtered in cool blood in their beds, and the school-building in which their offspring are instructed in Wisdom's ways is burned, as they tried to burn mine, may not this community expect retribution? The Crescent City is not alone in this display of the old spirit of rebellion. In Jackson, La., about two hundred miles from here, a gang, one of whom was a "*Justice of the Peace*," attempted the life of Mr. Geo. T. Ruby of Maine, because forsooth, as an agent of the Freedmen's Bureau, he attempted to establish a school in that community for the freed people. They beat, and were only deferred from killing this brave, trusty-colored educator, because they feared that some one of their party would *betray the secret of his death*. This party were brought before Judge Sherman, of the Military Commission of this city, and, after pleading "not guilty," were bailed $1,000 cash until November. In the mean time Mr. R is teaching steadily on, sublimely indifferent to the muttered threats against his life. We have some trusty men in the department and women, too, who "do and dare" for Freedom's cause. The estimable Rev. John Turner is on leave of absence from his charge for a few weeks. We need his calm, cheerful, powerful, executive arm in this disquieted region greatly.

E. GOODELLE H.

New Orleans, August 4th

On Horse Back—Saddle-Dash, No. 1 (1866)

Who that has taught school, the elementary branches year in and year out, don't know what teacher's *ennui* is? I always thought I did, but find that I have just found out. Here I am in the western interior of Louisiana trying with my might to instruct these very French, little and large creoles, in the simplest English, and in morals. But for my roan, I would break down as a harp unstrung; but as soon as day-school is out I am on his back, and off on a quick gallop for these grand old October woods. I took my first ride of six miles to a famous old spring, at which the rebel General Morton drank with his wretchedly demoralized command in their retreat after the battle of Shiloh. My horse, like every thing else here, was creole, and I am afraid rather *confederate* in his tendencies; for when I was feeling lost, almost to my surroundings in some meditations of an intensely union cast, he had the bad taste to get into a fence-leaping mood. Of course I conquered, and made myself mistress of the situation. Then I plunged into the thickest of the oak tree forest with its exquisite drapery of gray hanging moss. The old dame must have anticipated some children visitors, for she had swings ready made, formed of the thick interlaping vine-like branches, reaching from tree top to tree top all through these woods. What delightful order! Oh, if dear Henry D. Thoreau were here, wouldn't he go into a rhapsody! But he is here in spirit.

Nature's admiring children who perseveringly labor to know her secrets while in earth form, truly learn more after they "cross the river Jordan," and they hover around beautiful retreats. Yes, they are "ministering spirits." Then don't imagine me a modern spiritualist after the "affinity-seeking," "wife and husband leaving" strife. No, I detest "table rappings and crockery breaking," especially the last; for I have broken so much. But those who are of the same mind do coalesce whether in the spirit or out. Oh, what a cluster of scarlet blossoms! All negroes like red; so push on, pony, I must have those flowers! How I wish my Philadelphia friends had these! Why they are handsomer than either "fuchia's or bleeding heart." But I have left my botony in the city; so I can't trace their genera.

Oh, how independent one feels in the saddle! One thing, I can't imagine why one needs to wear such long riding skirts. They are so inconvenient when you have to ford streams or dash through briars. Oh, fashion, will no Emancipation Proclamation free us from thee!

My second ride was on an "American horse," so-called because he came from the North. Creole gents call northern horses *"American horses."* Really it is a compliment. They are so much more reliable than creole horses. One of the latter must have its own slow gait, like a mule's pace, or else run away on a wild gipsy chase.

Now for the matter in this saddle-dash. I had to keep off horse back for several days in order to recover from extreme fatigue and soreness, but my bay is at the door this glorious Saturday morning, and I am off till noon. Some rebel equestrians just passed, and fired four times almost in my face. But who is going to let grape[3] keep them off horse back or off duty? Hasn't He promised to keep His workers? "Then to doubt would be disloyal; to falter would be sin."

Oh! I forgot to say my roan did not understand English any better than my scholars do. When I said, "Whoa, pony," he would gallop. *Au revoir.*

I am home again from my canter. We passed through several cotton and corn-fields worked on shares. The former owners giving half what the crops yield to the hands in payment. Besides, there is five per cent tax levied to pay for the school privilege for the children of the hands. These men work well. Their employers say; "better than slaves did." But they work all day Sunday of their own accord on land they have rented; so anxious are they to get places of their own. Cotton is worth from 40 to 50 cents per pound here. One would soon get rich with one of these plantations. Oh! it is time for my night-school. Believe me, *Votre Amie Des Chevaux.*[4]

Oct. 13th, Vermillionville,
Lafayette Parish, La

SOURCES

Highgate, Edmonia Goodelle. "New Orleans Correspondence." *Christian Recorder*,
August 18, 1866, 1. Center for Research Libraries Global Resources Network.
———. "On Horse Back—Saddle-Dash, No. 1." *Christian Recorder*, November 3,
1866, 1. Center for Research Libraries Global Resources Network. All misspell-
ings are in the original.

NOTES

1. That is, the Louisiana Constitutional Convention of 1864. In July 1866, Louisiana Republicans reconvened the convention to protest the institution of black
codes in the state and to move to allow African American men to vote. The
suspicions and simmering racism of Democrats, many of them Confederate
veterans, resulted in a riot on July 30, culminating in the violent massacre of
forty-eight Republicans, forty-four of them African American.
2. Born free in Virginia, Louise De Mortie (1833–1867) was an African American
lecturer, singer, missionary, and advocate for Black children orphaned by the
U.S. Civil War. Just a year after Highgate's letter, De Mortie would die of yellow
fever in New Orleans, having managed and fundraised for the city's Colored
Orphans Home for several years.
3. Short for grapeshot, ammunition that consists of a collection of small round
shots packed together.
4. Your Friend of the Horses (French).

Harriet Jacobs

1813–1897

HARRIET JACOBS was born into slavery in Edenton, North Carolina. She was sexually harassed by her master and ran away in an attempt to get him to sell her children to their father. She hid for seven years in a tiny crawl space before she was finally able to escape to New York. Afterward, she worked as a nanny, joined up with abolitionist and feminist reformers, and helped found two schools for fugitive and freed slaves in the South. Her autobiography, *Incidents in the Life of a Slave Girl* (1861), was rediscovered in the civil rights era but thought to be fiction until it was authenticated in the 1980s. It is now considered a classic in the slave narrative genre. "Letter from a Fugitive Slave" is Jacobs's first published work, a response to former First Lady Julia Gardiner Tyler's defense of slavery, "The Women of England vs. the Women of America."

Letter from a Fugitive Slave (1853)

To the Editor of The N.Y. Tribune[1]

SIR: Having carefully read your paper for some months I became very much interested in some of the articles and comments written on Mrs. Tyler's Reply to the Ladies of England. Being a slave myself, I could not have felt otherwise. Would that I could write an article worthy of notice in your columns. As I never enjoyed the advantages of an education, therefore I could not study the arts of reading and writing, yet poor as it may be, I had rather give it from my own hand, than have it said that I employed others to do it for me. The truth can never be told so well through the second and third person as from yourself. But I am straying from the question. As Mrs. Tyler and her friend Bhains were so far used up, that he could not explain what those peculiar circumstances were, let one whose peculiar sufferings justifies her in explaining it for Mrs. Tyler.

I was born a slave, reared in the Southern hot-bed until I was the mother of two children, sold at the early age of two and four years old. I have been hunted through all of the Northern States, but no, I will not tell you of my own suffering—no, it would harrow up my soul, and defeat the object that I wish to pursue. Enough—the dregs of that bitter cup have been my bounty for many years.

And as this is the first time that I ever took my pen in hand to make such an attempt, you will not say that it is fiction, for had I the inclination I have neither the brain or talent to write it. But to this very peculiar circumstance under which slaves are sold.

My mother was held as property by a maiden lady; when she married, my younger sister was in her fourteenth year, whom they took into the family. She was as gentle as she was beautiful. Innocent and guileless child, the light of our desolate hearth! But oh, my heart bleeds to tell you of the misery and degradation she was forced to suffer in slavery. The monster who owned her had no humanity in his soul. The most sincere affection that his heart was capable of, could not make him faithful to his beautiful and wealthy bride the short time of three months, but every stratagem was used to seduce my sister. Mortified and tormented beyond endurance, this child came and threw herself on her mother's bosom, the only place where she could seek refuge from her persecutor; and yet she could not protect her child that she bore into the world. On that bosom with bitter tears she told her troubles, and entreated her mother to save her. And oh, Christian mothers! you that have daughters of your own, can you think of your sable sisters without offering a prayer to that God who created all in their behalf! My poor mother, naturally high-spirited, smarting under what she considered as the wrongs and outrages which her child had to bear, sought her master, entreating him to spare her child. Nothing could exceed his rage at this what he called impertinence. My mother was dragged to jail, there remained twenty-five days, with Negro traders to come in as they liked to examine her, as she was offered for sale. My sister was told that she must yield, or never expect to see her mother again. There were three younger children; on no other condition could she be restored to them, without the sacrifice of one. That child gave herself up to her master's bidding, to save one that was dearer to her than life itself. And can you, Christian, find it in your heart to despise her? Ah, no! not even Mrs. Tyler; for though we believe that the vanity of a name would lead her to bestow her hand where her heart could never go with it, yet, with all her faults and follies, she is nothing more than a woman. For if her domestic hearth is surrounded with slaves, ere long before this she has opened her eyes to the evils of slavery, and that the mistress as well as the slave must submit to the indignities and vices imposed on them by their lords of body and soul. But to one of those peculiar circumstances.

At fifteen, my sister held to her bosom an innocent offspring of her guilt and misery. In this way she dragged a miserable existence of two years, between the fires of her mistress's jealousy and her master's brutal passion. At seventeen, she gave birth to another helpless infant, heir to all the evils of slavery. Thus life and its sufferings was meted out to her until her twenty-first year. Sorrow and suffering has made its ravages upon her— she was less the object to be desired by the fiend who had crushed her to the earth; and as her children grew, they bore too strong a resemblance to him who desired to give them no other inheritance save Chains and Handcuffs, and in the dead hour of the night, when this young, deserted mother lay with her little ones clinging around her, little dreaming of the dark and inhuman plot that would be carried out into execution before another dawn, and when the sun rose on God's beautiful earth, that broken-hearted mother was far on her way to the capitol of Virginia. That day should have refused her light to so disgraceful and inhuman an act in your boasted country of Liberty. Yet, reader, it is true, those two helpless children were the sons of one of your sainted Members in Congress; that agonized mother, his victim and slave. And where she now is God only knows, who has kept a record on high of all that she has suffered on earth.

And, you would exclaim, Could not the master have been more merciful to his children? God is merciful to all of his children, but it is seldom that a slaveholder has any mercy for h[i]s slave child. And you will believe it when I tell you that mother and her children were sold to make room for another sister, who was now the age of that mother when she entered the family. And this selling appeased the mistress's wrath, and satisfied her desire for revenge, and made the path more smooth for her young rival at first. For there is a strong rivalry between a handsome mulatto girl and a jealous and faded mistress, and her liege lord sadly neglects his wife or doubles his attentions, to save him being suspected by his wife. Would you not think that Southern Women had cause to despise that Slavery which forces them to bear so much deception practiced by their husbands? Yet all this is true, for a slaveholder seldom takes a white mistress, for she is an expensive commodity, not as submissive as he would like to have her, but more apt to be tyrannical; and when his passion seeks another object, he must leave her in quiet possession of all the gewgaws that she has sold herself for. But not so with his poor slave victim, that he has robbed of everything that can make life desirable; she must be torn from the little that is left to bind her to life, and sold by her seducer and master, caring not where, so that it puts him in possession of enough to purchase another victim. And such are the peculiar circumstances of American Slavery—of all the evils in God's sight the most to be abhorred.

Perhaps while I am writing this you too, dear Emily, may be on your way to the Mississippi River, for those peculiar circumstances occur every day in the midst of my poor oppressed fellow-creatures in bondage. And oh ye Christians, while your arms are extended to receive the oppressed of all nations, while you exert every power of your soul to assist them to raise funds, put weapons in their hands, tell them to return to their own country to slay every foe until they break the accursed yoke from off their necks, not buying and selling; this they never do under any circumstances. But while Americans do all this, they forget the millions of slaves they have at home, bought and sold under very peculiar circumstances.

And because one friend of a slave has dared to tell of their wrongs you would annihilate her. But in Uncle Tom's Cabin she has not told the half.

Would that I had one spark from her store house of genius and talent I would tell you of my own sufferings—I would tell you of wrongs that Hungary has never inflicted, nor England ever dreamed of in this free country where all nations fly for liberty, equal rights and protection under your stripes and stars. It should be stripes and scars, for they go along with Mrs. Tyler's peculiar circumstances, of which I have told you only one.

A FUGITIVE SLAVE.

SOURCE

Jacobs, Harriet. "Letter from a Fugitive Slave." *New York Daily Tribune*, June 21, 1853, 6. *Chronicling America: Historic American Newspapers*, Library of Congress, https://chroniclingamerica.loc.gov/lccn/sn83030213/1853-06-21/ed-1/seq-6/.

NOTE

Chapter opening photo: The only known photograph of Harriet Jacobs, 1894.

1. The original publication of this letter is preceded by the following editorial note: "We publish the subjoined communication exactly as written by the author, with the exception of corrections in punctuation and spelling, and the omission of one or two passages."

Rebecca Cox Jackson

1795–1871

REBECCA COX JACKSON was born into a free Black family in Horns-
town, Pennsylvania. During a thunderstorm in 1830, she experienced
a religious awakening and thereafter had spiritual visions and supernatural experiences. She amassed a following of both men and women
and preached controversial views on holiness, including the necessity
of celibacy, even within marriage. This caused friction that ended not
only her marriage but also her relationships with her brother and the
A.M.E. Church. Jackson became an itinerant preacher and eventually
joined a New York Shaker community. Unsatisfied with their lack of
outreach to African Americans, Jackson and her lifelong companion
and protégé, Rebecca Perot, founded a Black Shaker community in
Philadelphia. After Jackson's death, Perot assumed the name of Mother
Rebecca Jackson and leadership of the community. Jackson's autobiography, *Gifts of Power*, was not published until the 1980s.

From *Gifts of Power* (ca. 1830–1864)

[*ON SPONTANEOUSLY LEARNING TO READ*]

A remarkable providence of God's love for me. After I received the blessing of God, I had a great desire to read the Bible. I am the only child of my
mother that had not learning. And now, having the charge of my brother
and his six children to see to, and my husband, and taking in sewing for
a living, I saw no way that I could now get learning without my brother
would give me one hour's lesson at night after supper or before he went to
bed. His time was taken up as well as mine. So I spoke to him about it. He
said he would give me one or two lessons, I being so desirous to learn. [He

was a tolerable scholar, so that he was able to teach his own children at home, without sending them to school. For a time, he fulfilled the offices of seven men in the Methodist church. And when he ceased from this, he worked hard and earned his bread by the sweat of his brow.][1] And my brother so tired when he would come home that he had not power so to do, and it would grieve me. Then I would pray to God to give me power over my feelings that I might not think hard of my brother. Then I would be comforted.

So I went to get my brother to write my letters and to read them. So he was awriting a letter in answer to one he had just read. I told him what to put in. Then I asked him to read. He did. I said, "Thee has put in more than I told thee." This he done several times. I then said, "I don't want thee to word my letter. I only want thee to write it." Then he said, "Sister, thee is the hardest one I ever wrote for!" These words, together with the manner that he had wrote my letter, pierced my soul like a sword. [As there was nothing I could do for him or his children that I thought was too hard for me to do for their comfort, I felt hurt, when he refused me these little things. And at this time,] I could not keep from crying. And these words were spoken in my heart, "Be faithful, and the time shall come when you can write." These words were spoken in my heart as though a tender father spoke them. My tears were gone in a moment.

One day I was sitting finishing a dress in haste and in prayer. This word was spoken in my mind, "Who learned the first man on earth?" "Why, God." "He is unchangeable, and if He learned the first man to read, He can learn you." I laid down my dress, picked up my Bible, ran upstairs, opened it, and kneeled down with it pressed to my breast, prayed earnestly to Almighty God if it was consisting to His holy will, to learn me to read His holy word. And when I looked on the word, I began to read. And when I found I was reading, I was frightened—then I could not read one word. I closed my eyes again in prayer and then opened my eyes, began to read. So I done, until I read the chapter. I came down. "Samuel, I can read the Bible." "Woman, you are agoing crazy!" "Praise the God of heaven and of earth, I can read His holy word!" Down I sat and read through. And it was in James. So Samuel praised the Lord with me. When my brother came to dinner I told him, "I can read the Bible! I have read a whole chapter!" "One thee has heard the children read, till thee has got it by heart." What a wound that was to me, to think he would make so light of a gift of God! But I did not speak. Samuel reproved him and told him all about it. He sat down very sorrowful. I then told him, "I had a promise, the day thee wrote my letter to sister Diges, that if I was faithful I would see the day when I can write." [I repeated this conditional promise to him at the time and said then "I will write thee a letter." He said, he had no doubt of it. This soon after took place.] So I tried, took my Bible daily and praying and read until I could read anywhere. The first chapter that I read I never could know it after that day. I only knowed it was in James, but what chapter I never can tell.

Oh how thankful I feel for this unspeakable gift of Almighty God to me! Oh may I make a good use of it all the days of my life!

[ON THE EXPERIENCE OF DYING]

I always had a dread on my mind about coming in contact with death. There seemed to be something in it fearful and frightful. I had witnessed the death of many, even little children. So I now felt to be coming to that trying scene. I felt I had done all that God required at my hand. I felt no condemnation as it regarded my future happiness. Therefore, I did not want to be interrupted, but to die in peace.

After encouraging Samuel to be faithful, then taking leave of him in prayer, I left, passing out at my feet. I went directly west, I turned neither to the right nor to the left. I passed through all substance—nothing impeded my way. I went a straight course, came down to a river. It run north and south, I stood on the bank. I then thought, "Here is Jordan—here I have got to suffer." I found, when I came out of the body it was with all ease and without any suffering, so I now found I had this suffering to go through.

As I stood on the bank looking across, I saw a large mountain, a path which went up from this river on to the top of this mountain. It was very narrow. I saw travelers going up this path. Some was further up the path than others [for two could not walk in it abreast]. They all walked as if they were tired.

On the south side of this mountain was a great deal of ice in great flakes. In the midst of it was a man with a boat, atrying to get it out. I thought he was the one that had taken them over and he was acoming for me. I seen his eyes were fastening upon me. And while I thus thought, I heard a voice from above say, "You must go around the Mediterranean first." This voice sounded over my right shoulder. It was a man's voice. I turned to go down this Jordan, which was south—I thought that was the way to the Mediterranean—but I was turned right around the way from whence I came and returned home.

I reentered my body. Samuel was weeping over me and said, "You have been dead some time." I spoke to him and then left as before. This I did three times, saw all and heard all, as at the first, spoke each time.

Then I passed out at my chest, going right through the ceiling and the roof. About twelve feet above the roof there was a cluster of angels on a cloud. They took me up a great height in the air, gave me much instruction, brought me back to the same place. Then I returned to the house, reentered my body, spoke to Samuel and he to me. This I done three times. The last time, when I returned, I found Samuel in prayer, crying to God in the bitterness of his spirit to only spare me a little longer. I spoke. He sprang to his feet. I said, "Turn me over." "Why, can you be turned?" "Yes. And I can use my right side." "Praise the God of heaven!" was his reply. So he turned me over. I went into sweet sleep and slept till morning.

Now, when my spirit left my body I was as sensible of it as I would be now to go out of this house and come in it again. All my senses and feeling and understanding was in my spirit. I found my body was no more than a chair to me, or any other piece of thing. The same fear I had in the body before my spirit left, I found I had when I stood on the banks of Jordan, and all that I had ever heard about Jordan rushed into my mind. I then saw the icy, chilly waters of this Jordan I had heard of from my childhood. And there I stood, under as much feeling and suffering of mind as I was able to endure. And when I heard I was to go around the Mediterranean first—why, my sorrows increased, for I had never heard that we had to come into contact with this Mediterranean Sea in death. And here I was plainly told that I must go around the Mediterranean first, which showed me that after I had went around this Mediterranean, I had to go across this Jordan. I saw thousands going up this path which had crossed, and they looked tired enough! And then this great mountain they had to ascend. I saw nothing that looked like heaven.

I went three times to this Jordan, three times into the air with these angels. This made six times I left the body. These were all new scenes to me. [Thus it pleased God to show me the difference between the man and the mold, in the beginning of my pilgrimage, for this was in the summer of 1831.] This was on a Sunday night.

[ON BEING A FREEDWOMAN IN A LAND OF SLAVERY]

Then I woke and found the burden of my people heavy upon me. I had borne a burden of my people for twelve years, but now it was double, and I cried unto the Lord and prayed this prayer, "Oh, Lord God of Hosts, if Thou art going to make me useful to my people, either temporal or spiritual,—for temporally they are held by their white brethren in bondage, not as bound man and bound woman, but as bought beasts, and spiritually they are held by their ministers, by the world, the flesh, and the devil. And if these are not a people in bondage, where are there any on the earth?—Oh, my Father and my God, make me faith[f]ul in this Thy work and give me wisdom that I may comply with Thy whole will."

[ON RECEIVING THE CALL TO PROPHESY]

March the 26th, 1843. As I got out of bed these words were spoken to me, "I have chosen thee to me, as I did Jeremiah and Ezekiel to speak to the house of Israel. So have I chosen thee to speak to this people. Be careful how thou does it." [Truly I can say, that was a word in time, and the Lord spoke it, for this has been a day of days in the battle of the Lord, but the Lord headed the army and God was glorified, and man abased.] I then entreated the Lord to give me understanding, power and wisdom and knowledge to enable me to do His holy will in all things, at all times, under all conditions, and to take the fear of man from me, and put His fear always before me that I may be able. And this was said to me at the same time, "Thou shall not speak to them. Only the words that I give thee." And in obedience to this word, it seemed that nothing was hid from my spirit eye, neither by night nor day, neither when I was asleep nor awake.

SOURCE

Jackson, Rebecca Cox. *Gifts of Power: The Writings of Rebecca Jackson, Black Visionary, Shaker Eldress*, edited by Jean McMahon Humez, 107–8, 111–12, 181–84. Amherst: University of Massachusetts Press, 1987. Reprinted by permission, the University of Massachusetts Press.

NOTE

1. Bracketed sections indicate manuscripts included by Alonzo G. Hollister (Shaker leader and early compiler of Cox Jackson's autobiography). These passages are not in Cox Jackson's handwriting and therefore may not reflect her original wording.

Belva Lockwood

1830–1917

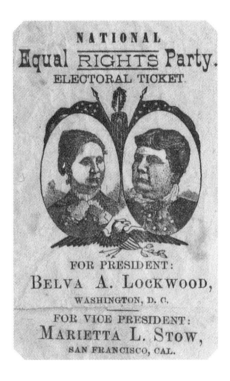

BELVA LOCKWOOD was a white attorney, politician, suffragist, and educator born in Royalton, New York. As headmistress of Lockport Union School, she expanded female students' curriculum to include courses that were normally reserved for young men. When she was in her forties, Lockwood fought to obtain her law degree when few schools would accept women. In 1880, she became the first female attorney to argue a case before the U.S. Supreme Court. She wrote and lobbied for women's rights legislation and ran for president in 1884 and 1888. She was the candidate of the National Equal Rights Party, which had nominated Victoria Woodhull for president in 1872. Lockwood was also an activist for peace, as the following selection shows.

The Growth of Peace Principles (1895)

Address delivered before the National Council of Women in Washington, Thursday evening, February 28th, [1895].

The woman of to-day needs both knowledge and wisdom, and this the Council is designed to develop. It must be a source of congratulation to all women that the Council idea has so broadened as to take into its fold the Jew and the Gentile; Catholic and Protestant; the affiliators with the Grand Army of the Republic; the Peace Union and the Red Cross.

Peace is a matter of education more largely than of legislation; although the latter is necessary.

The history of mankind has been one of war from the slaying of Abel in the Garden of Eden until the present time; and, strangely enough, the religious wars of the past, so contrary to the spirit of Christ and his teachings, have been the bitterest and most prolonged.

Mahomet thought to convert his fellows to his religious creed by making war upon them, ignoring the fact that the essential element of religion is love. One of the principal commandments contained in the Koran is "War against the infidel"; and the infidel has been in all ages, the man who does not believe as we do.

In the twelfth century the wars against heretics caused the death of millions of professed Christians, whose tenets did not precisely agree with those of their persecutors. During the reign of terror, which succeeded the horrid edicts of the Inquisition, wives testified against their husbands, and husbands against their wives; parents against their children, and children against their parents; until not only families, but communities were dismembered, and commerce ruined.

The slaughter of five thousand Huguenots in Paris and thirty thousand in the Provinces was the result of a religious war between Catholicism and Protestantism. In the three years of war which followed the Edict of Nantes, France is said to have lost nearly one million of inhabitants.

The Thirty Years' War in England during the same century had its origin in the same religious dissensions and jealousies; it created a bitterness between Catholics and Protestants, between Englishmen and Frenchmen, which two hundred years of peace have failed to eradicate, and which has recently found an outcropping in our own country in the birth of the A.P.A. It is the real cause of the lack of success of the movement for Home Rule in Ireland.

The Franco-Prussian War cost France besides the loss of territory five thousand million francs and five hundred thousand men. It engendered a hatred between Frenchmen and Germans that another century will not eradicate.

Our own civil war cost our nation one million men and three billion dollars, besides the waste of valuable records and countless treasure, and $145,000,000 yearly in pensions. It laid the foundation of the countless financial disasters of 1895, and created sectional prejudices and hatreds that will not entirely die out during the next fifty years.

The writers of war histories keep up this race and sectional prejudice by writing each from his own party standpoint. They suppress many facts, and belittle the strength, courage and magnanimity of their opponents, and too often color and magnify the usually very insignificant cause of the war itself. It is doubtful if a candid person, entirely unacquainted with the facts, who should read English history with an account of the seven years' war of the Revolution, and then read our American history of the same events, could believe that they related to the same events. The same may be said in reference to the historians of the Franco-German war or of our war of the Rebellion.

But we do not stop by putting these highly colored and erroneous histories into our libraries for the edification and instruction of mature readers. They are too often condensed into school books for the instruction of the young, who imbibe the hatreds and prejudices of ourselves and of our ancestors. We have ten statues to the soldier where we have one to the philanthropist.

A recital of their wars constitutes the largest portion of the history of Christian nations; while the strides that they have made in commerce, in manufactures, and the arts, constitute the least.

The love of home and country are undoubtedly meritorious attributes, and self-sacrifice for country has always been held in high esteem, but it is but another form of self-love, and it is quite possible to make this love not only excessive, but unjust. There is another and a higher love—the great love of humanity, of peace, of justice and equality—that should be taught to our youth as well. To die for one's country has been usually considered the highest order of patriotism; but to live for one's country is something higher.

We have another potent influence at work to foment war, and that is the war correspondent, and it is painful to see how his blood-curdling narratives stir up the war spirit in our young men.

By our Constitution we are pledged to neutrality. We do not need to increase our territory, and have publicly declared through the Pan-American Congress[1] that the right of conquest does not exist. We have gone further. We have invited the nations of the world, and particularly all of those with whom we are in treaty relations, to join with us in a series of permanent Treaties of Arbitration.

To bring about such a treaty between the United States and Great Britain, the Hon. Wm. Randal Cremer has recently visited our shores, bearing a petition to the President and the Congress of the United States, signed by 354 members of the British House of Commons, and assuring us that Her Majesty's Ministry are largely in favor of the measure. In doing this Mr. Cremer has ignored that old threadbare trick of so called diplomacy, which is always shifting responsibility by saying, let the other party make the overtures, and has had the moral courage to come to request that our Government take action in this very important matter. I am sorry to know that we have some legislators incapable of appreciating his motives, or the blessings that such a permanent state of international peace would give, but in spite of them our Government will by and by respond favorably to Mr. Cremer's memorial.

Our Congress, without any danger of war unless we provoke one by meddling, are continuously making appropriations for war ships to strengthen our Navy, in order to protect long stretches of sea coast, that no nation has the remotest idea of attacking, or to protect our foreign commerce, which has recently grown so small that one would need a microscope to discover it. These large naval appropriations furnish very good jobs for the young men who graduate at Annapolis; and glory for the Secretary of the Navy, who is usually anxious to magnify himself and his office. So the money of the people is spent for a costly vessel that will usually stand the strain of one peaceful cruise at sea, providing there are no storms, and then go to the dry dock for repairs. These appropriations are not only useless, but positively harmful, for they at once alarm our

European friends, and incite them to a greater increase of their military and naval appropriations.

All of this vast expenditure of money is made notwithstanding the present depleted condition of the Treasury, while the poor of Washington and other large cities are starving and business men are going to the wall.

The United States can afford to be generous and progressive along the line of peace legislation, even to taking the initiative in a permanent Treaty of Arbitration with a country as highly cultured as Great Britain, for the peace spirit is the cultured one, and the war spirit the savage side of human nature; other nationalities would be sure to follow. This would be the dawning of a new day, an epoch in history ever to be remembered.

The present industrial condition of the country, the struggle of labor against the greed of monopolies, of trusts, of vast aggregations of capital, is a far greater menace to the security and prosperity of the State than any foreign foe possibly can be. Canada and Mexico are bound to us by common interests and peaceful commercial treaties. There is no threat of violence from either.

But a great strike, that quarters on a community thousands of idle men, ties up the railroads, the great living arteries of a nation's life, impedes the mails and blocks the wheels of commerce, is a menace of which wise legislators should take note. A strike is a war whose blow is aimed at the very root of society.

Felix Adler says: "If we are not to rely upon mere brute force in quelling these disturbances; if we are not to depend upon bayonets and machine guns, we must find a way of peaceably solving these difficulties. We must see whether we cannot allay that keen sense of social justice which is far more operative to breed discontent than distress itself."[2]

Hon. Carroll D. Wright said recently before the Woman's National Press Club that the only true fighters and "the only true commanders are the captains of industry;"[3] that America's true greatness lies in her industrial world, in which all classes are engaged, and in which woman has now become an economic factor. He intimates that the cure for the strike is culture, education, moral suasion, and that the present tendency of organization in all classes of society is bringing about this result. A social organization like this Woman's Council may become a complicated machine as powerful for good as a standing army is for ill. All classes of labor are organized, constituting so many industrial armies, and newspapers and newspaper correspondents are by no means the last to wheel into line. When these ladies have presented their papers to this Council of Women their contents will be known at the same time to New York and London. Thought and handiwork have belted the globe. We are one people, with a community of interests, aspirations and desires. Why should we quarrel with each other?

The Red Cross follows after the army, binds up the wounds made by the sabre and the bullet, closes the eyes of the dying, and sends the parting message to the widow and mother; but the Peace Movement, with a broader charity, seeks to abolish guns and bayonets and to settle all difficulties by arbitration, or by judicial methods.

Women have nothing to gain by war, and the laboring man only a soldier's grave, or wasted health, with his sacrifices speedily forgotten or ignored by the Government and the masses.

The great war of to-day in this country is a war for bread and butter. The Congress of the United States, now at the close of its third heated term, finds itself unequal to cope with this great financial problem, in which capital and labor, silver and gold, are involved, while the Secretary of the Treasury has exhausted his financial ingenuity to protect the gold reserve, and the credit of a great and wealthy nation is being weighed in the balance, and battered on the markets of the world. Could a Woman's Council, with an upper and lower house, have plunged the country into a greater financial disaster?

I am here to tell what the advocates of peace are doing, and hope to do, and to ask your thought and co-operation; for no thoughtful person, no humane person, believes in war, which destroys everything and creates nothing but hatred.

We believe and teach peace and arbitration in the home, in the church, in society, in the State, and between nations. We believe in the sanctity of human life, the inalienable rights of individuals, in justice, in equality and fraternity. Our Government has already settled many serious difficulties with the various nations of the world by arbitration and by treaty, without resort to war and without bloodshed, and the expense of all of them combined has not been one-tenth that of the War of the Revolution.

Just now we are doing what you are doing. We are combining the work of all the Peace Societies, we are wiping out sectionalism; joining hands with our friends across the Atlantic and in far-off Asia; ignoring creeds and tongues, party lines and historical legends; affiliating with Professors of Colleges and Universities, and combining all of the friends of peace— and their name is legion—in one grand cordon for the suppression of war. The work of our Conventions and Conferences is sent to the crowned heads of the nations. Our resolutions and petitions are being introduced into the Parliaments of the world. We begin with the home, the school, the society, the university, the press, and then we go to the halls of legislation.

Our great aim to-day is permanent treaties of arbitration, a permanent International Arbitration Court, and gradual disarmament.

Peace Societies are springing up everywhere, not only in the United States, but in Europe. Organization is the hope of the world, and woman the elastic cement that is binding organizations together, and by them and through them we hope soon to hold the banner aloft to the nations of the world, proclaiming the Fatherhood of God and the brotherhood of man.

SOURCE

Lockwood, Belva. "The Growth of Peace Principles." *Advocate of Peace* 57, no. 4 (April 1895): 80–83.

NOTES

Chapter opening art: Detail from an 1884 National Equal Rights Party electoral ticket, with Belva Lockwood for president and Marietta Stow for vice president.

1. The First International Conference of American States (later called the first Pan-American Conference) was an 1889–90 meeting in Washington, DC, of delegates from thirteen countries in North and South America, to arbitrate trade, a customs union, and postwar acquisitions of sovereignty.

2. Felix Adler (1851–1933) was a German-American social reformer. The speech to which Lockwood refers was delivered before the Washington, DC, School of Ethics, date unknown.

3. Carroll Davidson Wright (1840–1909) was the first U.S. Commissioner of Labor. The date of the speech to which Lockwood refers is unknown.

Louisa Picquet

ca. 1828–1896

LOUISA PICQUET was born in Columbia, South Carolina, the child of an enslaved mother and her white master. At age thirteen, she was sold away from her mother and taken to New Orleans by her new master, who repeatedly raped and impregnated her. After his death in the 1840s, Picquet was freed and eventually able to move to Cincinnati, Ohio. She traveled around the country in the 1850s, working to raise enough money to buy her mother's freedom. In 1860, Hiram Mattison, a white minister, interviewed Picquet about her experiences in slavery as a very light-skinned "octoroon" woman, especially the sexual violence perpetrated against her by white men. The account, framed in Mattison's language, was published in 1861 as *Louisa Picquet, the Octoroon.*

From *Louisa Picquet, the Octoroon: Or Inside Views of Southern Domestic Life* (1861)

CHAPTER I. Illustrious Birth and Parentage

Louisa Picquet, the subject of the following narrative, was born in Columbia, South Carolina, and is apparently about thirty-three years of age. She is a little above the medium height, easy and graceful in her manners, of fair complexion and rosy cheeks, with dark eyes, a flowing head of hair with no perceptible inclination to curl, and every appearance, at first view, of an accomplished white lady.[1]

No one, not apprised of the fact, would suspect that she had a drop of African blood in her veins; indeed, few will believe it, at first, even when told of it.

But a few minutes' conversation with her will convince almost any one that she has, at least, spent most of her life in the South. A certain menial-like diffidence, her plantation expression and pronunciation, her inability to read or write, together with her familiarity with and readiness in describing plantation scenes and sorrows, all attest the truthfulness of her declaration that she has been most of her life a slave. Besides, her artless simplicity and sincerity are sufficient to dissipate the last doubt. No candid person can talk with her without becoming fully convinced that she is a truthful, conscientious, and Christian woman. She is now, and has been for the last eight years, a member of the Zion Baptist Church in Cincinnati, Ohio, of which Rev. Wallace Shelton is now (May, 1860) the pastor.

But, notwithstanding the fair complexion and lady-like bearing of Mrs. Picquet, she is of African descent on her mother's side—an octoroon, or eighth blood—and, consequently, one of the four millions in this land of Bibles, and churches, and ministers, and "liberty," who "have no rights that white men are bound to respect."

The story of her wrongs and sorrows will be recited, to a large extent, in her own language, as taken from her lips by the writer, in Buffalo, N.Y., in May, 1860.

CHAPTER II. Looks Too Much Like Madame Randolph's Children, and Is Sold Out of the Family

"I was born in Columbia, South Carolina. My mother's name was Elizabeth. She was a slave owned by John Randolph,[2] and was a seamstress in his family. She was fifteen years old when I was born. Mother's mistress had a child only two weeks older than me. Mother's master, Mr. Randolph, was my father. So mother told me. She was forbid to tell who was my father, but I looked so much like Madame Randolph's baby that she got dissatisfied, and mother had to be sold. Then mother and me was sent to Georgia, and sold. I was a baby—don't remember at all, but suppose I was about two months old, may be older."

[. . .]

CHAPTER VI. The Family Sold at Auction—Louisa Bought by a "New Orleans Gentleman," and What Came of It

Q.—"How did you say you come to be sold?"

A.—"Well, you see, Mr. Cook made great parties, and go off to watering-places, and get in debt, and had to break up, and then he took us to Mobile, and hired the most of us out, so the men he owe should not find us, and sell us for the debt. Then, after a while, the sheriff came from Georgia after Mr. Cook's debts, and found us all, and took us to auction, and sold us. My mother and brother was sold to Texas, and I was sold to New Orleans."

Q.—"How old were you, then?"

A.—"Well, I don't know exactly, but the auctioneer said I wasn't quite fourteen. I didn't know myself."

Q.—"How old was your brother?"

A.—"I suppose he was about two months old. He was little bit of baby."

Q.—"Where were you sold?"

A.—"In the city of Mobile."

Q.—"In a yard? In the city?"

A.—"No. They put all the men in one room, and all the women in another; and then whoever want to buy come and examine, and ask you whole lot of questions. They began to take the clothes off of me, and a gentleman said they needn't do that, and told them to take me out. He said he knew I was a virtuous girl, and he'd buy me, anyhow. He didn't strip me only just under my shoulders."

Q.—"Were there any others there white like you?"

A.—"Oh yes, plenty of them. There was only Lucy of our lot, but others!"

Q.—"Were others stripped and examined?"

A.—"Well, not quite naked, but just same."

Q.—"You say the gentleman told them to 'take you out.' What did he mean by that?"

A.—"Why, take me out of the room where the women and girls were kept; where they examine them—out where the auctioneer sold us."

Q.—"Where was that? In the street, or in a yard?"

A.—"At the market, where the block is?"

Q.—"What block?"

A.—"My! don't you know? The stand, where we have to get up?"

Q.—"Did you get up on the stand?"

A.—"Why, of course; we all have to get up to be seen."

Q.—"What else do you remember about it?"

A.—"Well, they first begin at upward of six hundred for me, and then some bid fifty more, and some twenty-five more, and that way."

Q.—"Do you remember any thing the auctioneer said about you when he sold you?"

A.—"Well, he said he could not recommend me for any thing else only

that I was a good-lookin' girl, and a good nurse, and kind and affectionate to children; but I was never used to any hard work. He told them they
could see that. My hair was quite short, and the auctioneer spoke about
it, but said, 'You see it good quality, and give it a little time, it will grew out
again.' You see Mr. Cook had my hair cut off. My hair grew fast, and look
so much better than Mr. Cook's daughter, and he fancy I had better hair
than his daughter, and so he had it cut off to make a difference."

Q.—"Well, how did they sell you and your mother? that is, which was
sold first?"

A.—"Mother was put up the first of our folks. She was sold for splendid
cook, and Mr. Horton, from Texas, bought her and the baby, my brother.
Then Henry, the carriage-driver, was put up, and Mr. Horton bought him,
and then two field-hands, Jim and Mary. The women there tend mills and
drive ox wagons, and plough, just like men. Then I was sold next. Mr. Horton run me up to fourteen hundred dollars. He wanted I should go with
my mother. Then some one said 'fifty.' Then Mr. Williams allowed that he
did not care what they bid, he was going to have me anyhow. Then he bid
fifteen hundred. Mr. Horton said 'twas no use to bid any more, and I was
sold to Mr. Williams. I went right to New Orleans then."

Q.—"Who was Mr. Williams?"

A.—"I didn't know then, only he lived in New Orleans. Him and his wife
had parted, some way—he had three children boys. When I was going
away I heard some one cryin', and prayin' the Lord to go with her only
daughter, and protect me. I felt pretty bad then, but hadn't no time only
to say good-bye. I wanted to go back and get the dress I bought with the
half-dollars, I thought a good deal of that; but Mr. Williams would not let
me go back and get it. He said he'd get me plenty of nice dresses. Then I
thought mother could cut it up and make dresses for my brother, the baby.
I knew she could not wear it; and I had a thought, too, that she'd have it
to remember me."

Q.—"It seems like a dream, don't it?"

A.—"No; it seems fresh in my memory when I think of it—no longer than
yesterday. Mother was right on her knees, with her hands up, prayin' to
the Lord for me. She didn't care who saw her: the people all lookin' at her. I
often thought her prayers followed me, for I never could forget her. Whenever I wanted any thing real bad after that, my mother was always sure to
appear to me in a dream that night, and have plenty to give me, always."

Q.—"Have you never seen her since?"

A.—"No, never since that time. I went to New Orleans, and she went to Texas. So I understood."

Q.—"Well, how was it with you after Mr. Williams bought you?"

A.—"Well, he took me right away to New Orleans."

Q.—"How did you go?"

A.—"In a boat, down the river. Mr. Williams told me what he bought me for, soon as we started for New Orleans. He said he was getting old, and when he saw me he thought he'd buy me, and end his days with me. He said if I behave myself he'd treat me well: but, if not, he'd whip me almost to death."

Q.—"How old was he?"

A.—"He was over forty; I guess pretty near fifty. He was gray headed. That's the reason he was always so jealous. He never let me go out anywhere."

Q.—"Did you never go to church?"

A.—"No, sir; I never darken a church door from the time he bought me till after he died. I used to ask him to let me go to church. He would accuse me of some object, and said there was more rascality done there than anywhere else. He'd sometimes say, 'Go on, I guess you've made your arrangements; go on, I'll catch up with you.' But I never dare go once."

Q.—"Had you any children while in New Orleans?"

A.—"Yes; I had four."

Q.—"Who was their father?"

A.—"Mr. Williams."

Q.—"Was it known that he was living with you?"

A.—"Every body knew I was housekeeper, but he never let on that he was the father of my children. I did all the work in his house—nobody there but me and the children."

Q.—"What children?"

A.—"My children and his. You see he had three sons."

Q.—"How old were his children when you went there?"

A.—"I guess the youngest was nine years old. When he had company, gentlemen folks, he took them to the hotel. He never have no gentlemen company home. Sometimes he would come and knock, if he stay out later than usual time; and if I did not let him in in a minute, when I would be asleep, he'd come in and take the light, and look under the bed, and in the wardrobe, and all over, and then ask me why I did not let him in sooner. I did not know what it meant till I learnt his ways."

Q.—"Were your children mulattoes?"

A.—"No, sir! They were all white. They look just like him. The neighbors all see that. After a while he got so disagreeable that I told him, one day, I wished he would sell me, or 'put me in his pocket'—that's the way we say—because I had no peace at all. I rather die than live in that way. Then he got awful mad, and said nothin' but death should separate us; and, if I run off, he'd blow my brains out. Then I thought, if that be the way, all I could do was just to pray for him to die."

Q.—"Where did you learn to pray?"

A.—"I first begin to pray when I was in Georgia, about whippin'—that the Lord would make them forget it, and not whip me: and it seems if when I pray I did not get so hard whippin'."

CHAPTER VIII. Octoroon Life in New Orleans

Q.—"Well, now tell me about your life in New Orleans."

A.—"Well, when Mr. Williams bought me he told me where I was goin', to New Orleans, and what he bought me for. Then I thought of what Mrs. Cook told me; and I thought, now I shall be committin' adultery, and there's no chance for me, and I'll have to die and be lost. Then I had this trouble with him and my soul the whole time."

Q.—"Did you ever say any thing to him about this trouble?"

A.—"Yes, sir; I told him often. Then he would dam' at it. He said he had all that to answer for himself. If I was only true to him, then I could get religion—that needn't hinder me from gettin' religion. But I knew better than that. I thought it was of no use to be prayin', and livin' in sin.

"I begin then, to pray that he might die, so that I might get religion; and then I promise the Lord one night, faithful, in prayer, if he would just take him out of the way, I'd get religion and be true to Him as long as I lived. If Mr. Williams only knew that, and get up out of his grave, he'd beat me half to death. Then it was some time before he got sick. Then, when he did get sick, he was sick nearly a year. Then he begin to get good, and talked kind to me. I could see there was a change in him. He was not all the time accusin' me of other people. Then, when I saw that he was sufferin' so, I begin to get sorry, and begin to pray that he might get religion first before he died. I felt sorry to see him die in his sins. I pray for him to have religion, when I did not have it myself. I thought if he got religion and then died, I knew that I could get religion.

"It seems he did get religion, because he was so much changed in his way; but he said he wanted to see his way clearer."

Q.—"Was he rich?"

A.—"Oh no, sir. He had to borrow some of the money of his brother to buy me."

Q.—"What kind of a house did you live in?"

A.—"Why, it was a rented house. When he got up, one mornin', I got him up in a chair by the fire—it was cold weather—then he told me he was goin' to die, and that he could not live; and he said that if I would promise him that I would go to New York, he would leave me and the children free. He was then writin' to a table—had a little table to the side of him. Then he told me how to conduct myself, and not to live as I had lived with him, with any person. He told me to come out this way (North), and not to let any one know who I was, or that I was colored. He said no person would know it, if I didn't tell it; and, if I conducted myself right, some one would want to marry me, but warned me not to marry any one but a mechanic—some one who had trade, and was able to take care of me and the children."

Q.—"How many children had you then?"

A.—"Only two. I had four, but two had died. Then I promised him to go to New York. Then he said, just as soon as he died I must go right to New York; and he said he would leave me the things. He hadn't any thing to leave me but the things."

Q.—"What things?"

A.—"The things in the house—the beds, and tables, and such things."

SOURCE

Mattison, H. *Louisa Picquet, the Octoroon: Or Inside Views of Southern Domestic Life*, edited by Rev. H. Mattison, 5, 16–20, 22–23. New York: published by the author, 1861.

NOTES

1. [Source editor's note.] The cut [i.e., woodcut illustration] on the outside title-page is a tolerable representation of the features of Mrs. P., though by no means a flattering picture.

2. [Original editor's note.] What "John Randolph" this was, we know not; but suppose it was not the celebrated "John Randolph of Roanoke," though it may have been, and probably was, one of the same family. A gentleman in Xenia, Ohio, told Mrs. P. that if she could only make it out that her mother was one of John Randolph's slaves, there was money somewhere, now, of John Randolph's estate, to buy her mother and brother.

Ora Eddleman Reed

1880–1968

ORA EDDLEMAN REED was born near Denton, Texas, but moved to
Muskogee, Indian Territory (now Oklahoma), when she was young. She
was of Cherokee descent on her mother's side and her father was white.
She gained experience working for her family's newspaper before co-
founding a monthly illustrated literary magazine in 1898. *Twin Territories: The Indian Magazine of Oklahoma* featured fiction written by Reed
under the pseudonym Mignon Schreiber ("Little Writer") and solicited
work from Native American writers. Reed was the editor and head fiction writer, curating content meant to dispel myths about Cherokee
culture, keep their stories alive, and share Native American history
with the country. The following essay appeared in *Sturm's Statehood
Magazine* (later *Sturm's Oklahoma Magazine*), whose "Indian Department" Reed edited for a year after selling *Twin Territories*.

Indian Tales between Pipes (1906)

Many are the amusing stories told by the field parties of the Dawes Commission[1] relative to their experiences with the full blood Indian. A party of these boys recently met at a corn dance down in the Hickory Grove district, and "swapped" experiences as they sat around the fire and smoked their pipes. In some of these stories it was evident that the ignorant (?)[2] full blood got the best of the white man, and demonstrates that his native wit and shrewdness to a large extent compensates his lack of learning acquired from school books.

Mr. H. Van Smith,[3] for several years disbursing clerk for the Commission, came in for a goodly share of the narratives, and said that more than once he was "bested" in an argument with a red man.

Mr. Smith was sent down in Mississippi a year ago to bring to the Territory the few remaining Choctaws who had successfully evaded former officials. After beating the brush for several weeks he succeeded in getting together sixty-four of the natives, and by promising to give them almost anything from a cap pistol to an upright piano, got their promise to be at the railroad station on a certain date. Everything appeared to be moving lovely and according to schedule until the day before the trip to the Territory was to take place. On this day a hungry looking wearer of the blanket approached Smith and after inspecting him for a few minutes said: "Maybe so, Injun take him dog." Smith was preoccupied and merely answered, "all right, take your dog if you want to." However, the Indian was not fully satisfied, and again said, this time with more emphasis "Maybe so, Injun take him dog." Smith replied with like emphasis that as far as he was concerned he could take all the dogs he wanted to, and then promptly dismissed the matter from his mind.

The next day Smith was detained in the town until nearly train time. When he arrived at the depot, however, he understood why his full blood friend had been so persistent on the day previous, for lo and behold— sixty-four Indians and sixty-five dogs. A dog for each Indian, and they had thoughtfully brought an extra one for Smith.

On another occasion a stalwart full blood, laboring under a fair load of Peruna,[4] or some other similar beverage that gives a man nerve to face a visit from his mother-in-law, entered one of the departments and without further ceremony announced that he wanted to file for his twenty-four children. As the applicant appeared scarcely more than thirty years of age himself, the clerk in charge told him there must be some mistake; that he surely did not have twenty-four children. The Indian insisted, and the clerk told him to go home and think it over a few days, then to come back when he felt better, and they would talk it over.

The Indian evidently recognized that he was properly equipped with that which cheers, for he promptly replied: "No, talk it over today. Maybe so come back when I feel better and I no talk any." Realizing it was best to hear him out, the clerk told him to go ahead and explain it to him. The Indian did so in this manner: "Maybe so I have four children, and squaw she die. I take another squaw with eight children. Then her children mine, maybe so?" The clerk agreed that when he married a widow with eight children, the children were then his. This pleased the Indian and he continued:

"Well so, my children hers, maybe so?"

The clerk also agreed that his new wife would be the mother of his own children. The Indian then promptly closed the argument with, "well so, she have twelve children, hers and mine, and I have twelve children, mine and hers. Maybe so you give land for twenty-four children."

A delegation had come in from the Eucha district to protest to the agent against a white man who would not keep his hogs fenced up, and consequently they were creating havoc with the crops being planted by the Indians. Some of the Creek Indians are great on oratory, and in this delegation was one of this kind—an old white headed King of the town. The younger members explained their mission and endeavored to demonstrate how very necessary it was that immediate steps be taken to compel this white man to pen up his hogs. The old King kept shaking his head in a dissatisfied manner, and finally demanded that he be heard. The younger members respectfully withdrew and the old fellow advanced to the center of the floor, pulled a bandana handkerchief of about the dimensions of an ordinary tablecloth from his pocket, deliberately wiped his mouth and hands, and striking a pose, commenced: "You young fellows don't know what you is talking about. You explanations you'se'f about as clear as mud. Talk about hogs! Why you don't know the first principle of a hog. Mr. Agent, let a man talk who has been raised among hogs."

It is needless to say the remainder of his speech was lost, owing to the office force being convulsed with laughter.

I. N. Ury,[5] a Kansas politician, an Indian Territory investor, a resident of Muskogee, and an all around good fellow, has also had some dealings with the full blood. Mr. Ury is gentleness itself wherever the weaker sex is concerned, but he is apt to lose patience when dealing with men, and especially if his feeding has not been up to the standard required by an active politician.

On one occasion Mr. Ury was driving overland in the Creek Nation with a party of friends. When they reached the north fork of the Canadian river, they found the water too high to ford with safety, so drove several miles up the river before crossing. Consequently, they lost their way and drove about aimlessly until sundown, when they pitched camp, relit their pipes for supper, and discussed their predicament. In the morning they tried another smoke for breakfast, and started out in the hope that they would soon meet someone who would direct them to their intended destination. They passed a number of houses, but being in the full blood settlement, the Indian women, according to custom in the absence of their husbands, grabbed their children and made for the brush.

Along about high noon the party was overjoyed by seeing a wagon, drawn by two fine mules, approaching them. Mr. Ury hailed the driver, who stopped his mules and politely waited. Ury asked him several questions, but was answered each time with "ugh," and the dull Indian shake of the head.

Finally Ury lost what little patience remained and began swearing, (and being a politician he has a fair "cussing" vocabulary, by the way). He cussed every Indian within the bounds of Indian Territory, then jumped from the Atlantic to the Pacific coast from Canada to the Gulf of Mexico and back. It is difficult to state just where he would have ended had he not exhausted his breath and stopped for a moment.

During this time the Indian had been sitting in his wagon, watching Ury with all interest possible. When the swearing ceased, he asked in excellent English and with the most bland manner, "what is the name of the town you gentlemen are desirous of reaching?"

He then directed them on their journey, which happily was of short duration, as they were within two miles of their desired destination. Ury, however, he who had fought many political campaigns to a finish, had bought and sold land of Freedmen, had met the Indian Territory lawyer on equal ground and been victorious,—Ury was the most subdued one of the party. Since then he has become wary of the "dull" full blood.

SOURCE

Reed, Ora Eddleman. "Indian Tales between Pipes." *Sturm's Oklahoma Magazine* 3, no. 3 (November 1906): 86–88. Oklahoma State University's Digital Collections. https://dc.library.okstate.edu/digital/collection/EOS/id/3119.

NOTES

Chapter opening photo: Ora Eddleman Reed, ca. 1910. Oklahoma Historical Society, *Twin Territories: The Indian Magazine* Collection, 21178.5.79.

1. Under the Dawes Act of 1887, the federal government seized, subdivided, and reallotted Native American landholdings to "full-blooded" Native families, in exchange for the abolition of their tribes' governments and courts. The "Five Civilized Tribes" (Cherokee, Chickasaw, Choctaw, Muscogee, and Seminole) were exempt from the act until 1893, when President Grover Cleveland established the Dawes Commission to seize their lands as well, applying the same racist criteria to Native Americans' "bloodedness." The Dawes Commission arrived in Muskogee, Oklahoma, in 1894, the same year Reed moved there with her family.

2. This editorial question mark appears in the original and is evidently Reed's.

3. Smith was indeed a special disbursing agent for the Dawes Commission.

4. Peruna was an 18 percent alcohol patent medicine, endorsed by politicians. The Southern Methodist University mascot is named after it.

5. Isaac Newton Ury was a land appraiser for the Dawes Commission.

Josephine St. Pierre Ruffin

1842–1924

JOSEPHINE ST. PIERRE RUFFIN was an African American activist, suffragist, and journalist, born into a prominent Boston family. In 1890, Ruffin founded the *Woman's Era*, the first newspaper by and for African American women. It included profiles of "eminent women," such as Harriet Tubman, and interviews with activists, such as Ida B. Wells-Barnett. She also launched the Woman's Era Club in Boston and went on to be a leading founder and proponent of African American women's organizations, including the National Federation of Afro-American Women and the National Association of Colored Women, of which she was vice president. The following selection is a call to her white counterparts in the South to do their part.

An Open Letter to the
Educational League of Georgia (1889)

Ladies of the Georgia Educational League:[1]

The telegram which you sent to Governor Northern to read to his audience, informing the people of the North of your willingness to undertake the moral training of the colored children of Georgia, merits more than a passing notice. It is the first time, we believe, in the history of the South where a body of representative Southern white women have shown such interest in the moral welfare of the children of their former slaves as to be willing to undertake to make them more worthy the duties and responsibilities of citizenship. True, there have been individual cases where courageous women have felt their moral responsibility, and have nobly met it, but one of the saddest things about the sad condition of affairs in the

South has been the utter indifference which Southern women, who were guarded with unheard of fidelity during the war, have manifested to the mental and moral welfare of the children of their faithful slaves, who, in the language of Henry Grady, placed a black mass of loyalty between them and dishonor. This was a rare opportunity for you to have shown your gratitude to your slaves and your interest in their future welfare.

The children would have grown up in utter ignorance had not the North sent thousands of her noblest daughters to the South on this mission of heroic love and mercy; and it is worthy of remark of those fair daughters of the North, that, often eating with Negroes, and in the earlier days sleeping in their humble cabins, and always surrounded by thousands of them, there is not one recorded instance where one has been the victim of violence or insult. If because of the bitterness of your feelings, of your deep poverty at the close of the war, conditions were such that you could not do this work yourselves, you might have give a Christian's welcome to the women who came a thousand miles to do the work, that, in all gratitude and obligation belonged to you,—but instead, these women were often persecuted, always they have been ruthlessly ostracised, even until this day; often they were lonely, often longed for a word of sympathy, often craved association with their own race, but for thirty years they have been treated by the Christian white women of the South,—simply because they were doing your work,—the work committed to you by your Saviour, when he said, "Inasmuch as you did it to one of the least of these my brethren, you did it unto me,"—with a contempt that would serve to justify a suspicion that instead of being the most cultured women, the purest, bravest missionaries in America, they were outcasts and lepers.

But at last a change has come. And so you have "decided to take up the work of moral and industrial training of the Negroes," as you "have been doing this work among the whites with splendid results." This is one of the most hopeful stars that have shot through the darkness of the Southern sky. What untold blessings might not the educated Christian women of the South prove to the Negro groping blindly in the darkness of the swamps and bogs of prejudice for a highway out of servitude, oppression, ignorance, and immorality!

* * * * *

The leading women of Georgia should not ask Northern charity to do what they certainly must have the means for making a beginning of themselves. If your heart is really in this work—and we do not question it—the very best way for you to atone for your negligence in the past is to make a start yourselves. Surely if the conditions are as serious as you represent them to be, your husbands, who are men of large means, who are able to run great expositions and big peace celebrations, will be willing to provide you with the means to protect your virtue and that of your daughters by the moral training you propose to give in the kindergartens.

There is much you might do without the contribution of a dollar from any pocket, Northern or Southern. On every plantation there are scores, if not hundreds, of little colored children who could be gathered about you on a Sabbath afternoon and given many helpful inspiring lessons in morals and good conduct.

*   *   *   *   *

It is a good augury of better days, let us hope, when the intelligent, broad-minded women of Georgia, spurning the incendiary advice of that human firebrand who would lynch a thousand Negroes a month, are willing to join in this great altruistic movement of the age and endeavor to lift up the degraded and ignorant, rather than to exterminate them. Your proposition implies that they may be uplifted and further, imports a tacit confession that if you had done your duty to them at the close of the war, which both gratitude and prudence should have prompted you to do, you would not now be confronted with a condition which you feel it necessary to check, in obedience to the great first law of nature—self-protection. If you enter upon this work you will doubtless be criticised by a class of your own people who think you are lowering your own dignity, but the South has suffered too much already from that kind of false pride to let it longer keep her recreant to the spirit of the age.

If, when you have entered upon it, you need the cooperation, either by advice or other assistance, of the colored women of the North, we beg to assure you that they will not be lacking,—until then, the earnest hope goes out that you will bravely face and sternly conquer your former prejudices and quickly undertake this missionary work which belongs to you.

SOURCE

Ruffin, Josephine St. Pierre. "An Open Letter to the Educational League of Georgia." *Masterpieces of Negro Eloquence: The Best Speeches Delivered by the Negro from the Days of Slavery to the Present Time*, edited by Alice Moore Dunbar, 173–76. New York: Bookery, 1914.

NOTE

1. The original text is preceded by the following byline: "By Josephine St. Pierre Ruffin, of Boston, Mass. Founder of the National Association of Negro Women. June, 1889."

Elizabeth Cady Stanton

1815–1902

Susan B. Anthony

1820–1906

Matilda Joslyn Gage

1826–1898

SUFFRAGISTS, ABOLITIONISTS, AND SOCIAL REFORMERS ALL,
Elizabeth Cady Stanton, Susan B. Anthony, and Matilda Joslyn Gage
were three of the most prominent women's rights advocates of the nineteenth century. Stanton is probably best known today for her early and
unwavering advocacy for women's suffrage, including coorganizing the
1848 Seneca Falls Convention and writing its landmark "Declaration of
Sentiments" (modeled on the Declaration of Independence). Anthony
likewise advocated for a wide range of women's rights, most especially
the right to vote, and famously cast an illegal vote in 1872, for which she
was briefly jailed. Lifelong friends, Stanton and Anthony spent decades
together advocating for women's suffrage and gender equality, though
not without controversy: the two famously tore the suffrage movement
asunder by declining to support the Fourteenth and Fifteenth Amendments, recoiling from the hypocrisy of enfranchising African American
men but not women of any race. The resulting schism yielded two parallel women's movements (and women's rights associations), which did
not reconcile until the creation of the National American Woman Suffrage Association in 1890. By then, the history of the suffrage movement

was already more than a half century old, and Stanton, Anthony, and the more radical, freethinking Gage—an outspoken critic of Christianity, advocate of women scientists, and founder of the splinter Woman's National Liberal Union—would spend the remaining years of their lives editing and contributing to the still standard *History of Woman Suffrage*.[1]

Introduction to *History of Woman Suffrage* (1889)

The prolonged slavery of woman is the darkest page in human history. A survey of the condition of the race through those barbarous periods, when physical force governed the world, when the motto, "might makes right," was the law, enables one to account, for the origin of woman's subjection to man without referring the fact to the general inferiority of the sex, or Nature's law.

Writers on this question differ as to the cause of the universal degradation of woman in all periods and nations.

One of the greatest minds of the century has thrown a ray of light on this gloomy picture by tracing the origin of woman's slavery to the same principle of selfishness and love of power in man that has thus far dominated all weaker nations and classes. This brings hope of final emancipation, for as all nations and classes are gradually, one after another, asserting and maintaining their independence, the path is clear for woman to follow. The slavish instinct of an oppressed class has led her to toil patiently through the ages, giving all and asking little, cheerfully sharing with man all perils and privations by land and sea, that husband and sons might attain honor and success. Justice and freedom for herself is her latest and highest demand.

Another writer asserts that the tyranny of man over woman has its roots, after all, in his nobler feelings; his love, his chivalry, and his desire to protect woman in the barbarous periods of pillage, lust, and war. But wherever the roots may be traced, the results at this hour are equally disastrous to woman. Her best interests and happiness do not seem to have been consulted in the arrangements made for her protection. She has been bought and sold, caressed and crucified at the will and pleasure of her master. But if a chivalrous desire to protect woman has always been the mainspring of man's dominion over her, it should have prompted him to place in her hands the same weapons of defense he has found to be most effective against wrong and oppression.

It is often asserted that as woman has always been man's slave— subject—inferior—dependent, under all forms of government and religion, slavery must be her normal condition. This might have some weight had not the vast majority of men also been enslaved for centuries to kings and popes, and orders of nobility, who, in the progress of civilization, have reached complete equality. And did we not also see the great changes in woman's condition, the marvelous transformation in her character, from a toy in the Turkish harem, or a drudge in the German fields, to a leader of thought in the literary circles of France, England, and America!

In an age when the wrongs of society are adjusted in the courts and at the ballot-box, material force yields to reason and majorities.

Woman's steady march onward, and her growing desire for a broader outlook, prove that she has not reached her normal condition, and that society has not yet conceded all that is necessary for its attainment.

Moreover, woman's discontent increases in exact proportion to her development. Instead of a feeling of gratitude for rights accorded, the wisest are indignant at the assumption of any legal disability based on sex, and their feelings in this matter are a surer test of what her nature demands, than the feelings and prejudices of the sex claiming to be superior. American men may quiet their consciences with the delusion that no such injustice exists in this country as in Eastern nations, though with the general improvement in our institutions, woman's condition must inevitably have improved also, yet the same principle that degrades her in Turkey, *insults* her in this republic. Custom forbids a woman there to enter a mosque, or call the hour for prayers; here it forbids her a voice in Church Councils or State Legislatures. The same taint of her primitive state of slavery affects both latitudes.

The condition of married women, under the laws of all countries, has been essentially that of slaves, until modified, in some respects, within the last quarter of a century in the United States. The change from the old Common Law of England, in regard to the civil rights of women, from 1848 to the advance legislation in most of the Northern States in 1880, marks an era both in the status of woman as a citizen and in our American system of jurisprudence. When the State of New York gave married women certain rights of property, the individual existence of the wife was recognized, and the old idea that "husband and wife are one, and that one the husband," received its death-blow. From that hour the statutes of the several States have been steadily diverging from the old English codes. Most of the Western States copied the advance legislation of New York, and some are now even more liberal.

The broader demand for political rights has not commanded the thought its merits and dignity should have secured. While complaining of many wrongs and oppressions, women themselves did not see that the political disability of sex was the cause of all their special grievances, and that to secure equality anywhere, it must be recognized everywhere. Like all disfranchised classes, they begun by asking to have certain wrongs redressed, and not by asserting their own right to make laws for themselves.

Overburdened with cares in the isolated home, women had not the time, education, opportunity, and pecuniary independence to put their thoughts clearly and concisely into propositions, nor the courage to compare their opinions with one another, nor to publish them, to any great extent, to the world.

It requires philosophy and heroism to rise above the opinion of the wise men of all nations and races, that to be unknown, is the highest testimonial woman can have to her virtue, delicacy and refinement.

A certain odium has ever rested on those who have risen above the conventional level and sought new spheres for thought and action, and especially on the few who demand complete equality in political rights. The leaders in this movement have been women of superior mental and physical organization, of good social standing and education, remarkable alike for their domestic virtues, knowledge of public affairs, and rare executive ability; good speakers and writers, inspiring and conducting the genuine reforms of the day; everywhere exerting themselves to promote the best interests of society; yet they have been uniformly ridiculed, misrepresented, and denounced in public and private by all classes of society.

Woman's political equality with man is the legitimate outgrowth of the fundamental principles of our Government, clearly set forth in the Declaration of Independence in 1776, in the United States Constitution adopted in 1784, in the prolonged debates on the origin of human rights in the anti-slavery conflict in 1840, and in the more recent discussions of the party in power since 1865, on the 13th, 14th, and 15th Amendments to the National Constitution; and the majority of our leading statesmen have taken the ground that suffrage is a natural right that may be regulated, but can not be abolished by State law.

Under the influence of these liberal principles of republicanism that pervades all classes of American minds, however vaguely, if suddenly called out, they might be stated, woman readily perceives the anomalous position she occupies in a republic, where the government and religion alike are based on individual conscience and judgment—where the natural rights of all citizens have been exhaustively discussed, and repeatedly declared equal.

From the inauguration of the government, representative women have expostulated against the inconsistencies between our principles and practices as a nation. Beginning with special grievances, woman's protests soon took a larger scope. Having petitioned State legislatures to change the statutes that robbed her of children, wages, and property, she demanded that the Constitutions—State and National—be so amended as to give her a voice in the laws, a choice in the rulers, and protection in the exercise of her rights as a citizen of the United States.

While the laws affecting woman's civil rights have been greatly improved during the past thirty years, the political demand has made but a questionable progress, though it must be counted as the chief influence in modifying the laws. The selfishness of man was readily enlisted in securing woman's civil rights, while the same element in his character antagonized her demand for political equality.

Fathers who had estates to bequeath to their daughters could see the advantage of securing to woman certain property rights that might limit the legal power of profligate husbands.

Husbands in extensive business operations could see the advantage of allowing the wife the right to hold separate property, settled on her in time of prosperity, that might not be seized for his debts. Hence in the several States able men championed these early measures. But political rights, involving in their last results equality everywhere, roused all the antagonism of a dominant power, against the self-assertion of a class hitherto subservient. Men saw that with political equality for woman, they could no longer keep her in social subordination, and "the majority of the male sex," says John Stuart Mill,[2] "can not yet tolerate the idea of living with an equal." The fear of a social revolution thus complicated the discussion. The Church, too, took alarm, knowing that with the freedom and education acquired in becoming a component part of the Government, woman would not only outgrow the power of the priesthood, and religious superstitions, but would also invade the pulpit, interpret the Bible anew from her own stand-point, and claim an equal voice in all ecclesiastical councils. With fierce warnings and denunciations from the pulpit, and false interpretations of Scripture, women have been intimidated and misled, and their religious feelings have been played upon for their more complete subjugation. While the general principles of the Bible are in favor of the most enlarged freedom and equality of the race, isolated texts have been used to block the wheels of progress in all periods; thus bigots have defended capital punishment, intemperance, slavery, polygamy, and the subjection of woman. The creeds of all nations make obedience to man the corner-stone of her religious character. Fortunately, however, more liberal minds are now giving us higher and purer expositions of the Scriptures.

As the social and religious objections appeared against the demand for political rights, the discussion became many-sided, contradictory, and as varied as the idiosyncrasies of individual character. Some said, "Man is woman's natural protector, and she can safely trust him to make laws for her."[3] She might with fairness reply, as he uniformly robbed her of all property rights to 1848, he can not safely be trusted with her personal rights in 1880, though the fact that he did make some restitution at last, might modify her distrust in the future. However, the calendars of our courts still show that fathers deal unjustly with daughters, husbands with wives, brothers with sisters, and sons with their own mothers. Though woman needs the protection of one man against his whole sex, in pioneer life, in threading her way through a lonely forest, on the highway, or in the streets of the metropolis on a dark night, she sometimes needs, too, the protection of all men against this one. But even if she could be sure, as she is not, of the ever-present, all-protecting power of one strong arm, that would be weak indeed compared with the subtle, all-pervading influence of just and equal laws for all women. Hence woman's need of the ballot, that she may hold in her own right hand the weapon of self-protection and self-defense.

Again it is said: "The women who make the demand are few in number, and their feelings and opinions are abnormal, and therefore of no weight in considering the aggregate judgment on the question." The number is larger than appears on the surface, for the fear of public ridicule, and the loss of private favors from those who shelter, feed, and clothe them, withhold many from declaring their opinions and demanding their rights. The ignorance and indifference of the majority of women, as to their status as citizens of a republic, is not remarkable, for history shows that the masses of all oppressed classes, in the most degraded conditions, have been stolid and apathetic until partial success had crowned the faith and enthusiasm of the few.

The insurrections on Southern plantations were always defeated by the doubt and duplicity of the slaves themselves. That little band of heroes who precipitated the American Revolution in 1776 were so ostracised that they walked the streets with bowed heads, from a sense of loneliness and apprehension. Woman's apathy to the wrongs of her sex, instead of being a plea for her remaining in her present condition, is the strongest argument against it. How completely demoralized by her subjection must she be, who does not feel her personal dignity assailed when all women are ranked in every State Constitution with idiots, lunatics, criminals, and minors; when in the name of Justice, man holds one scale for woman, another for himself; when by the spirit and letter of the laws she is made responsible for crimes committed against her, while the male criminal goes free; when from altars where she worships no woman may preach; when in the courts, where girls of tender age may be arraigned for the crime of infanticide, she may not plead for the most miserable of her sex; when colleges she is taxed to build and endow, deny her the right to share in their advantages; when she finds that which should be her glory—her possible motherhood—treated everywhere by man as a disability and a crime! A woman insensible to such indignities needs some transformation into nobler thought, some purer atmosphere to breathe, some higher stand-point from which to study human rights.

It is said, "the difference between the sexes indicates different spheres." It would be nearer the truth to say the difference indicates different duties in the same sphere, seeing that man and woman were evidently made for each other, and have shown equal capacity in the ordinary range of human duties. In governing nations, leading armies, piloting ships across the sea, rowing life-boats in terrific gales; in art, science, invention, literature, woman has proved herself the complement of man in the world of thought and action. This difference does not compel us to spread our tables with different food for man and woman, nor to provide in our common schools a different course of study for boys and girls. Sex pervades all nature, yet the male and female tree and vine and shrub rejoice in the same sunshine and shade. The earth and air are free to all the fruits and flowers, yet each absorbs what best ensures its growth. But whatever it is, it requires no special watchfulness on our part to see that it is maintained. This plea, when closely analyzed, is generally found to mean woman's inferiority.

The superiority of man, however, does not enter into the demand for suffrage, for in this country all men vote; and as the lower orders of men are not superior, either by nature or grace, to the higher orders of women, they must hold and exercise the right of self-government on some other ground than superiority to women.

Again it is said, "Woman when independent and self-asserting will lose her influence over man." In the happiest conditions in life, men and women will ever be mutually dependent on each other. The complete development of all woman's powers will not make her less capable of steadfast love and friendship, but give her new strength to meet the emergencies of life, to aid those who look to her for counsel and support. Men are uniformly more attentive to women of rank, family, and fortune, who least need their care, than to any other class. We do not see their protecting love generally extending to the helpless and unfortunate ones of earth. Wherever the skilled hands and cultured brain of woman have made the battle of life easier for man, he has readily pardoned her sound judgment and proper self-assertion. But the prejudices and preferences of man should be a secondary consideration, in presence of the individual happiness and freedom of woman. The formation of her character and its influence on the human race, is a larger question than man's personal liking. There is no fear, however, that when a superior order of women shall grace the earth, there will not be an order of men to match them, and influence over such minds will atone for the loss of it elsewhere.

An honest fear is sometimes expressed "that woman would degrade politics, and politics would degrade woman." As the influence of woman has been uniformly elevating in new civilizations, in missionary work in heathen nations, in schools, colleges, literature, and in general society, it is fair to suppose that politics would prove no exception. On the other hand, as the art of government is the most exalted of all sciences, and statesmanship requires the highest order of mind, the ennobling and refining influence of such pursuits must elevate rather than degrade woman. When politics degenerate into bitter persecutions and vulgar court-gossip, they are degrading to man, and his honor, virtue, dignity, and refinement are as valuable to woman as her virtues, are to him.

Again, it is said, "Those who make laws must execute them; government needs force behind it,—a woman could not be sheriff or a policeman." She might not fill these offices in the way men do, but she might far more effectively guard the morals of society, and the sanitary conditions of our cities. It might with equal force be said that a woman of culture and artistic taste can not keep house, because she can not wash and iron with her own hands, and clean the range and furnace. At the head of the police, a woman could direct her forces and keep order without ever using a baton or a pistol in her own hands. "The elements of sovereignty," says Blackstone, "are three: wisdom, goodness, and power." Conceding to woman wisdom and goodness, as they are not strictly masculine virtues, and substituting moral power for physical force, we have the necessary elements of government for most of life's emergencies. Women manage families, mixed schools, charitable institutions, large boarding-houses and hotels, farms and steam-engines, drunken and disorderly men and women, and stop street fights, as well as men do. The queens in history compare favorably with the kings.

But, "in the settlement of national difficulties," it is said, "the last resort is war; shall we summon our wives and mothers to the battle-field?" Women have led armies in all ages, have held positions in the army and navy for years in disguise. Some fought, bled, and died on the battle-field in our late war. They performed severe labors in the hospitals and sanitary department. Wisdom would dictate a division of labor in war as well as in peace, assigning each their appropriate department.

Numerous classes of men who enjoy their political rights are exempt from military duty. All men over forty-five, all who suffer mental or physical disability, such as the loss of an eye or a forefinger; clergymen, physicians, Quakers, school-teachers, professors, and presidents of colleges, judges, legislators, congressmen, State prison officials, and all county, State and National officers; fathers, brothers, or sons having certain relatives dependent on them for support,—all of these summed up in every State in the Union make millions of voters thus exempted.

In view of this fact there is no force in the plea, that "if women vote they must fight." Moreover, war is not the normal state of the human family in its higher development, but merely a feature of barbarism lasting on through the transition of the race, from the savage to the scholar. When England and America settled the *Alabama* Claims by the Geneva Arbitration, they pointed the way for the future adjustment of all national difficulties.

Some fear, "If women assume all the duties political equality implies, that the time and attention necessary to the duties of home life will be absorbed in the affairs of State." The act of voting occupies but little time in itself, and the vast majority of women will attend to their family and social affairs to the neglect of the State, just as men do to their individual interests. The virtue of patriotism is subordinate in most souls to individual and family aggrandizement. As to offices, it is not to be supposed that the class of men now elected will resign to women their chances, and if they should to any extent, the necessary number of women to fill the offices would make no apparent change in our social circles. If, for example, the Senate of the United States should be entirely composed of women, but two in each State would be withdrawn from the pursuit of domestic happiness. For many reasons, under all circumstances, a comparatively smaller proportion of women than men would actively engage in politics.

As the power to extend or limit the suffrage rests now wholly in the hands of man, he can commence the experiment with as small a number as he sees fit, by requiring any lawful qualification. Men were admitted on property and educational qualifications in most of the States, at one time, and still are in some—so hard has it been for man to understand the theory of self-government. Three-fourths of the women would be thus disqualified, and the remaining fourth would be too small a minority to precipitate a social revolution or defeat masculine measures in the halls of legislation, even if women were a unit on all questions and invariably voted together, which they would not. In this view, the path of duty is plain for the prompt action of those gentlemen who fear universal suffrage for women, but are willing to grant it on property and educational qualifications. While those who are governed by the law of expediency should give the measure of justice they deem safe, let those who trust the absolute right proclaim the higher principle in government, "equal rights to all."

Many seeming obstacles in the way of woman's enfranchisement will be surmounted by reforms in many directions. Co-operative labor and co-operative homes will remove many difficulties in the way of woman's success as artisan and housekeeper, when admitted to the governing power. The varied forms of progress, like parallel lines, move forward simultaneously in the same direction. Each reform, at its inception, seems out of joint with all its surroundings; but the discussion changes the conditions, and brings them in line with the new idea.

The isolated household is responsible for a large share of woman's ignorance and degradation. A mind always in contact with children and servants, whose aspirations and ambitions rise no higher than the roof that shelters it, is necessarily dwarfed in its proportions. The advantages to the few whose fortunes enable them to make the isolated household a more successful experiment, can not outweigh the difficulties of the many who are wholly sacrificed to its maintenance.

Quite as many false ideas prevail as to woman's true position in the home as to her status elsewhere. Womanhood is the great fact in her life; wifehood and motherhood are but incidental relations. Governments legislate for men; we do not have one code for bachelors, another for husbands and fathers; neither have the social relations of women any significance in their demands for civil and political rights. Custom and philosophy, in regard to woman's happiness, are alike based on the idea that her strongest social sentiment is love of children; that in this relation her soul finds complete satisfaction. But the love of offspring, common to all orders of women and all forms of animal life, tender and beautiful as it is, can not as a sentiment rank with conjugal love. The one calls out only the negative virtues that belong to apathetic classes, such as patience, endurance, self-sacrifice, exhausting the brain-forces, ever giving, asking nothing in return; the other, the outgrowth of the two supreme powers in nature, the positive and negative magnetism, the centrifugal and centripetal forces, the masculine and feminine elements, possessing the divine power of creation, in the universe of thought and action. Two pure souls fused into one by an impassioned love—friends, counselors—a mutual support and inspiration to each other amid life's struggles, must know the highest human happiness;—this is marriage; and this is the only corner-stone of an enduring home. Neither does ordinary motherhood, assumed without any high purpose or preparation, compare in sentiment with the lofty ambition and conscientious devotion of the artist whose pure children of the brain in poetry, painting, music, and science are ever beckoning her upward into an ideal world of beauty. They who give the world a true philosophy, a grand poem, a beautiful painting or statue, or can tell the story of every wandering star; a George Eliot, a Rosa Bonheur, an Elizabeth Barrett Browning, a Maria Mitchell—whose blood has flowed to the higher arches of the brain,—have lived to a holier purpose than they whose children are of the flesh alone, into whose minds they have breathed no clear perceptions of great principles, no moral aspiration, no spiritual life.

Her rights are as completely ignored in what is adjudged to be woman's sphere as out of it; the woman is uniformly sacrificed to the wife and mother. Neither law, gospel, public sentiment, nor domestic affection shield her from excessive and enforced maternity, depleting alike to mother and child;—all opportunity for mental improvement, health, happiness—yea, life itself, being ruthlessly sacrificed. The weazen, weary, withered, narrow-minded wife-mother of half a dozen children—her interests all centering at her fireside, forms a painful contrast in many a household to the liberal, genial, brilliant, cultured husband in the zenith of his power, who has never given one thought to the higher life, liberty, and happiness of the woman by his side; believing her self-abnegation to be Nature's law.

It is often asked, "if political equality would not rouse antagonisms between the sexes?" If it could be proved that men and women had been harmonious in all ages and countries, and that women were happy and satisfied in their slavery, one might hesitate in proposing any change whatever. But the apathy, the helpless, hopeless resignation of a subjected class can not be called happiness. The more complete the despotism, the more smoothly all things move on the surface. "Order reigns in Warsaw." In right conditions, the interests of man and woman are essentially one; but in false conditions, they must ever be opposed. The principle of equality of rights underlies all human sentiments, and its assertion by any individual or class must rouse antagonism, unless conceded. This has been the battle of the ages, and will be until all forms of slavery are banished from the earth. Philosophers, historians, poets, novelists, alike paint woman the victim ever of man's power and selfishness. And now all writers on Eastern civilization tell us, the one insurmountable obstacle to the improvement of society in those countries, is the ignorance and superstition of the women. Stronger than the trammels of custom and law, is her religion, which teaches that her condition is Heaven-ordained. As the most ignorant minds cling with the greatest tenacity to the dogmas and traditions of their faith, a reform that involves an attack on that stronghold can only be carried by the education of another generation. Hence the self-assertion, the antagonism, the rebellion of woman, so much deplored in England and the United States, is the hope of our higher civilization. A woman growing up under American ideas of liberty in government and religion, having never blushed behind a Turkish mask, nor pressed her feet in Chinese shoes, can not brook any disabilities based on sex alone, without a deep feeling of antagonism with the power that creates it. The change needed to restore good feeling can not be reached by remanding woman to the spinning-wheel, and the contentment of her grandmother, but by conceding to her every right which the spirit of the age demands. Modern inventions have banished the spinning-wheel, and the same law of progress makes the woman of to-day a different woman from her grandmother.

With these brief replies to the oft-repeated objections made by the opposition, we hope to rouse new thoughts in minds prepared to receive them. That equal rights for woman have not long ago been secured, is due to causes beyond the control of the actors in this reform. "The success of a movement," says Lecky, "depends much less upon the force of its arguments, or upon the ability of its advocates, than the predisposition of society to receive it."

SOURCE

Introduction to *History of Woman Suffrage*, edited by Elizabeth Cady Stanton, Susan B. Anthony, and Matilda Joslyn Gage, 1:13–24. Rochester, NY: Charles Mann, 1889.

NOTES

1. The full *History*, which would eventually span six volumes, was published piece-meal between 1881 and 1922.
2. British utilitarian philosopher and liberal political theorist John Stuart Mill (1806–1873) was a suffragist and early (male) advocate for gender equality.
3. This quotation, as well as a number of those that follow, exemplifies a general antisuffragist stance rather than the words of a specific person.

Maria W. Stewart

1803–1879

MARIA W. STEWART was born to two free Black parents in Hartford, Connecticut, but orphaned and put into indentured servitude at age five. She became an essayist, abolitionist, and women's rights activist. William Lloyd Garrison published her first pamphlet, *Religion and the Pure Principles of Morality* (1831), which called on African Americans in the North and South to organize against slavery and stand up for their rights and education. In a time when it was taboo for women to give public addresses to audiences including men, Stewart was perhaps the first to do so. She gave four speeches on equality and civil rights before going back to writing and teaching, and the third is included here. The response to them was overwhelmingly negative, as the "audacity" of her speaking in public was condemned.

An Address Delivered at the African Masonic Hall, Boston, February 27, 1833

African rights and liberty is a subject that ought to fire the breast of every free man of color in these United States, and excite in his bosom a lively, deep, decided and heart-felt interest. When I cast my eyes on the long list of illustrious names that are enrolled on the bright annals of fame among the whites, I turn my eyes within, and ask my thoughts, "Where are the names of *our* illustrious ones?" It must certainly have been for the want of energy on the part of the free people of color, that they have been long willing to bear the yoke of oppression. It must have been the want of ambition and force that has given the whites occasion to say, that our natural abilities are not as good, and our capacities by nature inferior to theirs. They boldly assert, that, did we possess a natural independence of soul, and feel a love for liberty within our breasts, some one of our sable race, long before this, would have testified it, notwithstanding the disadvantages under which we labor. We have made ourselves appear altogether unqualified to speak in our own defence, and are therefore looked upon as objects of pity and commiseration. We have been imposed upon, insulted and derided on every side; and now, if we complain, it is considered as the height of impertinence. We have suffered ourselves to be considered as dastards, cowards, mean, faint-hearted wretches; and on this account, (not because of our complexion) many despise us, and would gladly spurn us from their presence.

These things have fired my soul with a holy indignation, and compelled me thus to come forward; and endeavor to turn their attention to knowledge and improvement; for knowledge is power. I would ask, is it blindness of mind, or stupidity of soul, or the want of education, that has caused our men who are 60 to 70 years of age, never to let their voices be heard, or nor their hands be raised in behalf of their color? Or has it been for the fear of offending the whites? If it has, O ye fearful ones, throw off your fearfulness, and come forth in the name of the Lord, and in the strength of the God of Justice, and make yourselves useful and active members in society; for they admire a noble and patriotic spirit in others; and should they not admire it in us? If you are men, convince them that you possess the spirit of men; and as your day, so shall your strength be. Have the sons of Africa no souls? feel they no ambitious desires? shall the chains of ignorance forever confine them? shall the insipid appellation of "clever negroes," or "good creatures," any longer content them? Where can we find among ourselves the man of science, or a philosopher, or an able statesman, or a counsellor at law? Show me our fearless and brave, our noble and gallant ones. Where are our lecturers on natural history, and our critics in useful knowledge? There may be a few such men among us, but they are rare. It is true, our fathers bled and died in the revolutionary war, and others fought bravely under the command of Jackson, in defence of liberty. But where is the man that has distinguished himself in these modern days by acting wholly in the defence of African rights and liberty? There was one, although he sleeps, his memory lives.

I am sensible that there are many highly intelligent gentlemen of color in those United States, in the force of whose arguments, doubtless, I should discover my inferiority; but if they are blest with wit and talent, friends and fortune, why have they not made themselves men of eminence, by striving to take all the reproach that is cast upon the people of color, and in endeavoring to alleviate the woes of their brethren in bondage? Talk, without effort, is nothing; you are abundantly capable, gentlemen, of making yourselves men of distinction; and this gross neglect, on your part, causes my blood to boil within me. Here is the grand cause which hinders the rise and progress of the people of color. It is their want of laudable ambition and requisite courage.

Individuals have been distinguished according to their genius and talents, ever since the first formation of man, and will continue to be while the world stands. The different grades rise to honor and respectability as their merits may deserve. History informs us that we sprung from one of the most learned nations of the whole earth; from the seat, if not the parent of science; yes, poor, despised Africa was once the resort of sages and legislators of other nations, was esteemed the school for learning, and the most illustrious men in Greece flocked thither for instruction. But it was our gross sins and abominations that provoked the Almighty to frown thus heavily upon us, and give our glory unto others. Sin and prodigality have caused the downfall of nations, kings and emperors; and were it not that God in wrath remembers mercy; we might indeed despair; but a promise is left us; "Ethiopia shall again stretch forth her hands unto God."

But it is of no use for us to boast that we sprung from this learned and enlightened nation, for this day a thick mist of moral gloom hangs over millions of our race. Our condition as a people has been low for hundreds of years, and it will continue to be so, unless, by true piety and virtue, we strive to regain that which we have lost. White Americans, by their prudence, economy and exertions, have sprung up and become one of the most flourishing nations in the world, distinguished for their knowledge of the arts and sciences, for their polite literature. While our minds are vacant, and starving for want of knowledge, theirs are filled to overflowing. Most of our color have been taught to stand in fear of the white man, from their earliest infancy, to work as soon as they could walk, and call "master," before they scarce could lisp the name of *mother*. Continual fear and laborious servitude have in some degree lessened in us that natural force and energy which belong to man; or else, in defiance of opposition, our men, before this, would have nobly and boldly contended for their rights. But give the man of color an equal opportunity with the white from the cradle to manhood, and from manhood to the grave, and you would discover the dignified statesman, the man of science, and the philosopher. But there is no such opportunity for the sons of Africa, and I fear that our powerful ones are fully determined that there never shall be. Forbid, ye Powers on High, that it should any longer be said that our men possess no force. O ye sons of Africa, when will your voices be heard in our legislative halls, in defiance of your enemies, contending for equal rights and liberty? How can you, when you reflect from what you have fallen, refrain from crying mightily unto God, to turn away from us the fierceness of his anger, and remember our transgressions against us no more forever. But a God of infinite purity will not regard the prayers of those who hold religion in one hand, and prejudice, sin and pollution in the other; he will not regard the prayers of self-righteousness and hypocrisy. Is it possible, I exclaim, that for the want of knowledge, we have labored for hundreds of years to support others, and been content to receive what they chose to give us in return? Cast your eyes about, look as far as you can see; all, all is owned by the lordly white, except here and there a lowly dwelling which the man of color, midst deprivations, fraud and opposition, has been scarce able to procure. Like king Solomon, who put neither nail nor hammer to the temple, yet received the praise; so also have the white Americans gained themselves a name, like the names of the great men that are in the earth, while in reality we have been their principal foundation and support. We have pursued the shadow, they have obtained the substance; we have performed the labor, they have received the profits; we have planted the vines, they have eaten the fruits of them.

I would implore our men, and especially our rising youth, to flee from the gambling board and the dance hall; for we are poor, and have no money to throw away. I do not consider dancing as criminal in itself, but it is astonishing to me that our young men are so blind to their own interest and the future welfare of their children, as to spend their hard earnings for this frivolous amusement; for it has been carried on among us to such an unbecoming extent, that it has became absolutely disgusting. "Faithful are the wounds of a friend, but the kisses of an enemy are deceitful." Had those men among us, who have had an opportunity, turned their attention as assiduously to mental and moral improvement as they have to gambling and dancing, I might have remained quietly at home, and they stood contending in my place. These polite accomplishments will never enrol your names on the bright annals of tune, who admire the belle void of intellectual knowledge, or applaud the dandy that talks largely on politics, without striving to assist his fellow in the revolution, when the nerves and muscles of every other man forced him into the field of action. You have a right to rejoice, and to let your hearts cheer you in the days of your youth; yet remember that for all these things, God will bring you into judgment. Then, O ye sons of Africa, turn your mind from these perishable objects, and contend for the cause of God and the rights of man. Form yourselves into temperance societies. There are temperate men among you; then why will you any longer neglect to strive, by your example, to suppress vice in all its abhorrent forms? You have been told repeatedly of the glorious results arising from temperance, and can you bear to see the whites arising in honor and respectability, without endeavoring to grasp after that honor and respectability also?

But I forbear. Let our money, instead of being thrown away as heretofore, be appropriated for schools and seminaries of learning for our children and youth. We ought to follow the example of the whites in this respect. Nothing would raise our respectability, add to our peace and happiness, and reflect so much honor upon us, as to be ourselves the promoters of temperance, and the supporters, as far as we are able, of useful and scientific knowledge. The rays of light and knowledge have been hid from our view; we have been taught to consider ourselves as scarce superior to the brute creation; and have performed the most laborious part of American drudgery. Had we as a people received one half the early advantages the whites have received, I would defy the government of these United States to deprive us any longer of our rights.

I am informed that the agent of the Colonization Society has recently formed an association of young men, for the purpose of influencing those of us to go to Liberia who may feel disposed. The colonizationists are blind to their own interest, for should the nations of the earth make war with America, they would find their forces much weakened by our absence; or should we remain here, can our "brave soldiers," and "fellow citizens," as they were termed in time of calamity, condescend to defend the rights of the whites, and be again deprived of their own, or sent to Liberia in return? Or, if the colonizationists are real friends to Africa, let them expend the money which they collect, in erecting a college to educate her injured sons in this land of gospel light and liberty; for it would be most thankfully received on our part, and convince us of the truth of their professions, and save time, expense and anxiety. Let them place before us noble objects, worthy of pursuit, and see if we prove ourselves to be those unambitious negroes they term us. But ah! methinks their hearts are so frozen towards us, they had rather their money should be sunk in the ocean than to administer it to our relief; and I fear, if they dared, like Pharaoh, king of Egypt, they would order every male child among us to be drowned. But the most high God is still as able to subdue the lofty pride of these white Americans, as He was the heart of that ancient rebel. They say, though we are looked upon as things, yet we sprang from a scientific people. Had our men the requisite force and energy, they would soon convince them by their efforts both in public and private, that they were men, or things in the shape of men. Well may the colonizationists laugh us to scorn for our negligence; well may they cry, "Shame to the sons of Africa." As the burden of the Israelites was too great for Moses to bear, so also is our burden too great for Moses to bear, so also is our burden too great for our noble advocate to bear. You must feel interested, my brethren, in what he undertakes, and hold up his hands by your good works, or in spite of himself, his soul will become discouraged, and his heart will die within him; for he has, as it were, the strong bulls of Bashan to contend with.

It is of no use for us to wait any longer for a generation of well educated men to arise. We have slumbered and slept too long already; the day is far spent; the night of death approaches; and you have sound sense and good judgement sufficient to begin with, if you feel disposed to make a right use of it. Let every man of color throughout the United States, who possesses the spirit and principles of a man, sign a petition to Congress, to abolish slavery in the District of Columbia, and grant you the rights and privileges of common free citizens; for if you had had faith as a grain of mustard seed, long before this the mountains of prejudice might have been removed. We are all sensible that the Anti-Slavery Society has taken hold of the arm of our whole population, in order to raise them out of the mire. Now all we have to do is, by a spirit of virtuous ambition to strive to raise ourselves; and I am happy to have it in my power thus publicly to say, that the colored inhabitants of this city, in some respects, are beginning to improve. Had the free people of color in these United States nobly and boldly contended for their rights, and showed a natural genius and talent, although not so brilliant as some; had they held up, encouraged and patronized each other, nothing could have hindered us from being a thriving and flourishing people. There has been a fault among us. The reason why our distinguished men have not made themselves more influential is, because they fear that the strong current of opposition through which they must pass, would cause their downfall and prove their overthrow. And what gives rise to this opposition? Envy. And what has it amounted to? Nothing. And who are the cause of it? Our whited sepulchers, who want to be great, and don't know how; who love to be called of men "Rabbi, Rabbi," who put on false sanctity, and humble themselves to their brethren, for the sake of acquiring the highest place in the synagogue, and the uppermost seats at the feast. You, dearly beloved, who are the genuine followers of our Lord Jesus Christ, the salt of the earth and the light of the world, are not so culpable. As I told you, in the very first of my writing, I tell you again, I am but as a drop in the bucket—as one particle of the small dust of the earth. God will surely raise up those among us who will plead the cause of virtue, and the pure principles of morality, more eloquently than I am able to do.

It appears to me that America has become like the great city of Babylon, for she has boasted in her heart,—"I sit a queen, and am no widow, and shall see no sorrow." She is indeed a seller of slaves and the souls of men; she has made the Africans drunk with the wine of her fornication; she has put them completely beneath her feet, and she means to keep them there; her right hand supports the reins of government, and her left hand the wheel of power, and she is determined not to let go her grasp. But many powerful sons and daughters of Africa will shortly arise, who will put down vice and immorality among us, and declare by Him that sitteth upon the throne, that they will have their rights; and if refused, I am afraid they will spread horror and devastation around. I believe that the oppression of injured Africa has come up before the Majesty of Heaven; and when our cries shall have reached the ears of the Most High, it will be a tremendous day for the people of this land; for strong is the arm of the Lord God Almighty.

Life has almost lost its charms for me; death has lost its sting and the grave its terrors; and at times I have a strong desire to depart and dwell with Christ, which is far better. Let me entreat my white brethren to awake and save our sons from dissipation, and our daughters from ruin. Lend the hand of assistance to feeble merit, plead the cause of virtue among our sable race; so shall our curses upon you be turned into blessings; and though you should endeavor to drive us from these shores, still we will cling to you the more firmly; nor will we attempt to rise above you: we will presume to be called your equals only.

The unfriendly whites first drove the native American from his much loved home. Then they stole our fathers from their peaceful and quiet dwellings, and brought them hither, and made bond men and bond women of them and their little ones; they have obliged our brethren to labor, kept them in utter ignorance, nourished them in vice, and raised them in degradation; and now that we have enriched their soil, and filled their coffers, they say that we are not capable of becoming like white men, and that we never can rise to respectability in this country. They would drive us to a strange land. But before I go, the bayonet shall pierce me through. African rights and liberty is a subject that ought to fire the breast of every free man of color in these United States, and excite in his bosom a lively, deep, decided and heartfelt interest.

SOURCE

Stewart, Maria W. "An Address Delivered at the African Masonic Hall, Boston, February 27, 1833." *Liberator* 3, no. 17 (April 27, 1833): 68; no. 18 (May 4, 1833): 72.

Lucy Stone

1818–1893

LUCY STONE was a white orator and editor born in West Brookfield, Massachusetts. A naturally gifted speaker, she was appointed a lecturer for the Massachusetts Anti-Slavery Society. In 1850, Stone organized the first national women's rights convention in Worcester, Massachusetts, and gave an address that won over Susan B. Anthony to the cause. She famously kept her own surname when she married Henry Blackwell, as documented in "Marriage of Lucy Stone under Protest." Together, they founded and edited the *Woman's Journal*, considered by many the voice of the women's movement. Stone organized the American Woman Suffrage Association, which was the most moderate wing of the movement, in conflict with leaders such as Elizabeth Cady Stanton and Susan B. Anthony over policy and strategy until the organizations merged into the National American Woman Suffrage Association in 1890.

From Lucy Stone (1850)
Letter to the *Liberator*

For the Woman's Rights Convention:

DEAR FRIENDS,—The friends of human freedom in Massachusetts rejoice that a Woman's Rights Convention is to be held in Ohio. We hail it as
a sign of progress, and deem it especially fitting that such a Convention
should be held *now*, when a new State Constitution is to be formed. It is
easier, when the old is destroyed, to build the new right than to right it
after it is built.

The statute books of every State in the Union are disgraced by an article
which limits the right to the elective franchise to "*male* citizens, of twenty-
one years of age and upwards," thus excluding one-half the population of
the country from all political influence—subjecting woman to laws, in
the making of which she has neither vote nor voice. The lowest drunkard
may come up from his wallowing in the gutter, and, covered with filth,
reel up to the ballot-box and deposit his vote, and *his* right to do so is not
questioned. The meanest foreigner who comes to our shores—who cannot speak his mother tongue correctly—has secured for him the right of
suffrage.

The negro—crushed and degraded as if he were not a brother man—
made the lowest of the low—even he, in *some* of the States, can vote; but
woman, in *every* State, is politically plunged in a degradation lower than
his lowest deep.

Woman is taxed under laws made by those who profess to believe that
taxation and representation are inseparable, while in the use and imposition of the taxes, as in representation, she is absolutely without influence.
Should she hint that profession and practice do not agree, she is gravely
told that "women should not talk politics." In most of the States, the married woman loses, by her marriage, the control of her person and the right
to property, and if she is a mother, the right to her children also; while she
secures what the town paupers have, the right to be maintained. The legal
disabilities under which women labor have no end; I will not attempt to
enumerate them. Let the earnest women who speak in your Convention
enter into the detail of this question, nor stop to "patch fig-leaves for the
naked truth;" but "before all Israel and the sun," expose the atrocity of the

laws relative to women, until the ears of those who hear shall tingle, and so that the men, who meet in Convention to form the new Constitution for Ohio, shall, for very shame's sake, make haste to put away the last remnant of the barbarism which your statute-book (in common with those of the other States) retains, in its inequality, and injustice to woman. We know too well the stern reform spirit of those who have called this Women's Rights Convention, to doubt for a moment that what can be done by you, to secure equal rights for all, will be done.

Massachusetts *ought* to have taken the lead in the work you are now doing, but if she chooses to linger, let her young sister of the West set her a worthy example; and if "the Pilgrim spirit is not dead," *we'll pledge Massachusetts to follow her.*

Yours for justice and equal rights,

LUCY STONE.

At Southampton, April 10th, 1850.

Marriage of Lucy Stone under Protest (1855)

T. W. Higginson sends to the Worcester *Spy* the following:

It was my privilege to celebrate May-Day by officiating at a wedding, in a farm-house among the hills of West Brookfield. The bridegroom was a man of tried worth, a leader in the Western anti-slavery movement; and the bride was one whose fair fame is known throughout the nation—one whose rare intellectual qualities are excelled by the private beauty of her heart and life.

I never perform the marriage ceremony without a renewed sense of the iniquity of our present system of laws, in respect to marriage;—a system by which "man and wife are one, and that one is the husband." It was with my hearty concurrence, therefore, that the following protest was read and signed, as a part of the nuptial ceremony, and I send it to you, that others may be induced to do likewise.

PROTEST.

While we acknowledge our mutual affection, by publicly assuming the sacred relationship of husband and wife, yet in justice to ourselves and a great principle, we deem it a duty to declare that this act on our part implies no sanction of, nor promise of voluntary obedience to, such of the present laws of marriage, as refuse to recognize the wife as an independent rational being, while they confer upon the husband an injurious and unnatural superiority, investing him with legal powers which no honorable man would exercise, and which no man should possess.

We protest especially against the laws which give to the husband—

1. The custody of his wife's person.
2. The exclusive control and guardianship of their children.
3. The sole ownership of her personal, and use of her real estate, unless previously settled upon her, or placed in the hands of trustees, as in the case of minors, lunatics and idiots.
4. The absolute right to the product of her industry.
5. Also against laws which give to the widower so much larger and more permanent an interest in the property of his deceased wife, than they give to the widow in that of her deceased husband.
6. Finally, against the whole system by which "the legal existence of the wife is suspended during marriage," so that in most States she neither has a legal part in the choice of her residence, nor can she make a will, nor sue or be sued in her own name, nor inherit property.

We believe that personal independence and equal human rights can never be forfeited, except for crime; that marriage should be an equal and permanent partnership, and so recognized by law; that until it is so recognized, married partners should provide against the radical injustice of present laws, by every means in their power.

We believe that where domestic difficulties arise, no appeal should be made to legal tribunals under existing laws, but that all difficulties should be submitted to the equitable adjustment of arbitrators mutually chosen.

Thus reverencing law, we enter our protest against rules and customs which are unworthy of the name, since they violate justice, the essence of Law.

(Signed,) HENRY B. BLACKWELL,
LUCY STONE.[1]

SOURCES

Higginson, T. W. "Marriage of Lucy Stone under Protest." *Liberator* 25, no. 18 (May 4, 1855): 71. ProQuest Historical Newspapers.

Stone, Lucy. "From Lucy Stone." *Liberator* 20, no. 20 (May 17, 1850): 80. ProQuest Historical Newspapers.

NOTE

Chapter opening photo: Lucy Stone, ca. 1840–60. Library of Congress, Prints & Photographs Division, LC-USZ62-29701.

1. The editor of the *Liberator*'s rather tone-deaf follow-up to this letter reads as follows: "We are very sorry (as will be a host of others) to lose Lucy Stone, and certainly no less glad to gain Lucy Blackwell. Our most fervent benediction upon the heads of the parties thus united!"

Mary Church Terrell

1863–1954

MARY CHURCH TERRELL was born in Memphis, Tennessee, to formerly enslaved parents who had become small business owners. Terrell became an activist in 1892, after a friend was lynched. She joined Ida B. Wells in antilynching efforts but focused on racial uplift as her strategy for gaining African American rights and equality. Her phrase "lifting as we climb" became the motto of the National Association of Colored Women, which she helped found in 1896 and led until 1901. She campaigned tirelessly for both women's suffrage and civil rights, drawing attention to the intersectional issues that African American women faced. In 1909, Terrell helped found the NAACP. She published her autobiography, *A Colored Woman in a White World*, in 1940.

Lynching from a Negro's Point of View (1904)

Before 1904 was three months old, thirty-one negroes had been lynched.[1] Of this number, fifteen were murdered within one week in Arkansas, and one was shot to death in Springfield, Ohio, by a mob composed of men who did not take the trouble to wear masks. Hanging, shooting and burning black men, women and children in the United States have become so common that such occurrences create but little sensation and evoke but slight comment now. Those who are jealous of their country's fair name feel keenly the necessity of extirpating this lawlessness, which is so widespread and has taken such deep root. But means of prevention can never be devised, until the cause of lynching is more generally understood.

The reasons why the whole subject is deeply and seriously involved in error are obvious. Those who live in the section where nine-tenths of the lynchings occur do not dare to tell the truth, even if they perceive it. When men know that the death-knell of their aspirations and hopes will be sounded as soon as they express views to which the majority in their immediate vicinage are opposed, they either suppress their views or trim them to fit the popular mind. Only martyrs are brave and bold enough to defy the public will, and the manufacture of martyrs in the negro's behalf is not very brisk just now. Those who do not live in the section where most of the lynchings occur borrow their views from their brothers who do, and so the errors are continually repeated and inevitably perpetuated.

In the discussion of this subject, four mistakes are commonly made.

In the first place, it is a great mistake to suppose that rape is the real cause of lynching in the South. Beginning with the Ku-Klux Klan, the negro has been constantly subjected to some form of organized violence ever since he became free. It is easy to prove that rape is simply the pretext and not the cause of lynching. Statistics show that, out of every hundred negroes who are lynched, from seventy-five to eighty-five are not even accused of this crime, and many who are accused of it are innocent. And, yet, men who admit the accuracy of these figures gravely tell the country that lynching can never be suppressed, until negroes cease to commit a crime with which less than one-fourth of those murdered by mobs are charged.

The prevailing belief that negroes are not tortured by mobs unless they are charged with the "usual" crime, does not tally with the facts. The savagery which attended the lynching of a man and his wife the first week in March of the present year was probably never exceeded in this country or anywhere else in the civilized world. A white planter was murdered at Doddsville, Miss., and a negro was charged with the crime. The negro fled, and his wife, who was known to be innocent, fled with him to escape the fate which she knew awaited her, if she remained. The two negroes were pursued and captured, and the following account of the tragedy by an eye-witness appeared in the "Evening Post," a Democratic daily of Vicksburg, Miss.

"When the two negroes were captured, they were tied to trees, and while the funeral pyres were being prepared they were forced to suffer the most fiendish tortures. The blacks were forced to hold out their hands while one finger at a time was chopped off. The fingers were distributed as souvenirs. The ears of the murderers were cut off. Holbert was beaten severely, his skull was fractured, and one of his eyes, knocked out with a stick, hung by a shred from the socket. Neither the man nor the woman begged for mercy, nor made a groan or plea. When the executioner came forward to lop off fingers, Holbert extended his hand without being asked. The most excruciating form of punishment consisted in the use of a large corkscrew in the hands of some of the mob. This instrument was bored into the flesh of the man and the woman, in the arms, legs and body, and then pulled out, the spirals tearing out big pieces of raw, quivering flesh every time it was withdrawn. Even this devilish torture did not make the poor brutes cry out. When finally they were thrown on the fire and allowed to be burned to death, this came as a relief to the maimed and suffering victims."

The North frequently sympathizes with the Southern mob, because it has been led to believe the negro's diabolical assaults upon white women are the chief cause of lynching. In spite of the facts, distinguished representatives from the South are still insisting, in Congress and elsewhere, that "whenever negroes, cease committing the crime of rape, the lynchings and burnings will cease with it." But since three-fourths of the negroes who have met a violent death at the hands of Southern mobs have not been accused of this crime, it is evident that, instead of being the "usual" crime, rape is the most unusual of all the crimes for which negroes are shot, hanged and burned.

Although Southern men of prominence still insist that "this crime is more responsible for mob violence than all other crimes combined," it is gratifying to observe that a few of them, at least, are beginning to feel ashamed to pervert the facts. During the past few years, several Southern gentlemen, of unquestioned ability and integrity, have publicly exposed the falsity of this plea. Two years ago, in a masterful article on the race problem, Professor Andrew Sledd,[2] at that time an instructor in a Southern college, admitted that only a small number of the negroes who are lynched are even accused of assaulting white women. Said he:

> "On the contrary, a frank consideration of all the facts, with no other desire than to find the truth, the whole truth and nothing but the truth, however contrary to our wishes and humiliating to our section the truth may be, will show that by far the most of our Southern lynchings are carried through in *sheer, unqualified and increasing brutality.*"

But a heavy penalty was paid by this man who dared to make such a frank and fearless statement of facts. He was forced to resign his position as professor, and lost prestige in his section in various ways. In the summer of 1903, Bishop Candler of Georgia made a strong protest against lynching, and called attention to the fact that, out of 128 negroes who had been done to death in 1901, only 16 were even accused of rape.

In the second place, it is a mistake to suppose that the negro's desire for social equality sustains any relation whatsoever to the crime of rape. According to the testimony of eye-witnesses, as well as the reports of Southern newspapers, the negroes who are known to have been guilty of assault have, as a rule, been ignorant, repulsive in appearance and as near the brute creation as it is possible for a human being to be. It is safe to assert that, among the negroes who have been guilty of ravishing white women, not one had been taught that he was the equal of white people or had ever heard of social equality. And if by chance he had heard of it, he had no clearer conception of its meaning than he had of the principle of the binomial theorem. In conversing with a large number of ignorant negroes, the writer has never found one who seemed to have any idea of what social equality means, or who expressed a desire to put this theory into practice when it was explained to him.

Negroes who have been educated in Northern institutions of learning with white men and women, and who for that reason might have learned the meaning of social equality and have acquired a taste for the same, neither assault white women nor commit other crimes, as a rule. A careful review of the facts will show that negroes who have the "convention habit" developed to a high degree, or who are able to earn their living by editing newspapers, do not belong to the criminal class, although such negroes are always held up by Southern gentlemen as objects of ridicule, contempt and scorn. Strange as it may appear, illiterate negroes, who are the only ones contributing largely to the criminal class, are coddled and caressed by the South. To the educated, cultivated members of the race, they are held up as bright and shining examples of what a really good negro should be. The dictionary is searched in vain by Southern gentlemen and gentle-women for words sufficiently ornate and strong to express their admiration for a dear old "mammy" or a faithful old "uncle," who can neither read nor write, and who assure their white friends they would not, if they could.

On the other hand, no language is sufficiently caustic, bitter and severe, to express the disgust, hatred and scorn which Southern gentlemen feel for what is called the "New Issue," which, being interpreted, means, negroes who aspire to knowledge and culture, and who have acquired a taste for the highest and best things in life. At the door of this "New Issue," the sins and shortcomings of the whole race are laid. This "New Issue" is beyond hope of redemption, we are told, because somebody, nobody knows who, has taught it to believe in social equality, something, nobody knows what. The alleged fear of social equality has always been used by the South to explain its unchristian treatment of the negro and to excuse its many crimes. How many crimes have been committed, and how many falsehoods have been uttered, in the name of social equality by the South! Of all these, the greatest is the determination to lay lynching at its door. In the North, which is the only section that accords the negro the scrap of social equality enjoyed by him in the United States, he is rarely accused of rape. The only form of social equality ever attempted between the two races, and practised to any considerable extent, is that which was originated by the white masters of slave women, and which has been perpetuated by them and their descendants even unto the present day. Of whatever other crime we may accuse the big, black burly brute, who is so familiar a figure in the reports of rape and lynching-bees sent out by the Southern press, surely we cannot truthfully charge him with an attempt to introduce social equality into this republican form of government, or to foist it upon a democratic land. There is no more connection between social equality and lynching to-day than there was between social equality and slavery before the war, or than there is between social equality and the convict-lease system, or any other form of oppression to which the negro has uniformly been subjected in the South.

The third error on the subject of lynching consists of the widely circulated statement that the moral sensibilities of the best negroes in the United States are so stunted and dull, and the standard of morality among even the leaders of the race is so low, that they do not appreciate the enormity and heinousness of rape. Those who claim to know the negro best and to be his best friends declare, that he usually sympathizes with the black victim of mob violence rather than with the white victim of the black fiend's lust, even when he does not go so far as to condone the crime of rape. Only those who are densely ignorant of the standards and sentiments of the best negroes, or who wish wilfully to misrepresent and maliciously to slander a race already resting under burdens greater than it can bear, would accuse its thousands of reputable men and women of sympathizing with rapists, either black or white, or of condoning their crime. The negro preachers and teachers who have had the advantage of education and moral training, together with others occupying positions of honor and trust, are continually expressing their horror of this one particular crime, and exhorting all whom they can reach by voice or pen to do everything in their power to wash the ugly stain of rape from the race's good name. And whenever the slightest pity for the victim of mob violence is expressed by a negro who represents the intelligence and decency of his race, it is invariably because there is a reasonable doubt of his innocence, rather than because there is condonation of the alleged crime.

Everybody who is well informed on the subject of lynching knows that many a negro who has been accused of assault or murder, or other violation of the law, and has been tortured to death by a mob, has afterward been proved innocent of the crime with which he was charged. So great is the thirst for the negro's blood in the South, that but a single breath of suspicion is sufficient to kindle into an all-consuming flame the embers of hatred ever smouldering in the breasts of the fiends who compose a typical mob. When once such a bloodthirsty company starts on a negro's trail, and the right one cannot be found, the first available specimen is sacrificed to their rage, no matter whether he is guilty or not.

A white man who died near Charleston, South Carolina, in March of the present year, confessed on his death-bed that he had murdered his wife, although three negroes were lynched for this crime at Ravenel, South Carolina, in May, 1902. This murder was one of the most brutal ever committed in the State, and the horrible tortures to which the three innocent negroes were subjected indicated plainly that the mob intended the punishment to fit the crime. In August, 1901, three negroes, a mother, her daughter and her son, were lynched in Carrollton, Miss., because it was rumored that they had heard of a murder before it was committed, and had not reported it. A negro was accused of murdering a woman, and was lynched in Shreveport, Louisiana, in April, 1902, who was afterward proved innocent. The woman who was lynched in Mississippi this year was not even accused of a crime. The charge of murder had not been proved against her husband, and, as the white man who was murdered had engaged in an altercation with him, it is quite likely that, if the negro had been tried in a court of law, it would have been shown to be a case of justifiable homicide. And so other cases might easily be cited to prove that the charge that innocent negroes are sometimes lynched is by no means without foundation. It is not strange, therefore, that even reputable, law-abiding negroes should protest against the tortures and cruelties inflicted by mobs which wreak vengeance upon the guilty and innocent and upon the just and unjust of their race alike. It is to the credit and not to the shame of the negro that he tries to uphold the sacred majesty of the law, which is so often trailed in the dust and trampled under foot by white mobs.

In the fourth place, it is well to remember, in discussing the subject of lynching, that it is not always possible to ascertain the facts from the accounts in the newspapers. The facts are often suppressed, intentionally or unintentionally, or distorted by the press. The case of Sam Hose, to which reference has so often been made, is a good illustration of the unreliability of the press in reporting the lynching of negroes. Sam Hose, a negro, murdered Alfred Cranford, a white man, in a dispute over wages which the white employer refused to pay the colored workman. It was decided to make an example of a negro who dared to kill a white man. A well-known, influential newspaper immediately offered a reward of $500 for the capture of Sam Hose. This same newspaper predicted a lynching, and stated that, though several modes of punishment had been suggested, it was the consensus of opinion that the negro should be burned at the stake and tortured before being burned. A rumor was started, and circulated far and wide by the press, that Sam Hose had assaulted the wife of Alfred Cranford, after the latter had been killed. One of the best detectives in Chicago was sent to Atlanta to investigate the affair. After securing all the information it was possible to obtain from black and white alike, and carefully weighing the evidence, this white detective declared it would have been a physical impossibility for the negro to assault the murdered man's wife, and expressed it as his opinion that the charge of assault was an invention intended to make the burning a certainty.

The Sunday on which Sam Hose was burned was converted into a holiday. Special trains were made up to take the Christian people of Atlanta to the scene of the burning, a short distance from the city. After the first train moved out with every inch of available space inside and out filled to overflowing, a second had to be made up, so as to accommodate those who had just come from church. After Sam Hose had been tortured and burned to death, the great concourse of Christians who had witnessed the tragedy scraped for hours among his ashes in the hope of finding a sufficient number of his bones to take to their friends as souvenirs. The charge has been made that Sam Hose boasted to another negro that he intended to assault Alfred Cranford's wife. It would be difficult for anybody who understands conditions in the South to believe that a sane negro would announce his purpose to violate a white woman there, then deliberately enter her husband's house, while all the family were present, to carry out his threat.

Two years ago a riot occurred in Atlanta, Georgia, in which four white policemen were killed and several wounded by a colored man named Richardson, who was himself finally burned to death. Through the press the public was informed that the negro was a desperado. As a matter of fact, Richardson was a merchant, well to do and law-abiding. The head and front of his offending was that he dared to reprimand an ex-policeman for living in open adultery with a colored woman. When it was learned that this negro had been so impudent to a white man, the sheriff led out a posse, consisting of the city police, to arrest Richardson. Seeing the large number of officers surrounding his house, and knowing what would be his fate, if caught, the negro determined to sell his life dear, and he did. With the exception of the Macon "Telegraph," but few white newspapers ever gave the real cause of the riot, and so Richardson has gone down to history as a black desperado, who shot to death four officers of the law and wounded as many more. Several years ago, near New Orleans, a negro was at work in a corn-field. In working through the corn he made considerable noise, which frightened a young white woman, who happened to be passing by. She ran to the nearest house, and reported that a negro had jumped at her. A large crowd of white men immediately shouldered guns and seized the negro, who had no idea what it meant. When told why he was taken, the negro protested that he had not even seen the girl whom he was accused of frightening, but his protest was of no avail and he was hanged to the nearest tree. The press informed the country that this negro was lynched for attempted rape. Instance after instance might be cited to prove that facts bearing upon lynching, as well as upon other phases of the race problem, are often garbled—without intention, perhaps—by the press.

What, then, is the cause of lynching? At the last analysis, it will be discovered that there are just two causes of lynching. In the first place, it is due to race hatred, the hatred of a stronger people toward a weaker who were once held as slaves. In the second place, it is due to the lawlessness so prevalent in the section where nine-tenths of the lynchings occur. View the question of lynching from any point of view one may, and it is evident that it is just as impossible for the negroes of this country to prevent mob violence by any attitude of mind which they may assume, or any course of conduct which they may pursue, as it is for a straw dam to stop Niagara's flow. Upon the same spirit of intolerance and of hatred the crime of lynching must be fastened as that which called into being the Ku-Klux Klan, and which has prompted more recent exhibitions of hostility toward the negro, such as the disfranchisement acts, the Jim Crow Car Laws, and the new slavery called "peonage," together with other acts of oppression which make the negro's lot so hard.

Lynching is the aftermath of slavery. The white men who shoot negroes to death and flay them alive, and the white women who apply flaming torches to their oil-soaked bodies to-day, are the sons and daughters of women who had but little, if any, compassion on the race when it was enslaved. The men who lynch negroes today are, as a rule, the children of women who sat by their firesides happy and proud in the possession and affection of their own children, while they looked with unpitying eye and adamantine heart upon the anguish of slave mothers whose children had been sold away, when not overtaken by a sadder fate. If it be contended, as it often is, that negroes are rarely lynched by the descendants of former slaveholders, it will be difficult to prove the point. According to the reports of lynchings sent out by the Southern press itself, mobs are generally composed of the "best citizens" of a place, who quietly disperse to their homes as soon as they are certain that the negro is good and dead. The newspaper who predicted that Sam Hose would be lynched, which offered a reward for his capture and which suggested burning at the stake, was neither owned nor edited by the poor whites. But if it be conceded that the descendants of slaveholders do not shoot and burn negroes, lynching must still be regarded as the legitimate offspring of slavery. If the children of the poor whites of the South are the chief aggressors in the lynching-bees of that section, it is because their ancestors were brutalized by their slaveholding environment. In discussing the lynching of negroes at the present time, the heredity and the environment, past and present, of the white mobs are not taken sufficiently into account. It is as impossible to comprehend the cause of the ferocity and barbarity which attend the average lynching-bee without taking into account the brutalizing effect of slavery upon the people of the section where most of the lynchings occur, as it is to investigate the essence and nature of fire without considering the gases which cause the flame to ignite. It is too much to expect, perhaps, that the children of women who for generations looked upon the hardships and the degradation of their sisters of a darker hue with few if any protests, should have mercy and compassion upon the children of that oppressed race now. But what a tremendous influence for law and order, and what a mighty foe to mob violence Southern white women might be, if they would arise in the purity and power of their womanhood to implore their fathers, husbands and sons no longer to stain their hands with the black man's blood!

While the men of the South were off fighting to keep the negro in bondage, their mothers, wives and daughters were entrusted to the black man's care. How faithfully and loyally he kept his sacred trust the records of history attest! Not a white woman was violated throughout the entire war. Can the white women of the South forget how black men bore themselves throughout that trying time? Surely it is not too much to ask that the daughters of mothers who were shielded from harm by the black man's constancy and care should requite their former protectors, by at least asking that, when the children of the latter are accused of crime, they should be treated like human beings and not like wild animals to be butchered and shot.

If there were one particularly heinous crime for which an infuriated people took vengeance upon the negro, or if there were a genuine fear that a guilty negro might escape the penalty of the law in the South, then it might be possible to explain the cause of lynching on some other hypothesis than that of race hatred. It has already been shown that the first supposition has no foundation in fact. It is easy to prove that the second is false. Even those who condone lynching do not pretend to fear the delay or the uncertainty of the law, when a guilty negro is concerned. With the courts of law entirely in the hands of the white man, with judge and jury belonging to the superior race, a guilty negro could no more extricate himself from the meshes of the law in the South than he could slide from the devil-fish's embrace or slip from the anaconda's coils. Miscarriage of justice in the South is possible only when white men transgress the law.

In addition to lynching, the South is continually furnishing proof of its determination to wreak terrible vengeance upon the negro. The recent shocking revelations of the extent to which the actual enslavement of negroes has been carried under the peonage system of Alabama and Mississippi, and the unspeakable cruelties to which men, women and children are alike subjected, all bear witness to this fact. In January of the present year, a government detective found six negro children ranging in age from six to sixteen years working on a Georgia plantation in bare feet, scantily clad in rags, although the ground was covered with snow. The owner of the plantation is one of the wealthiest men in northeast Georgia, and is said to have made his fortune by holding negroes in slavery. When he was tried it was shown that the white planter had killed the father of the six children a few years before, but was acquitted of the murder, as almost invariably happens, when a white man takes a negro's life. After the death of their father, the children were treated with incredible cruelty. They were often chained in a room without fire and were beaten until the blood streamed from their backs, when they were unable to do their stint of work. The planter was placed under $5,000 bail, but it is doubtful whether he will ever pay the penalty of his crime. Like the children just mentioned hundreds of negroes are to-day groaning under a bondage more crushing and more cruel than that abolished forty years ago.

This same spirit manifests itself in a variety of ways. Efforts are constantly making to curtail the educational opportunities of colored children. Already one State has enacted a law by which colored children in the public schools are prohibited from receiving instruction higher than the sixth grade, and other States will, doubtless, soon follow this lead. It is a well-known fact that a Governor recently elected in one of the Southern States owes his popularity and his votes to his open and avowed opposition to the education of negroes. Instance after instance might be cited to prove that the hostility toward the negro in the South is bitter and pronounced, and that lynching is but a manifestation of this spirit of vengeance and intolerance in its ugliest and most brutal form.

To the widespread lawlessness among the white people of the South lynching is also due. In commenting upon the blood-guiltiness of South Carolina, the Nashville "American" declared some time ago that, if the killings in the other States had been in the same ratio to population as in South Carolina, a larger number of people would have been murdered in the United States during 1902 than fell on the American side in the Spanish and Philippine wars.

Whenever Southern white people discuss lynching, they are prone to slander the whole negro race. Not long ago, a Southern writer of great repute declared without qualification or reservation that "the crime of rape is well-nigh wholly confined to the negro race," and insisted that "negroes furnish most of the ravishers." These assertions are as unjust to the negro as they are unfounded in fact. According to statistics recently published, only one colored male in 100,000 over five years of age was accused of assault upon a white woman in the South in 1902, whereas one male out of every 20,000 over five years of age was charged with rape in Chicago during the same year. If these figures prove anything at all, they show that the men and boys in Chicago are many times more addicted to rape than are the negroes in the South. Already in the present year two white men have been arrested in the national capital for attempted assault upon little children. One was convicted and sentenced to six years in the penitentiary. The crime of which the other was accused was of the most infamous character. A short account of the trial of the convicted man appeared in the Washington dailies, as any other criminal suit would have been reported; but if a colored man had committed the same crime, the newspapers from one end of the United States to the other would have published it broadcast. Editorials upon the total depravity and the hope-less immorality of the negro would have been written, based upon this particular case as a text. With such facts to prove the falsity of the charge that "the crime of rape is well-nigh wholly confined to the negro race," it is amazing that any writer of repute should affix his signature to such a slander.

But even if the negro's morals were as loose and as lax as some claim them to be, and if his belief in the virtue of women were as slight as we are told, the South has nobody to blame but itself. The only object lesson in virtue and morality which the negro received for 250 years came through the medium of slavery, and that peculiar institution was not calculated to set his standards of correct living very high. Men do not gather grapes of thorns nor figs of thistles. Throughout their entire period of bondage colored women were debauched by their masters. From the day they were liberated to the present time, prepossessing young colored girls have been considered the rightful prey of white gentlemen in the South, and they have been protected neither by public sentiment nor by law. In the South, the negro's home is not considered sacred by the superior race. White men are neither punished for invading it, nor lynched for violating colored women and girls. In discussing this phase of the race problem last year, one of the most godly and eloquent ministers in the Methodist Episcopal Church (white) expressed himself as follows: "The negro's teachers have been white. It is from the white man the negro has learned to lie and steal. If you wish to know who taught the negro licentiousness, you have only to look into the faces of thousands of mulatto people and get your an-swer." When one thinks how the negro was degraded in slavery, which discouraged, when it did not positively forbid, marriage between slaves, and considers the bad example set them by white masters, upon whom the negroes looked as scarcely lower than the angels, the freedman's self-control seems almost like a miracle of modern times. In demanding so much of the negro, the South places itself in the anomalous position of insisting that the conduct of the inferior race shall be better, and its stan-dards higher, than those of the people who claim to be superior.

The recent lynching in Springfield, Ohio, and in other cities of the North, show how rapidly this lawlessness is spreading throughout the United States. If the number of Americans who participate in this wild and diabolical carnival of blood does not diminish, nothing can prevent this country from becoming a by-word and a reproach throughout the civilized world. When Secretary Hay appealed to Roumania in behalf of the Jews, there were many sarcastic comments made by the press of that country and of other foreign lands about the inhuman treatment of the negro in the United States. In November, 1903, a manifesto signed by delegates from all over the world was issued at Brussels, Belgium, by the International Socialist Bureau, protesting against the lynching of negroes in the United States.

It is a source of deep regret and sorrow to many good Christians in this country that the church puts forth so few and such feeble protests against lynching. As the attitude of many ministers on the question of slavery greatly discouraged the abolitionists before the war, so silence in the pulpit concerning the lynching of negroes to-day plunges many of the persecuted race into deep gloom and dark despair. Thousands of dollars are raised by our churches every year to send missionaries to Christianize the heathen in foreign lands, and this is proper and right. But in addition to this foreign missionary work, would it not be well for our churches to inaugurate a crusade against the barbarism at home, which converts hundreds of white women and children into savages every year, while it crushes the spirit, blights the hearth and breaks the heart of hundreds of defenceless blacks? Not only do ministers fail, as a rule, to protest strongly against the hanging and burning of negroes, but some actually condone the crime without incurring the displeasure of their congregations or invoking the censure of the church. Although the church court which tried the preacher in Wilmington, Delaware, accused of inciting his community to riot and lynching by means of an incendiary sermon, found him guilty of "unministerial and unchristian conduct," of advocating mob murder and of thereby breaking down the public respect for the law, yet it simply admonished him to be "more careful in the future" and inflicted no punishment at all. Such indifference to lynching on the part of the church recalls the experience of Abraham Lincoln, who refused to join church in Springfield, Illinois, because only three out of twenty-two ministers in the whole city stood with him in his effort to free the slave. But, however unfortunate may have been the attitude of some of the churches on the question of slavery before the war, from the moment the shackles fell from the black man's limbs to the present day, the American Church has been most kind and generous in its treatment of the backward and struggling race. Nothing but ignorance or malice could prompt one to disparage the efforts put forth by the churches in the negro's behalf. But, in the face of so much lawlessness today, surely there is a role for the Church Militant to play. When one reflects upon the large number of negroes who are yearly hurled into eternity, unshriven by priest and untried by law, one cannot help realizing that as a nation we have fallen upon grave times, indeed. Surely, it is time for the ministers in their pulpits and the Christians in their pews to fall upon their knees and pray for deliverance from this rising tide of barbarism which threatens to deluge the whole land.

How can lynching be extirpated in the United States? There are just two ways in which this can be accomplished. In the first place, lynching can never be suppressed in the South, until the masses of ignorant white people in that section are educated and lifted to a higher moral plane. It is difficult for one who has not seen these people to comprehend the density of their ignorance and the depth of their degradation. A well-known white author who lives in the South describes them as follows:

"Wholly ignorant, absolutely without culture, apparently without even the capacity to appreciate the nicer feelings or higher sense, yet conceited on account of their white skin which they constantly dishonor, they make, when aroused, as wild and brutal a mob as ever disgraced the face of the earth."[3]

In lamenting the mental backwardness of the white people of the South, the Atlanta "Constitution" expressed itself as follows two years ago: "We have as many illiterate white men over the age of twenty-one years in the South to-day as there were fifty-two years ago, when the census of 1850 was taken." Over against these statistics stands the record of the negro, who has reduced his illiteracy 44.5 per cent, in forty years. The hostility which has always existed between the poor whites and the negroes of the South has been greatly intensified in these latter days, by the material and intellectual advancement of the negro. The wrath of a Spanish bull, before whose maddened eyes a red flag is flaunted, is but a feeble attempt at temper compared with the seething, boiling rage of the average white man in the South who beholds a well-educated negro dressed in fine or becoming clothes. In the second place, lynching cannot be suppressed in the South until all classes of white people who dwell there, those of high as well as middle and low degree, respect the rights of other human beings, no matter what may be the color of their skin, become merciful and just enough to cease their persecution of a weaker race and learn a holy reverence for the law.

It is not because the American people are cruel, as a whole, or indifferent on general principles to the suffering of the wronged or oppressed, that outrages against the negro are permitted to occur and go unpunished, but because many are ignorant of the extent to which they are carried, while others despair of eradicating them. The South has so industriously, persistently and eloquently preached the inferiority of the negro, that the North has apparently been converted to this view—the thousands of negroes of sterling qualities, moral worth and lofty patriotism to the contrary notwithstanding. The South has insisted so continuously and belligerently that it is the negro's best friend, that it understands him better than other people on the face of the earth and that it will brook interference from nobody in its method of dealing with him, that the North has been persuaded or intimidated into bowing to this decree.

Then, too, there seems to be a decline of the great convictions in which this government was conceived and into which it was born. Until there is a renaissance of popular belief in the principles of liberty and equality upon which this government was founded, lynching, the Convict Lease System, the Disfranchisement Acts, the Jim Crow Car Laws, unjust discriminations in the professions and trades and similar atrocities will continue to dishearten and degrade the negro, and stain the fair name of the United States. For there can be no doubt that the greatest obstacle in the way of extirpating lynching is the general attitude of the public mind toward this unspeakable crime. The whole country seems tired of hearing about the black man's woes. The wrongs of the Irish, of the Armenians, of the Roumanian and Russian Jews, of the exiles of Russia and of every other oppressed people upon the face of the globe, can arouse the sympathy and fire the indignation of the American public, while they seem to be all but indifferent to the murderous assaults upon the negroes in the South.

MARY CHURCH TERRELL.

What It Means to Be Colored in the Capital of the United States (1907)

Washington, D.C., has been called "The Colored Man's Paradise."[4] Whether this sobriquet was given to the national capital in bitter irony by a member of the handicapped race, as he reviewed some of his own persecutions and rebuffs, or whether it was given immediately after the war by an ex-slave-holder who for the first time in his life saw colored people walking about like freemen, minus the overseer and his whip, history saith not. It is certain that it would be difficult to find a worse misnomer for Washington than "The Colored Man's Paradise" if so prosaic a consideration as veracity is to determine the appropriateness of a name.

For fifteen years I have resided in Washington, and while it was far from being a paradise for colored people, when I first touched these shores it has been doing its level best ever since to make conditions for us intolerable. As a colored woman I might enter Washington any night, a stranger in a strange land, and walk miles without finding a place to lay my head. Unless I happened to know colored people who live here or ran across a chance acquaintance who could recommend a colored boarding-house to me, I should be obliged to spend the entire night wandering about. Indians, Chinamen, Filipinos, Japanese and representatives of any other dark race can find hotel accommodations, if they can pay for them. The colored man alone is thrust out of the hotels of the national capital like a leper.

As a colored woman I may walk from the Capitol to the White House, ravenously hungry and abundantly supplied with money with which to purchase a meal, without finding a single restaurant in which I would be permitted to take a morsel of food, if it was patronized by white people, unless I were willing to sit behind a screen. As a colored woman I cannot visit the tomb of the Father of this country, which owes its very existence to the love of freedom in the human heart and which stands for equal opportunity to all, without being forced to sit in the Jim Crow section of an electric car which starts from the very heart of the city—midway between the Capitol and the White House. If I refuse thus to be humiliated, I am cast into jail and forced to pay a fine for violating the Virginia laws. Every hour in the day Jim Crow cars filled with colored people, many of whom are intelligent and well to do, enter and leave the national capital.

As a colored woman I may enter more than one white church in Washington without receiving that welcome which as a human being I have the right to expect in the sanctuary of God. Sometimes the color blindness of the usher takes on that particular form which prevents a dark face from making any impression whatsoever upon his retina, so that it is impossible for him to see colored people at all. If he is not so afflicted, after keeping a colored man or woman waiting a long time, he will ungraciously show these dusky Christians who have had the temerity to thrust themselves into a temple where only the fair of face are expected to worship God to a seat in the rear, which is named in honor of a certain personage, well known in this country, and commonly called Jim Crow.

Unless I am willing to engage in a few menial occupations, in which the pay for my services would be very poor, there is no way for me to earn an honest living, if I am not a trained nurse or a dressmaker or can secure a position as teacher in the public schools, which is exceedingly difficult to do. It matters not what my intellectual attainments may be or how great is the need of the services of a competent person, if I try to enter many of the numerous vocations in which my white sisters are allowed to engage, the door is shut in my face.

From one Washington theater I am excluded altogether. In the remainder certain seats are set aside for colored people, and it is almost impossible to secure others. I once telephoned to the ticket seller just before a matinee and asked if a neat-appearing colored nurse would be allowed to sit in the parquet with her little white charge, and the answer rushed quickly and positively thru the receiver—NO. When I remonstrated a bit and told him that in some of the theaters colored nurses were allowed to sit with the white children for whom they cared, the ticket seller told me that in Washington it was very poor policy to employ colored nurses, for they were excluded from many places where white girls would be allowed to take children for pleasure.

If I possess artistic talent, there is not a single art school of repute which will admit me. A few years ago a colored woman who possessed great talent submitted some drawings to the Corcoran Art School, of Washington, which were accepted by the committee of awards, who sent her a ticket entitling her to a course in this school. But when the committee discovered that the young woman was colored they declined to admit her, and told her that if they had suspected that her drawings had been made by a colored woman they would not have examined them at all. The efforts of Frederick Douglass and a lawyer of great repute who took a keen interest in the affair were unavailing. In order to cultivate her talent this young woman was forced to leave her comfortable home in Washington and incur the expense of going to New York. Having entered the Woman's Art School of Cooper Union, she graduated with honor, and then went to Paris to continue her studies, where she achieved signal success and was complimented by some of the greatest living artists in France.

With the exception of the Catholic University, there is not a single white college in the national capital to which colored people are admitted, no matter how great their ability, how lofty their ambition, how unexceptionable their character or how great their thirst for knowledge may be.

A few years ago the Columbian Law School admitted colored students, but in deference to the Southern white students the authorities have decided to exclude them altogether.

Some time ago a young woman who had already attracted some attention in the literary world by her volume of short stories answered an advertisement which appeared in a Washington newspaper, which called for the services of a skilled stenographer and expert typewriter. It is unnecessary to state the reasons why a young woman whose literary ability was so great as that possessed by the one referred to should decide to earn money in this way. The applicants were requested to send specimens of their work and answer certain questions concerning their experience and their speed before they called in person. In reply to her application the young colored woman, who, by the way, is very fair and attractive indeed, received a letter from the firm stating that her references and experience were the most satisfactory that had been sent and requesting her to call. When she presented herself there was some doubt in the mind of the man to whom she was directed concerning her racial pedigree, so he asked her point-blank whether she was colored or white. When she confessed the truth the merchant expressed great sorrow and deep regret that he could not avail himself of the services of so competent a person, but frankly admitted that employing a colored woman in his establishment in any except a menial position was simply out of the question.

Another young friend had an experience which, for some reasons, was still more disheartening and bitter than the one just mentioned. In order to secure lucrative employment she left Washington and went to New York. There she worked her way up in one of the largest dry goods stores till she was placed as saleswoman in the cloak department. Tired of being separated from her family she decided to return to Washington, feeling sure that, with her experience and her fine recommendation from the New York firm, she could easily secure employment. Nor was she overconfident, for the proprietor of one of the largest dry goods stores in her native city was glad to secure the services of a young woman who brought such hearty credentials from New York. She had not been in this store very long, however, before she called upon me one day and asked me to intercede with the proprietor in her behalf, saying that she had been discharged that afternoon because it had been discovered that she was colored. When I called upon my young friend's employer he made no effort to avoid the issue, as I feared he would. He did not say he had discharged the young saleswoman because she had not given satisfaction, as he might easily have done. On the contrary, he admitted without the slightest hesitation that the young woman he had just discharged was one of the best clerks he had ever had. In the cloak department, where she had been assigned, she had been a brilliant success, he said. "But I cannot keep Miss Smith in my employ," he concluded. "Are you not master of your own store?" I ventured to inquire. The proprietor of this store was a Jew, and I felt that it was particularly cruel, unnatural and cold-blooded for the representative of one oppressed and persecuted race to deal so harshly and unjustly with a member of another. I had intended to make this point when I decided to intercede for my young friend, but when I thought how a reference to the persecution of his own race would wound his feelings, the words froze on my lips. "When I first heard your friend was colored," he explained, "I did not believe it and said so to the clerks who made the statement. Finally, the girls who had been most pronounced in their opposition to working in a store with a colored girl came to me in a body and threatened to strike. 'Strike away,' said I, 'your places will be easily filled.' Then they started on another tack. Delegation after delegation began to file down to my office, some of the women my very best customers, to protest against my employing a colored girl. Moreover, they threatened to boycott my store if I did not discharge her at once. Then it became a question of bread and butter and I yielded to the inevitable—that's all. Now," said he, concluding, "if I lived in a great, cosmopolitan city like New York, I should do as I pleased, and refuse to discharge a girl simply because she was colored." But I thought of a similar incident that happened in New York. I remembered that a colored woman, as fair as a lily and as beautiful as a Madonna, who was the head saleswoman in a large department store in New York, had been discharged, after she held this position for years, when the proprietor accidentally discovered that a fatal drop of African blood was percolating somewhere thru her veins.

Not only can colored women secure no employment in the Washington stores, department and otherwise, except as menials, and such positions, of course, are few, but even as customers they are not infrequently treated with discourtesy both by the clerks and the proprietor himself. Following the trend of the times, the senior partner of the largest and best department store in Washington, who originally hailed from Boston, once the home of Wm. Lloyd Garrison, Wendell Phillips and Charles Sumner, if my memory serves me right, decided to open a restaurant in his store. Tired and hungry after her morning's shopping a colored school teacher, whose relation to her African progenitors is so remote as scarcely to be discernible to the naked eye, took a seat at one of the tables in the restaurant of this Boston store. After sitting unnoticed a long time the colored teacher asked a waiter who passed her by if she would not take her order. She was quickly informed that colored people could not be served in that restaurant and was obliged to leave in confusion and shame, much to the amusement of the waiters and the guests who had noticed the incident. Shortly after that a teacher in Howard University, one of the best schools for colored youth in the country, was similarly insulted in the restaurant of the same store.

In one of the Washington theaters from which colored people are excluded altogether, members of the race have been viciously assaulted several times, for the proprietor well knows that colored people have no redress for such discriminations against them in the District courts. Not long ago a colored clerk in one of the departments who looks more like his paternal ancestors who fought for the lost cause than his grandmothers who were victims of the peculiar institution, bought a ticket for the parquet of this theater in which colored people are nowhere welcome, for himself and mother, whose complexion is a bit swarthy. The usher refused to allow the young man to take the seats for which his tickets called and tried to snatch from him the coupons. A scuffle ensued and both mother and son were ejected by force. A suit was brought against the proprietor and the damages awarded the injured man and his mother amounted to the munificent sum of one cent. One of the teachers in the Colored High School received similar treatment in the same theater.

Not long ago one of my little daughter's bosom friends figured in one of the most pathetic instances of which I have ever heard. A gentleman who is very fond of children promised to take six little girls in his neighborhood to a matinee. It happened that he himself and five of his little friends were so fair that they easily passed muster, as they stood in judgment before the ticket-seller and the ticket taker. Three of the little girls were sisters, two of whom were very fair and the other a bit brown. Just as this little girl, who happened to be last in the procession, went by the ticket taker, that argus-eyed sophisticated gentleman detected something which caused a deep, dark frown to mantle his brow and he did not allow her to pass. "I guess you have made a mistake," he called to the host of this theater party. "Those little girls," pointing to the fair ones, "may be admitted, but this one," designating the brown one, "can't." But the colored man was quite equal to the emergency. Fairly frothing at the mouth with anger he asked the ticket taker what he meant, what he was trying to insinuate about that particular little girl. "Do you mean to tell me," he shouted in rage, "that I must go clear to the Philippine Islands to bring this child to the United States and then I can't take her to the theater in the National Capital?" The little ruse succeeded brilliantly, as he knew it would. "Beg your pardon," said the ticket taker, "don't know what I was thinking about. Of course she can go in."

"What was the matter with me this afternoon? mother," asked the little brown girl innocently, when she mentioned the affair at home. "Why did the man at the theater let my two sisters and the other girls in and try to keep me out?" In relating this incident, the child's mother told me her little girl's question, which showed such blissful ignorance of the depressing, cruel conditions which confronted her, completely unnerved her for a time.

Altho white and colored teachers are under the same Board of Education and the system for the children of both races is said to be uniform, prejudice against the colored teachers in the public schools is manifested in a variety of ways. From 1870 to 1900 there was a colored superintendent at the head of the colored schools. During all that time the directors of the cooking, sewing, physical culture, manual training, music and art departments were colored people. Six years ago a change was inaugurated. The colored superintendent was legislated out of office and the directorships, without a single exception, were taken from colored teachers and given to the whites. There was no complaint about the work done by the colored directors no more than is heard about every officer in every school. The directors of the art and physical culture departments were particularly fine. Now, no matter how competent or superior the colored teachers in our public schools may be, they know that they can never rise to the height of a directorship, can never hope to be more than an assistant and receive the meager salary therefor, unless the present regime is radically changed.

Not long ago one of the most distinguished kindergartners in the country came to deliver a course of lectures in Washington. The colored teachers were eager to attend, but they could not buy the coveted privilege for love or money. When they appealed to the director of kindergartens, they were told that the expert kindergartner had come to Washington under the auspices of private individuals, so that she could not possibly have them admitted. Realizing what a loss colored teachers had sustained in being deprived of the information and inspiration which these lectures afforded, one of the white teachers volunteered to repeat them as best she could for the benefit of her colored co-laborers for half the price she herself had paid, and the proposition was eagerly accepted by some.

Strenuous efforts are being made to run Jim Crow cars in the national capital. "Resolved, that a Jim Crow law should be adopted and enforced in the District of Columbia," was the subject of a discussion engaged in last January by the Columbian Debating Society of the George Washington University in our national capital, and the decision was rendered in favor of the affirmative. Representative Heflin, of Alabama, who introduced a bill providing for Jim Crow street cars in the District of Columbia last winter, has just received a letter from the president of the East Brookland Citizens' Association "indorsing the movement for separate street cars and sincerely hoping that you will be successful in getting this enacted into a law as soon as possible." Brookland is a suburb of Washington.

The colored laborer's path to a decent livelihood is by no means smooth. Into some of the trades unions here he is admitted, while from others he is excluded altogether. By the union men this is denied, altho I am personally acquainted with skilled workmen who tell me they are not admitted into the unions because they are colored. But even when they are allowed to join the unions they frequently derive little benefit, owing to certain tricks of the trade. When the word passes round that help is needed and colored laborers apply, they are often told by the union officials that they have secured all the men they needed, because the places are reserved for white men, until they have been provided with jobs, and colored men must remain idle, unless the supply of white men is too small.

I am personally acquainted with one of the most skilful laborers in the hardware business in Washington. For thirty years he has been working for the same firm. He told me he could not join the union, and that his employer had been almost forced to discharge him, because the union men threatened to boycott his store if he did not. If another man could have been found at the time to take his place he would have lost his job, he said. When no other human being can bring a refractory chimney or stove to its senses, this colored man is called upon as the court of last appeal. If he fails to subdue it, it is pronounced a hopeless case at once. And yet this expert workman receives much less for his services than do white men who cannot compare with him in skill.

And so I might go on citing instance after instance to show the variety of ways in which our people are sacrificed on the altar of prejudice in the Capital of the United States and how almost insurmountable are the obstacles which block his path to success. Early in life many a colored youth is so appalled by the helplessness and hopelessness of his situation in this country that in a sort of stoical despair he resigns himself to his fate. "What is the good of our trying to acquire an education? We can't all be preachers, teachers, doctors, and lawyers. Besides those professions there is almost nothing for colored people to do but engage in the most menial occupations, and we do not need an education for that." More than once such remarks, uttered by young men and women in our public schools who possess brilliant intellects, have wrung my heart.

It is impossible for any white person in the United States, no matter how sympathetic and broad, to realize what life would mean to him if his incentive to effort were suddenly snatched away. To the lack of incentive to effort, which is the awful shadow under which we live, may be traced the wreck and ruin of scores of colored youth. And surely nowhere in the world do oppression and persecution based solely on the color of the skin appear more hateful and hideous than in the capital of the United States, because the chasm between the principles upon which this Government was founded, in which it still professes to believe, and those which are daily practiced under the protection of the flag, yawn so wide and deep.

WASHINGTON, D.C.

SOURCES

Terrell, Mary Church. "Lynching from a Negro's Point of View." *North American Review* 178, no. 571 (June 1, 1904): 853–68. https://www.jstor.org/stable/25150991.
———. "What It Means to Be Colored in the Capital of the United States." *Independent* 62, no. 3034 (January 24, 1907): 181–86. Oberlin College Archives. Collections of the Five Colleges of Ohio. https://ohio5.contentdm.oclc.org/digital/collection/p15963coll16/id/566.

NOTES

Chapter opening photo: Mary Church Terrell, ca. 1880–1900. Library of Congress, Prints & Photographs Division, LC-DIG-ppmsca-68742.

1. In the original publication, the byline that precedes this essay is "By Mary Church Terrell, Honorary President of the National Association of Colored Women."
2. American theologian Andrew Sledd (1870–1939) was a white university professor at Emory College (Oxford, Georgia) when, in 1899, he witnessed the lynching and burning of Sam Hose, an African American man. His descriptions of gruesome lynchings, including Hose's, appear in "The Negro: Another View," an article Sledd published in the July 1902 issue of *Atlantic Monthly*, in which he nevertheless advocates for segregation. Shortly after its publication, Sledd was forced to resign from Emory.
3. Terrell quotes Sledd's "The Negro: Another View," *Atlantic Monthly* (July 1902), 70.
4. This speech was delivered on October 10, 1906, at the United Women's Club, Washington, DC. It originally appeared in print with the following note from the editor: "The special interest in the present article rests in the fact that it describes conditions in Washington, a city governed solely by the United States Congress. It is our only city which represents the whole country. It lies between the two sections, North and South, and has a very large negro population. The article is timely now that Senator Foraker has brought before the Senate the dismissal without honor of the negro battalion. The writer is a colored woman of much culture and recognized standing."

Katherine Davis Chapman Tillman

1870–unknown

KATHERINE DAVIS CHAPMAN TILLMAN was an African American writer born in Mound City, Illinois. She started writing poetry and corresponding with newspapers at a young age, publishing her first poem in the *Christian Recorder* in 1888. Her poetry and essays frequently appeared in religious publications, such as the *A.M.E. Church Review*, and she authored two historical plays and two novellas, *Beryl Weston's Ambition: The Story of an Afro-American Girl's Life* (1893) and *Clancy Street* (serialized, 1898–99). In 1902, she published her book of poetry, *Recitations*. Tillman's avowed mission was to uplift African American women and girls with her writing, encouraging them to believe in their own abilities and their equality with men.

The Negro among Anglo-Saxon Poets (1898)

The type of Negro oftenest depicted by modern fiction writers, is a genuine Southern production, a race of ante-bellum days—the simple-hearted, affectionate negro, who has no higher ambition than to serve faithfully the children of his former master. Isabel A. Mallon's story entitled, "The Colonel and Me," in the recent issue of the *Ladies' Home Journal*, is an example of this class of literature of which thinking Negroes are becoming heartily tired.

While these stories occasionally interest, they never inspire the Negro reader, and besides, give the Anglo-Saxon reader false ideas concerning the race. It is praiseworthy to be a good servant, but all Negroes are not content to be merely hewers of wood and drawers of water. Out of the Negro race must come soldiers, statesmen, poets, authors, financiers and reformers, and fiction that is written with Negro men and women as heroes and heroines must keep these facts in mind.

In sharp contrast with the narrowness of the majority of prose writers, especially those of American descent, are the lines which have written of the Negro by some of the world's greatest poets.

"The poet," says Ralph Waldo Emerson, "is the sayer, the namer. He is a sovereign and stands on the centre.... the end of expression.... The signs and credentials are that he announces that which no man foretold."[1]

Viewing the poet through the eyes of America's foremost essayist, it is extremely interesting to note the place occupied by the Negro in Anglo-Saxon poetry.

Beginning with the poet who declared "Ethiopia shall soon stretch forth her hands unto God," we find a more inspiring ideal of Negro manhood.

If we go to Shakespeare, the king of poets, and the acknowledged master of English prose, we shall find among his marvelous delineations of character a type of Negro manhood both generous and brave.

Othello, a brave Moorish general of undeniably black complexion, by the bewitching tales and exploits on the "tented field," woos and wins Desdemona, the only daughter of Brabantio, a Venetian. To use Othello's words:

"She loved me for the danger I had passed,
And I loved her that she did pity them." (Act I, Scene 2.)

"I fetch my life and being
From men of royal siege and my demerits
May speak unbonneted to as fair a fortune
As this that I have reached." (Act I, Scene 2)

Following the reading of this interesting tragedy, we see how a noble, unsuspicious nature is gradually poisoned and disturbed by the crafty Iago, until the gentle Desdemona is believed by Othello to be untrue to her marriage vows and dies a victim to the Moor's unfounded jealousy.

There seems little doubt to unprejudiced minds that Othello had Negro blood flowing through his veins. Shakespeare refers to this fact several times in the play, and of all the writers who have lived none knew better than Shakespeare how to say exactly what he wished. Iago, alluding to Othello's color, calls him an "old black ram," and Brabantio says that Desdemona

"Runs from her guardage to the sooty
Bosom of such a thing as thou."[2]

Desdemona says in extenuation of her love for the Moor: "I saw Othello's visage in his mind" (Act I, Scene 3).

For another spirited tale, let us read "The Runaway Slave at Pilgrim's Point," written by Elizabeth Barrett Browning. A slave girl loved a fellow slave. Her affection was returned, and they pledged themselves to be true to each other, but alas, as the slave girl says:

"We were black, we were black,
We had no claim to love and bliss;
What marvel if each went to wrack?
They wrung my cold hands out of his,
They dragged him where I crawled
To touch his blood's mark in the dust.

A wrong followed by a deeper wrong,
Mere grief's too good for such as I,
So the white man brought the shame ere long,
To strangle the sob of my agony,
They would not leave me with dull wet eye,
It was too merciful to let me weep pure tears and die."

Time passed, and an unwelcome child with the master's likeness stamped upon its little face, looked up into its slave mother's face and demanded nourishment.

"For hark! I will tell you low, low
I am black you see,
And the babe who lay on my bosom so
Was far too white for me;
As white as the ladies who scorned to pray
Beside me at church but yesterday,
Though my tears had washed a place for my knee."

Crazed by her wrongs, the poor girl took her baby's life, and afterward buried it in the quiet woods that surrounded the plantation. To her pursuers she cried:

"I am not mad; I am black,
I see you staring in my face,
Ye are born of the Washington race,
And this land is the free America;
And this mark on my wrist (I prove what I say)
Ropes tied me up here to the flogging place."

"You think I shrieked then? Not a sound!
I hung as a gourd hangs in the sun,
I only cursed them all around
As softly as I might have done
My very own child! From these sands
Up to the mountains, lift up your hands,
O slaves, and end what I begun."

The next poem to which the reader's attention is invited, is Whittier's Toussaint l'Ouverture, founded upon an incident in real life. Toussaint l'Ouverture, the black chieftain of Hayti, formerly a slave on the plantation "de Libertas," belonging to M. Bayou, successfully led an insurrection against the slaveholders and won freedom for his enslaved countrymen. Remembering the kindness of his former owner, Toussaint generously assisted the family to escape to Baltimore. The Island of Hayti, under the rule of Toussaint was happy and prosperous, until, in 1801, the brave leader was treacherously betrayed by order of Napoleon and conveyed to France, where he died, April, 1803, about eight months after his arrival.

Says Godwin, "The West Indies since their first discovery by Columbus cannot boast of a single name which deserves comparison with that of Toussaint l'Ouverture."

"Brief was the silence, once again
Pealed to the skies that frantic yell;
Glowed on the Heavens a fiery strain,
And flashes rose and fell;
And painted on the blood red sky
Dark naked arms were tossed on high
And round the white man's lordly hall
Trode fierce and free the brute he made,
And those who crept along the wall,

And answered to his lightest call
    With more than spaniel dread—
The creatures of his lawless beck
Were trampling on his very neck!
Then, injured Afric—for the shame
Of thy own daughters, vengeance came
Full on the scornful hearts of those
Who mocked thee in thy nameless woes,
And to thy hapless children gave
One choice—pollution or the grave!
Dark-browed Toussaint!—the storm had risen,
Obedient to his master-call,
The Negro's mind had burst its prison,
    His hand its iron thrall."

In concluding this grand tribute Whittier feelingly says:

"Sleep calmly in thy dungeon tomb
Beneath Bensancon's alien sky,
Dark Haytien! for the time shall come,
    Yea, even now is nigh,
When everywhere thy name shall be,
Redeemed from color's infamy,
And men shall learn to speak of thee,
As one of earth's great spirits, born
In servitude and nursed in scorn,
Casting aside the weary weight
And fetters of its low estate,
In that strong majesty which knows
No color, tongue or clime."

Another poem that appeals to all bold, courageous souls in "The Warning," by Henry Wadsworth Longfellow, who, some critics aver, won more English hearts over to the anti-slavery cause than did the "Quaker Poet."

"Beware! The Israelite of old who tore
The lion in his path, when poor and blind,
He saw the blessed light of heaven no more,
Shorn of his noble strength and forced to grind

In prison at last led forth to be
A panderer to Philistine revelry!
Upon the pillars of the temple laid
His desperate hands, and in its overthrow
Destroyed himself, and with him, those who made
A cruel mockery of his sightless woe
The poor blind slave, the scoff, the pest of all,
Expired and thousands perished in the fall.
Shorn of his strength and bound with chains of steel,
Who may in some grim revel raise his hand,
And shake the pillars of the Commonwealth,
Till the vast temples of our liberties,
A shapeless mass of wreck and rubbish lies."

Once more and I am done. Some time ago in the columns of the *Judge*, appeared the thoughtful face of a Negro woman. Underneath the portrait was a poem by A. T. Worden, entitled, "An American type."

Behold in their calm face,
The modern Sphinx with such a thoughtful mien
As bids us pause, when like a Frankenstein
A nation dares create another race.

No longer here the crude
And unformed features of a savage face;
But in those pleading eyes a kindred race,
Asks for the highway out of servitude.

Like as the Amazon
With mighty currents marks the ocean hue
Until her leagues of tide blend with the blue,
So do these patient millions still press on.

Such at the cradle side
Have crooned as foster-mothers, sung and wept,
Across the chamber doors of pain have slept,
And for their sisters pale have gladly died.

Two hundred weary years
Of burden-bearing in a shadowed path,

And yet no hand is raised in cruel wrath,
And all their wrongs evoke as yet but tears.

Study the problem well
For in this sphinx a message somewhere lies;
A nation's glory or its shame may rise
From out the reading what these features tell.

It is from perusing poems like these that our sorely tried spirits arise refreshed, and we are enabled to go on from "strength to strength."

SOURCE

Tillman, Katherine Davis Chapman. "The Negro among Anglo-Saxon Poets." *A.M.E. Church Review* 14 (July 1898): 106–12.

NOTES

1. Tillman quotes "The Poet" (1844), a lecture-turned-essay by American transcendentalist Ralph Waldo Emerson (1803–1882).
2. [Original editor's note.] The labored effort to prove that Shakespeare did not intend Othello as a Negro must in time give way to fairness, common sense, and the Shakespearean text itself. In speaking of the passage in Act I, Scene 1, where Shakespeare makes Roderigo, the Venetian gentleman, call Othello "the thick-lips," Edward Knight, the editor of Collier's edition of Shakespeare, exercises a plethora of ingenuity upon a paucity of material to disprove this intention. He says the popular notion of the difference between a Moor and an uncivilized African was in Shakespeare's day somewhat confused. Mr. Knight confesses that "it is by no means impossible that Othello was represented as a Negro" on the stage of that time, but thinks it impossible that Shakespeare conformed to that idea. He cites Coleridge as coinciding with his views, though not denying that there would have been nothing unusual in the presentation of a Negro character in such a role.

The answer to all this is that by their own admission such a thing would have been no innovation and that no antagonism would have interfered; that Shakespeare, "the myriad-minded," was not fettered by latter-day prejudices against the Negro; that whatever may have been the motive of Roderigo in calling Othello "thick-lipped," the designation could only have point by specifying a physical peculiarity actually existing, and one, too, considered characteristic of the Negro; that to this day Negroes are called in Europe black-a-moors; and by the historical fact that in Venice all colors and nationalities mingled, including

Negroes, on terms of perfect equality; that it was a regular policy of the Venetian Republic to employ foreign officers in places of command in order to lessen the danger of intrigues at home. These last two points are fully and strongly brought out by a writer as follows:

Rymer, certainly no friend to the Negro, in his "Short View of Tragedy," admits this custom in Venice and also, with censure, accepts the view that Shakespeare certainly did intend to make Othello a Negro. Here are his exact words (p. 91): "With us [the English] a black-a-moor might rise to be a trumpeter; but Shakespeare would not have him less than a lieutenant-general. With us a Moor might mean some little drab, or small-coal wench: Shakespeare would provide him the daughter and heir of some great lord or privy councilor; and all the town shall reckon it a very suitable match."

Literary honesty requires that the truth be told.

While not a part of the argument, it is an interesting "aside" to say that a negro, Ira F. Aldridge, was long considered in Europe as the best impersonator of the character Othello on the stage.

Sojourner Truth

1797–1883

SOJOURNER TRUTH was born Isabella Baumfree, an enslaved person in Ulster County, New York. She escaped to freedom in 1826 and became an itinerant preacher as well as a lecturer on the horrors of slavery and the need for women's rights. We have included selections from her 1828 memoir, as well as a lesser-known but probably more accurate version of what has become known as her "Ain't I a Woman?" speech, transcribed by reporter and close friend Marius Robinson, who was present at the event and published the speech less than a month later. Robinson and Truth also went over his transcription together before it was printed. Note that it does not include the phrase "ain't I a woman?" nor is it in the Southern dialect that Frances Gage imposed upon it when she published her more popular version of the speech in 1863.

From *Narrative of Sojourner Truth, a Northern Slave* (1850)

HER ESCAPE

The question in her mind, and one not easily solved, now was, "How can I get away?" So, as was her usual custom, she "told God she was afraid to go in the night, and in the day every body would see her." At length, the thought came to her that she could leave just before the day dawned, and get out of the neighborhood where she was known before the people were much astir. "Yes," said she, fervently, "that's a good thought! Thank you, God, for *that* thought!" So, receiving it as coming direct from God, she acted upon it, and one fine morning, a little before day-break, she might have been seen stepping stealthily away from the rear of Master Dumont's house, her infant on one arm and her wardrobe on the other; the bulk and weight of which, probably, she never found so convenient as on the present occasion, a cotton handkerchief containing both her clothes and her provisions.

As she gained the summit of a high hill, a considerable distance from her master's, the sun offended her by coming forth in all his pristine splendor. She thought it never was so light before; indeed, she thought it much too light. She stopped to look about her, and ascertain if her pursuers were yet in sight. No one appeared, and, for the first time, the question came up for settlement, "Where, and to whom, shall I go?" In all her thoughts of getting away, she had not once asked herself whither she should direct her steps. She sat down, fed her infant, and again turning her thoughts to God, her only help, she prayed him to direct her to some safe asylum. And soon it occurred to her, that there was a man living somewhere in the direction she had been pursuing, by the name of Levi Rowe, whom she had known, and who, she thought, would be likely to befriend her. She accordingly pursued her way to his house, where she found him ready to entertain and assist her, though he was then on his death-bed. He bade her partake of the hospitalities of his house, said he knew of two good places where she might get in, and requested his wife to show her where they were to be found. As soon as she came in sight of the first house, she recollected having seen it and its inhabitants before, and instantly exclaimed, "That's the place for me; I shall stop there." She went there, and found the good people of the house, Mr. and Mrs. Van Wagener, absent, but was kindly received and hospitably entertained by their excellent mother, till the return of her children. When they arrived, she made her case known to them. They listened to her story, assuring her they never turned the needy away, and willingly gave her employment.

She had not been there long before her old master, Dumont, appeared, as she had anticipated; for when she took French leave of him, she resolved not to go too far from him, and not put him to as much trouble in looking her up—for the latter he was sure to do—as Tom and Jack had done when they ran away from him, a short time before. This was very considerate in her, to say the least, and a proof that "like begets like." He had often considered *her* feelings, though not always, and she was equally considerate.

When her master saw her, he said, "Well, Bell, so you've run away from me." "No, I did not *run away*; I walked away by day-light, and all because you had promised me a year of my time." His reply was, "You must go back with me." Her decisive answer was, "No, I *won't* go back with you." He said, "Well, I shall take the *child.*" *This* also was as stoutly negatived.

Mr. Isaac S. Van Wagener then interposed, saying, he had never been in the practice of buying and selling slaves; he did not believe in slavery; but, rather than have Isabella taken back by force, he would buy her services for the balance of the year—for which her master charged twenty dollars, and five in addition for the child. The sum was paid, and her master Dumont departed; but not till he had heard Mr. Van Wagener tell her not to call him master—adding, "there is but *one* master; and he who is *your* master is *my* master." Isabella inquired what she *should* call him? He answered, "call me Isaac Van Wagener, and my wife is Maria Van Wagener." Isabella could not understand this, and thought it a *mighty change,* as it most truly was from a master whose word was law, to simple Isaac S. Van Wagener, who was master to *no* one. With these noble people, who, though they could not be the masters of slaves, were undoubtedly a portion of God's nobility, she resided one year, and from them she derived the name of Van Wagener; he being her last master in the eye of the law, and a slave's surname is ever the same as his master; that is, if he is allowed to have any other name than Tom, Jack, or Guffin. Slaves have sometimes been severely punished for adding their master's name to their own. But when they have no particular title to it, it is no particular offence.

[. . .]

GLEANINGS

There are some hard things that crossed Isabella's life while in slavery, that she has no desire to publish, for various reasons. First, because the parties from whose hands she suffered them have rendered up their account to a higher tribunal, and their innocent friends alone are living, to have their feelings injured by the recital; secondly, because they are not all for the public ear, from their very nature; thirdly, and not least, because, she says, were she to tell all that happened to her as a slave—all that she knows is "God's truth"—it would seem to others, especially the uninitiated, so unaccountable, so unreasonable, and what is usually called so unnatural, (though it may be questioned whether people do not always act naturally,) they would not easily believe it. "Why, no!" she says, "they'd call me a liar! they would, indeed! and I do not wish to say anything to destroy my own character for veracity, though what I say is strictly true."

Some things have been omitted through forgetfulness, which not having been mentioned in their places, can only be briefly spoken of here;—such as, that her father Bomefree had had two wives before he took Mau-mau Bett; one of whom, if not both, were torn from him by the iron hand of the ruthless trafficker in human flesh;—that her husband, Thomas, after one of *his* wives had been sold away from him, ran away to New York City, where he remained a year or two, before he was discovered and taken back to the prison-house of slavery;—that her master Dumont, when he promised Isabella one year of her time, before the State should make her free, made the same promise to her husband, and in addition to freedom, they were promised a log cabin for a home of their own; all of which, with the one-thousand-and-one day-dreams resulting therefrom, went into the repository of unfulfilled promises and unrealized hopes;—that she had often heard her father repeat a thrilling story of a little slave-child, which, because it annoyed the family with its cries, was caught up by a white man, who dashed its brains out against the wall. An Indian (for Indians were plenty in that region then) passed along as the bereaved mother washed the bloody corpse of her murdered child, and learning the cause of its death, said, with characteristic vehemence, "If I had been here, I would have put my tomahawk in his head!" meaning the murderer's.

Of the cruelty of one Hasbrouck.—He had a sick slave-woman, who was lingering with a slow consumption, whom he made to spin, regardless of her weakness and suffering; and this woman had a child, that was un-able to walk or talk, at the age of five years, neither could it cry like other children, but made a constant, piteous moaning sound. This exhibition of helplessness and imbecility, instead of exciting the master's pity, stung his cupidity, and so enraged him, that he would kick the poor thing about like a foot-ball.

Isabella's informant had seen this brute of a man, when the child was curled up under a chair, innocently amusing itself with a few sticks, drag it hence, that he might have the pleasure of tormenting it. She had seen him, with one blow of his foot, send it rolling quite across the room, and down the steps at the door. Oh, how she wished it might instantly die! "But," she said, "it seemed as tough as a moccasin." Though it *did* die at last, and made glad the heart of its friends; and its persecutor, no doubt, rejoiced with them, but from very different motives. But the day of his retribution was not far off—for he sickened, and his reason fled. It was fearful to hear his old slave soon tell how, in the day of his calamity, she treated *him.*

She was very strong, and was therefore selected to support her master, as he sat up in bed, by putting her arms around, while she stood behind him. It was then that she did her best to wreak her vengeance on him. She would clutch his feeble frame in her iron grasp, as in a vice; and, when her mistress did not see, would give him a squeeze, a shake, and lifting him up, set him down again, as *hard as possible.* If his breathing betrayed too tight a grasp, and her mistress said, "Be careful, don't hurt him, Soan!" her ever-ready answer was, "Oh no, Missus, no," in her most pleasant tone— and then, as soon as Missus's eyes and ears were engaged away, another grasp—another shake—another bounce. She was afraid the disease alone would let him recover,—an event she dreaded more than to do wrong herself. Isabella asked her, if she were not afraid his spirit would haunt her. "Oh, no," says Soan; "he was *so* wicked, the devil will never let him out of hell long enough for that."

Many slaveholders boast of the love of their slaves. How would it freeze the blood of some of them to know what kind of love rankles in the bosoms of slaves for them! Witness the attempt to poison Mrs. Calhoun, and hundreds of similar cases. Most *"surprising"* to every body, because committed by slaves supposed to be so *grateful* for their chains.

These reflections bring to mind a discussion on this point, between the writer and a slaveholding friend in Kentucky, on Christmas morning, 1846. We had asserted, that until mankind were far in advance of what they are now, irresponsible power over our fellow-beings would be, as it is, abused. Our friend declared it was *his* conviction, that the cruelties of slavery existed chiefly in imagination, and that no person in D— County, where we then were, but would be above ill-treating a helpless slave. We answered, that if his belief was well-founded, the people in Kentucky were greatly in advance of the people of New England—for we would not dare say as much as that of any school-district there, letting alone counties. No, we would not answer for our own conduct even on so delicate a point.

The next evening, he very magnanimously overthrew his own position and established ours, by informing us that, on the morning previous, and as near as we could learn, at the very hour in which we were earnestly discussing the probabilities of the case, a young woman of fine appearance, and high standing in society, the pride of her husband, and the mother of an infant daughter, only a few miles from us, ay, in D— County, too, was actually beating in the skull of a slave-woman called Tabby; and not content with that, had her tied up and whipped, after her skull was broken, and she died hanging to the bedstead, to which she had been fastened. When informed that Tabby was dead, she answered, "I am *glad of it*, for she has worried my life out of me." But Tabby's highest good was probably not the end proposed by Mrs. M—, for no one supposed she meant to kill her. Tabby was considered quite lacking in good sense, and no doubt belonged to that class at the South, that are silly enough to "die of moderate correction."

A mob collected around the house for an hour or two, in that manner expressing a momentary indignation. But was she treated as a murderess? Not at all! She was allowed to take boat (for her residence was near the beautiful Ohio) that evening, to spend a few months with her absent friends, after which she returned and remained with her husband, no one to "molest or make her afraid."

Had she been left to the punishment of an outraged conscience from right motives, I would have "rejoiced with exceeding joy." But to see the life of one woman, and she a murderess, put in the balance against the lives of three millions of innocent slaves, and to contrast her punishment with what I felt would be the punishment of one who was merely suspected of being an equal friend of all mankind, regardless of color or condition, caused my blood to stir within me, and my heart to sicken at the thought. The husband of Mrs. M— was absent from home, at the time alluded to; and when he arrived, some weeks afterwards, bringing beautiful presents to his cherished companion, he beheld his once happy home deserted, Tabby murdered and buried in the garden, and the wife of his bosom, and the mother of his child, the doer of a dreadful deed, a *murderess!*

When Isabella went to New York City, she went in company with a Miss Grear, who introduced her to the family of Mr. James Latourette, a wealthy merchant, and a Methodist in religion; but who, the latter part of his life, felt that he had outgrown ordinances, and advocated free meetings, holding them at his own dwelling-house for several years previous to his death. She worked for them, and they generously gave her a home while she labored for others, and in their kindness made her as one of their own.

At that time, the "moral reform" movement was awakening the attention of the benevolent in that city. Many women, among whom were Mrs. Latourette and Miss Grear, became deeply interested in making an attempt to reform their fallen sisters, even the most degraded of them; and in this enterprise of labor and danger, they enlisted Isabella and others, who for a time put forth their most zealous efforts, and performed the work of missionaries with much apparent success. Isabella accompanied those ladies to the most wretched abodes of vice and misery, and sometimes she went where they dared not follow. They even succeeded in establishing prayer-meetings in several places, where such a thing might least have been expected.

But these meetings soon became the most noisy, shouting, ranting, and boisterous of gatherings; where they became delirious with excitement, and then exhausted from over-action. Such meetings Isabel had not much sympathy with, at best. But one evening she attended one of them, where the members of it, in a fit of ecstasy, jumped upon her cloak in such a manner as to drag her to the floor—and then, thinking she had fallen in a spiritual trance, they increased their glorifications on her account,—jumping, shouting, stamping, and clapping of hands; rejoicing so much over her spirit, and so entirely overlooking her body, that she suffered much, both from fear and bruises; and ever after refused to attend any more such meetings, doubting much whether God had any thing to do with such worship.

[...]

HER LAST INTERVIEW WITH HER MASTER

In the spring of 1849, Sojourner made a visit to her eldest daughter, Diana, who has ever suffered from ill health, and remained with Mr. Dumont, Isabella's humane master. She found him still living, though advanced in age, and reduced in property, (as he had been for a number of years,) but greatly enlightened on the subject of slavery. He said he could then see that "slavery was the wickedest thing in the world, the greatest curse the earth had ever felt—that it was then very clear to his mind that it was so, though, while he was a slaveholder himself, he did not see it so, and thought it was as right as holding any other property." Sojourner remarked to him, that it might be the same with those who are now slaveholders.

"O, no," replied he, with warmth, "it cannot be. For, now, the sin of slavery is so clearly written out, and so much talked against,—(why, the whole world cries out against it!)—that if any one says he don't know, and has not heard, he must, I think, be a liar. In my slaveholding days, there were few that spoke against it, and these few made little impression on any one. Had it been as it is now, think you I could have held slaves? No! I should not have dared to do it, but should have emancipated every one of them. Now, it is very different; all may hear if they will."

Yes, reader, if any one feels that the tocsin of alarm, or the anti-slavery trump, must sound a louder note before they can hear it, one would think they must be very hard of hearing,—yea, that they belong to that class, of whom it may be truly said, "they have stopped their ears that they may not hear."

She received a letter from her daughter Diana, dated Hyde Park, December 19, 1849, which informed her that Mr. Dumont had "gone West" with some of his sons—that he had taken along with him, probably through mistake, the few articles of furniture she had left with him. "Never mind," says Sojourner, "what we give to the poor, we lend to the Lord." She thanked the Lord with fervor, that she had lived to hear her master say such blessed things! She recalled the lectures he used to give his slaves, on speaking the truth and being honest, and laughing, she says he taught us not to lie and steal, when *he* was stealing all the time himself, and did not know it! Oh! how sweet to my mind was this confession! And what a confession for a master to make to a slave! A slaveholding master turned to a brother! Poor old man, may the Lord bless him, and all slave-holders partake of his spirit!

Speech to the Women's Rights Convention in Akron, Ohio, on May 29, 1851

May I say a few words?[1] I want to say a few words about this matter. I am a woman's rights. I have as much muscle as any man, and can do as much work as any man. I have plowed and reaped and husked and chopped and mowed, and can any man do more than that? I have heard much about the sexes being equal; I can carry as much as any man, and can eat as much too, if I can get it. I am as strong as any man that is now. As for intellect, all I can say is, if women have a pint and man a quart—why can't she have her little pint full? You need not be afraid to give us our rights for fear we will take too much, for we can't take more than our pint'll hold. The poor men seem to be all in confusion, and don't know what to do. Why children, if you have woman's rights, give it to her and you will feel better. You will have your own rights, and they won't be so much trouble. I can't read, but I can hear. I have heard the bible and have learned that Eve caused man to sin. Well if woman upset the world, do give her a chance to set it right side up again. The Lady has spoken about Jesus, how he never spurned woman from him, and she was right. When Lazarus died, Mary and Martha came to him with faith and love and besought him to raise their brother. And Jesus wept—and Lazarus came forth. And how came Jesus into the world? Through God who created him and woman who bore him. Man, where is your part?

But the women are coming up blessed be God and a few of the men are coming up with them. But man is in a tight place, the poor slave is on him, woman is coming on him, and he is surely between a hawk and a buzzard.

SOURCES

Truth, Sojourner. *Narrative of Sojourner Truth, a Northern Slave, Emancipated from Bodily Servitude by the State of New York, in 1828*, edited by Olive Gilbert, 41–43, 81–86, 124–26. Boston: published by the author, 1850.

———. "Women's Rights Convention." *Anti-Slavery Bugle* 6, no. 41 (June 21, 1851): 4. *Chronicling America: Historic American Newspapers*. Library of Congress. https://chroniclingamerica.loc.gov/lccn/sn83035487/1851-06-21/ed-1/seq-4/.

NOTE

1. This is the earliest known version of the famous "Ain't I a Woman?" speech, transcribed by Truth's friend Marius Robinson and approved by Truth before publication. Note that it doesn't have the Southern dialect and "Ain't I a woman?" refrain that was imposed twelve years later by Frances Gage in the *New York Independent*. The transcription in the *Anti-Slavery Bugle* is preceded by an editorial note: "One of the most unique and interesting speeches of the Convention was made by Sojourner Truth, an emancipated slave. It is impossible to transfer it to paper, or convey any adequate idea of the effect it produced upon the audience. Those only can appreciate it who saw her powerful form, her whole-souled, earnest gestures, and listened to her strong and truthful tones. She came forward to the platform and addressing the President said with great simplicity:" (the text follows).

Ida B. Wells-Barnett

1862–1931

IDA B. WELLS-BARNETT was one of the most prominent investigative journalists of her generation, an outspoken opponent of lynching, and one of the cofounders of the NAACP. A leading voice among African Americans and women alike, Wells-Barnett spent decades writing and lecturing in favor of civil rights and women's suffrage; in 2020, she was posthumously awarded the Pulitzer Prize for her antilynching journalism. Wells-Barnett regularly risked her life for her work; at one point, after she had published her position against lynching in her Memphis newspaper, the *Free Speech*, a mob destroyed the newspaper's office. In this pamphlet, she draws on this example and many others dealing with lynching.

From *Southern Horrors:*
Lynch Law in All Its Phases (1892)

PREFACE

The greater part of what is contained in these pages was published in the *New York Age* June 25, 1892, in explanation of the editorial which the Memphis whites considered sufficiently infamous to justify the destruction of my paper, *The Free Speech.*

Since the appearance of that statement, requests have come from all parts of the country that "Exiled," (the name under which it then appeared) be issued in pamphlet form. Some donations were made, but not enough for that purpose. The noble effort of the ladies of New York and Brooklyn Oct 5 have enabled me to comply with this request and give the world a true, unvarnished account of the causes of lynch law in the South.

This statement is not a shield for the despoiler of virtue, nor altogether a defense for the poor blind Afro-American Sampsons who suffer themselves to be betrayed by white Delilahs. It is a contribution to truth, an array of facts, the perusal of which it is hoped will stimulate this great American Republic to demand that justice be done though the heavens fall.

It is with no pleasure I have dipped my hands in the corruption here exposed. Somebody must show that the Afro-American race is more sinned against than sinning, and it seems to have fallen upon me to do so. The awful death-roll that Judge Lynch is calling every week is appalling, not only because of the lives it takes, the rank cruelty and outrage to the victims, but because of the prejudice it fosters and the stain it places against the good name of a weak race.

The Afro-American is not a bestial race. If this work can contribute in any way toward proving this, and at the same time arouse the conscience of the American people to a demand for justice to every citizen, and punishment by law for the lawless, I shall feel I have done my race a service. Other considerations are of minor importance.

New York City, Oct. 26, 1892.

Ida B. Wells.

CHAPTER II. The Black and White of It

The "Cleveland Gazette" of January 16, 1892, publishes a case in point. Mrs. J. S. Underwood, the wife of a minister of Elyria, Ohio, accused an

Afro-American of rape. She told her husband that during his absence in 1888, stumping the State for the Prohibition Party, the man came to the kitchen door, forced his way in the house and insulted her. She tried to drive him out with a heavy poker, but he overpowered and chloroformed her, and when she revived her clothing was torn and she was in a horrible condition. She did not know the man but could identify him. She pointed out William Offett, a married man, who was arrested and, being in Ohio, was granted a trial.

The prisoner vehemently denied the charge of rape, but confessed he went to Mrs. Underwood's residence at her invitation and was criminally intimate with her at her request. This availed him nothing against the sworn testimony of a minister's wife, a lady of the highest respectability. He was found guilty, and entered the penitentiary, December 14, 1888, for fifteen years. Some time afterwards the woman's remorse led her to confess to her husband that the man was innocent.

These are her words: "I met Offett at the Post Office. It was raining. He was polite to me, and as I had several bundles in my arms he offered to carry them home for me, which he did. He had a strange fascination for me, and I invited him to call on me. He called, bringing chestnuts and candy for the children. By this means we got them to leave us alone in the room. Then I sat on his lap. He made a proposal to me and I readily consented. Why I did so, I do not know, but that I did is true. He visited me several times after that and each time I was indiscreet. I did not care after the first time. In fact I could not have resisted, and had no desire to resist."

When asked by her husband why she told him she had been outraged, she said: "I had several reasons for telling you. One was the neighbors saw the fellows here, another was, I was afraid I had contracted a loathsome disease, and still another was that I feared I might give birth to a Negro baby. I hoped to save my reputation by telling you a deliberate lie." Her husband horrified by the confession had Offett, who had already served four years, released and secured a divorce.

There are thousands of such cases throughout the South, with the difference that the Southern white men in insatiate fury wreak their vengeance without intervention of law upon the Afro-Americans who consort with their women. A few instances to substantiate the assertion that some white women love the company of the Afro-American will not be out of place. Most of these cases were reported by the daily papers of the South.

In the winter of 1885-6 the wife of a practicing physician in Memphis, in good social standing whose name has escaped me, left home, husband and children, and ran away with her black coachman. She was with him a month before her husband found and brought her home. The coachman could not be found. The doctor moved his family away from Memphis, and is living in another city under an assumed name.

In the same city last year a white girl in the dusk of evening screamed at the approach of some parties that a Negro had assaulted her on the street. He was captured, tried by a white judge and jury, that acquitted him of the charge. It is needless to add if there had been a scrap of evidence on which to convict him of so grave a charge he would have been convicted.

Sarah Clark of Memphis loved a black man and lived openly with him. When she was indicted last spring for miscegenation, she swore in court that she was *not* a white woman. This she did to escape the penitentiary and continued her illicit relation undisturbed. That she is of the lower class of whites, does not disturb the fact that she is a white woman. "The leading citizens" of Memphis are defending the "honor" of *all* white women, *demi-monde*[1] included.

Since the manager of the "Free Speech" has been run away from Memphis by the guardians of the honor of Southern white women, a young girl living on Poplar St., who was discovered in intimate relations with a handsome mulatto young colored man, Will Morgan by name, stole her father's money to send the young fellow away from that father's wrath. She has since joined him in Chicago.

The Memphis "Ledger" for June 8th has the following; "If Lillie Bailey, a rather pretty white girl seventeen years of age, who is now at the City Hospital, would be somewhat less reserved about her disgrace there would be some very nauseating details in the story of her life. She is the mother of a little coon. The truth might reveal fearful depravity or it might reveal the evidence of a rank outrage. She will not divulge the name of the man who has left such black evidence of her disgrace, and, in fact, says it is a matter in which there can be no interest to the outside world. She came to Memphis nearly three months ago and was taken in at the Woman's Refuge in the southern part of the city. She remained there until a few weeks ago, when the child was born. The ladies in charge of the Refuge were horrified. The girl was at once sent to the City Hospital, where she has been since May 30th. She is a country girl. She came to Memphis from her father's farm, a short distance from Hernando, Miss. Just when she left there she would not say. In fact she says she came to

Memphis from Arkansas, and says her home is in that State. She is rather good looking, has blue eyes, a low forehead and dark red hair. The ladies at the Woman's Refuge do not know anything about the girl further than what they learned when she was an inmate of the institution; and she would not tell much. When the child was born an attempt was made to get the girl to reveal the name of the Negro who had disgraced her, she obstinately refused and it was impossible to elicit any information from her on the subject."

Note the wording. "The truth might reveal fearful depravity or rank outrage." If it had been a white child or Lillie Bailey had told a pitiful story of Negro outrage, it would have been a case of woman's weakness or assault and she could have remained at the Woman's Refuge. But a Negro child and to withhold its father's name and thus prevent the killing of another Negro "rapist." A case of "fearful depravity."

The very week the "leading citizens" of Memphis were making a spectacle of themselves in defense of all white women of every kind, an Afro-American, Mr. Stricklin, was found in a white woman's room in that city. Although she made no outcry of rape, he was jailed and would have been lynched, but the woman stated she bought curtains of him (he was a furniture dealer) and his business in her room that night was to put them up. A white woman's word was taken as absolutely in this case as when the cry of rape is made, and he was freed.

What is true of Memphis is true of the entire South. The daily papers last year reported a farmer's wife in Alabama had given birth to a Negro child. When the Negro farm hand who was plowing in the field heard it he took the mule from the plow and fled. The dispatches also told of a woman in South Carolina who gave birth to a Negro child and charged three men with being its father, *every one of whom has since disappeared.* In Tuscumbia, Ala., the colored boy who was lynched there last year for assaulting a white girl told her before his accusers that he had met her there in the woods often before.

Frank Weems of Chattanooga who was not lynched in May only because the prominent citizens became his body guard until the doors of the penitentiary closed on him, had letters in his pocket from the white woman in the case, making the appointment with him. Edward Coy who was burned alive in Texarkana, January 1, 1892, died protesting his innocence. Investigation since as given by the Bystander in the Chicago Inter-Ocean, October 1, proves:

1. The woman who was paraded as a victim of violence was of bad character; her husband was a drunkard and a gambler.

2. She was publicly reported and generally known to have been criminally intimate with Coy for more than a year previous.

3. She was compelled by threats, if not by violence, to make the charge against the victim.

4. When she came to apply the match Coy asked her if she would burn him after they had "been sweethearting" so long.

5. A large majority of the "superior" white men prominent in the affair are the reputed fathers of mulatto children.

These are not pleasant facts, but they are illustrative of the vital phase of the so-called "race question," which should properly be designated an earnest inquiry as to the best methods by which religion, science, law and political power may be employed to excuse injustice, barbarity and crime done to a people because of race and color. There can be no possible belief that these people were inspired by any consuming zeal to vindicate God's law against miscegenationists of the most practical sort. The woman was a willing partner in the victim's guilt, and being of the "superior" race must naturally have been more guilty.

In Natchez, Miss., Mrs. Marshall, one of the *creme de la creme* of the city, created a tremendous sensation several years ago. She has a black coachman who was married, and had been in her employ several years. During this time she gave birth to a child whose color was remarked, but traced to some brunette ancestor, and one of the fashionable dames of the city was its godmother. Mrs. Marshall's social position was unquestioned, and wealth showered every dainty on this child which was idolized with its brothers and sisters by its white papa. In course of time another child appeared on the scene, but it was unmistakably dark. All were alarmed, and "rush of blood, strangulation" were the conjectures, but the doctor, when asked the cause, grimly told them it was a Negro child. There was a family conclave, the coachman heard of it and leaving his own family went West, and has never returned. As soon as Mrs. Marshall was able to travel she was sent away in deep disgrace. Her husband died within the year of a broken heart.

Ebenzer Fowler, the wealthiest colored man in Issaquena County, Miss., was shot down on the street in Mayersville, January 30, 1885, just before dark by an armed body of white men who filled his body with bullets. They charged him with writing a note to a white woman of the place, which they intercepted and which proved there was an intimacy existing between them.

Hundreds of such cases might be cited, but enough have been given to prove the assertion that there are white women in the South who love the Afro-American's company even as there are white men notorious for their preference for Afro-American women.

There is hardly a town in the South which has not an instance of the kind which is well-known, and hence the assertion is reiterated that "nobody in the South believes the old thread bare lie that negro men rape white women." Hence there is a growing demand among Afro-Americans that the guilt or innocence of parties accused of rape be fully established. They know the men of the section of the country who refuse this are not so desirous of punishing rapists as they pretend. The utterances of the leading white men show that with them it is not the crime but the *class.* Bishop Fitzgerald has become apologist for lynchers of the rapists of *white* women only. Governor Tillman, of South Carolina, in the month of June, standing under the tree in Barnwell, S.C., on which eight Afro-Americans were hung last year, declared that he would lead a mob to lynch a *negro* who raped a *white* woman. So say the pulpits, officials and newspapers of the South. But when the victim is a colored woman it is different.

Last winter in Baltimore, Md., three white ruffians assaulted a Miss Camphor, a young Afro-American girl, while out walking with a young man of her own race. They held her escort and outraged the girl. It was a deed dastardly enough to arouse Southern blood, which gives its horror of rape as excuse for lawlessness, but she was an Afro-American. The case went to the courts, an Afro-American lawyer defended the men and they were acquitted.

In Nashville, Tenn., there is a white man, Pat Hanifan, who outraged a little Afro-American girl, and, from the physical injuries received, she has been ruined for life. He was jailed for six months, discharged, and is now a detective in that city. In the same city, last May, a white man outraged an Afro-American girl in a drug store. He was arrested, and released on bail at the trial. It was rumored that five hundred Afro-Americans had organized to lynch him. Two hundred and fifty white citizens armed themselves with Winchesters and guarded him. A cannon was placed in front of his home, and the Buchanan Rifles (State Militia) ordered to the scene for his protection. The Afro-American mob did not materialize. Only two weeks before Eph. Grizzard, who had only been *charged* with rape upon a white woman, had been taken from the jail, with Governor Buchanan and the police and militia standing by, dragged through the streets in broad daylight, knives plunged into him at every step, and with every fiendish cruelty a frenzied mob could devise, he was at last swung out on the bridge with hands cut to pieces as he tried to climb up the stanchions. A naked, bloody example of the blood-thirstiness of the nineteenth century civilization of the Athens of the South! No cannon or military was called out in his defense. He dared to visit a white woman.

At the very moment these civilized whites were announcing their determination "to protect their wives and daughters," by murdering Grizzard, a white man was in the same jail for raping eight-year-old Maggie Reese, an Afro-American girl. He was not harmed. The "honor" of grown women who were glad enough to be supported by the Grizzard boys and Ed Coy, as long as the liaison was not known, needed protection; they were white. The outrage upon helpless childhood needed no avenging in this case; she was black.

A white man in Guthrie, Oklahoma Territory, two months ago inflicted such injuries upon another Afro-American child that she died. He was not punished, but an attempt was made in the same town in the month of June to lynch an Afro-American who visited a white woman.

In Memphis, Tenn., in the month of June, Ellerton L. Dorr, who is the husband of Russell Hancock's widow, was arrested for attempted rape on Mattie Cole, a neighbor's cook; he was only prevented from accomplishing his purpose, by the appearance of Mattie's employer. Dorr's friends say he was drunk and not responsible for his actions. The grand jury refused to indict him and he was discharged.

[…]

CHAPTER VI. Self Help

In the creation of this healthier public sentiment, the Afro-American can do for himself what no one else can do for him, The world looks on with wonder that we have conceded so much and remain law-abiding under such great outrage and provocation.

To Northern capital and Afro-American labor the South owes its rehabilitation. If labor is withdrawn capital will not remain. The Afro-

American is thus the backbone of the South. A thorough knowledge and judicious exercise of this power in lynching localities could many times effect a bloodless revolution. The white man's dollar is his god, and to stop this will be to stop outrages in many localities.

The Afro[-]Americans of Memphis denounced the lynching of three of their best citizens, and urged and waited for the authorities to act in the matter and bring the lynchers to justice. No attempt was made to do so, and the black men left the city by thousands, bringing about great stagnation in every branch of business. Those who remained so injured the business of the street car company by staying off the cars, that the superintendent, manager and treasurer called personally on the editor of the "Free Speech," asked them to urge our people to give them their patronage again. Other business men became alarmed over the situation and the "Free Speech" was run away that the colored people might be more easily controlled. A meeting of white citizens in June, three months after the lynching, passed resolutions for the first time, condemning it. *But they did not punish the lynchers.* Every one of them was known by name, because they had been selected to do the dirty work, by some of the very citizens who passed these resolutions. Memphis is fast losing her black population, who proclaim as they go that there is no protection for the life and property of any Afro-American citizen in Memphis who is not a slave.

The Afro-American citizens of Kentucky, whose intellectual and financial improvement has been phenomenal, have never had a separate car law until now. Delegations and petitions poured into the Legislature against it, yet the bill passed and the Jim Crow Car of Kentucky is a legalized institution. Will the great mass of Negroes continue to patronize the railroad? A special from Covington, Ky., says:

Covington, June 13th.—The railroads of the State are beginning to feel very markedly, the effects of the separate coach bill recently passed by the Legislature. No class of people in the State have so many and so largely attended excursions as the blacks. All these have been abandoned, and regular travel is reduced to a minimum. A competent authority says the loss to the various roads will reach $1,000,000 this year.

A call to a State Conference in Lexington, Ky., last June had delegates from every county in the State. Those delegates, the ministers, teachers, heads of secret and others orders, and the head of every family should pas[s] the word around for every member of the race in Kentucky to stay off railroads unless obliged to ride. If they did so, and their advice was followed persistently the convention would not need to petition the Legislature to repeal the law or raise money to file a suit. The railroad corporations would be so effected they would in self-defense lobby to have the separate car law repealed. On the other hand, as long as the railroads can get Afro-American excursions they will always have plenty of money to fight all the suits brought against them. They will be aided in so doing by the same partisan public sentiment which passed the law. White men passed the law, and white judges and juries would pass upon the suits against the law, and render judgment in line with their prejudices and in deference to the greater financial power.

The appeal to the white man's pocket has ever been more effectual than all the appeals ever made to his conscience. Nothing, absolutely nothing, is to be gained by a further sacrifice of manhood and self-respect. By the right exercise of his power as the industrial factor of the South, the Afro-American can demand and secure his rights, the punishment of lynchers, and a fair trial for accused rapists.

Of the many inhuman outrages of this present year, the only case where the proposed lynching did *not* occur, was where the men armed themselves in Jacksonville, Fla., and Paducah, Ky., and prevented it. The only times an Afro-American who was assaulted got away has been when he had a gun and used it in self-defense.

The lesson this teaches and which every Afro-American should ponder well, is that a Winchester rifle should have a place of honor in every black home, and it should be used for that protection which the law refuses to give. When the white man who is always the aggressor knows he runs as great a risk of biting the dust every time his Afro-American victim does, he will have greater respect for Afro-American life. The more the Afro-American yields and cringes and begs, the more he has to do so, the more he is insulted, outraged and lynched.

The assertion has been substantiated throughout these pages that the press contains unreliable and doctored reports of lynchings, and one of the most necessary things for the race to do is to get these facts before the public. The people must know before they can act, and there is no educator to compare with the press.

The Afro-American papers are the only ones which will print the truth, and they lack means to employ agents and detectives to get at the facts. The race must rally a mighty host to the support of their journals, and thus enable them to do much in the way of investigation.

A lynching occurred at Port Jarvis, N.Y., the first week in June. A white and colored man were implicated in the assault upon a white girl. It was charged that the white man paid the colored boy to make the assault, which he did on the public highway in broad day time, and was lynched. This, too was done by "parties unknown." The white man in the case still lives. He was imprisoned and promises to fight the case on trial. At the preliminary examination, it developed that he had been a suitor of the girl's. She had repulsed and refused him, yet had given him money, and he had sent threatening letters demanding more.

The day before this examination she was so wrought up, she left home and wandered miles away. When found she said she did so because she was afraid of the man's testimony. Why should she be afraid of the prisoner? Why should she yield to his demands for money if not to prevent him exposing something he knew? It seems explainable only on the hypothesis that a *liason* existed between the colored boy and the girl, and the white man knew of it. The press is singularly silent. Has it a motive? We owe it to ourselves to find out.

The story comes from Larned, Kansas, Oct. 1st, that a young white lady held at bay until daylight, without alarming any one in the house, "a burly Negro" who entered her room and bed. The "burly Negro" was promptly lynched without investigation or examination of inconsistant stories.

A house was found burned down near Montgomery, Ala., in Monroe County, Oct. 13th, a few weeks ago; also the burned bodies of the owners and melted piles of gold and silver.

These discoveries led to the conclusion that the awful crime was not prompted by motives of robbery. The suggestion of the whites was that "brutal lust was the incentive, and as there are nearly 200 Negroes living within a radius of five miles of the place the conclusion was inevitable that some of them were the perpetrators."

Upon this "suggestion" probably made by the real criminal, the mob acted upon the "conclusion" and arrested ten Afro-Americans, four of whom, they tell the world, confessed to the deed of murdering Richard L. Johnson and outraging his daughter, Jeanette. These four men, Berrell

260 · IDA B. WELLS-BARNETT

Jones, Moses Johnson, Jim and John Packer, none of them 25 years of age, upon this conclusion, were taken from jail, hanged, shot, and burned while yet alive the night of Oct. 12th. The same report says Mr. Johnson was on the best of terms with his Negro tenants.

The race thus outraged must find out the facts of this awful hurling of men into eternity on supposition, and give them to the indifferent and apathetic country. We feel this to be a garbled report, but how can we prove it?

Near Vicksburg, Miss., a murder was committed by a gang of burglars. Of course it must have been done by Negroes, and Negroes were arrested for it. It is believed that 2 men, Smith Tooley and John Adams belonged to a gang controlled by white men and, fearing exposure, on the night of July 4th, they were hanged in the Court House yard by those interested in silencing them. Robberies since committed in the same vicinity have been known to be by white men who had their faces blackened. We strongly believe in the innocence of these murdered men, but we have no proof. No other news goes out to the world save that which stamps us as a race of cut-throats, robbers and lustful wild beasts. So great is Southern hate and prejudice, they legally (?) hung poor little thirteen year old Mildrey Brown at Columbia, S.C., Oct. 7th, on the circumstantial evidence that she poisoned a white infant. If her guilt had been proven unmistakably, had she been white, Mildrey Brown would never have been hung.

The country would have been aroused and South Carolina disgraced forever for such a crime. The Afro[-]American himself did not know as he should have known as his journals should be in a position to have him know and act.

Nothing is more definitely settled than he must act for himself. I have shown how he may employ the boycott, emigration and the press, and I feel that by a combination of all these agencies can be effectually stamped out lynch law, that last relic of barbarism and slavery. "The gods help those who help themselves."

SOURCE

Wells, Ida B. *Southern Horrors: Lynch Law in All Its Phases*, i, 7–12, 22–24. New York: New York Age Print, 1892.

NOTE

Chapter opening photo: Ida B. Wells-Barnett, ca. 1893. National Portrait Gallery, Smithsonian Institution.

1. A female courtesan or prostitute (from the French *demi-monde* ["half-world"], a coinage often credited to French author Alexandre Dumas *fils* because of the title of his comic 1855 play, *Le Demi Monde*).

Frances Willard

1839–1898

FRANCES WILLARD was a white woman born in Churchville, New York. She was president of the Evanston College for Ladies, which was later absorbed by Northwestern University, which made Willard dean of women. She was a talented speaker and lobbyist and became one of her time's leading reformers. For nineteen years, Willard was president of the National Women's Christian Temperance Union (whose "Do Everything" reform policy appears in the second selection); she was also a leader of the national Prohibition Party. In the attempt to merge supporters of the separate causes of suffrage and temperance, Willard had a public disagreement with Ida B. Wells-Barnett, who called on her and the WCTU to take an antilynching stance and stop using racist rhetoric to win Southern support for temperance. The first selection comes from Willard's account of learning to ride a bicycle, a somewhat scandalous activity for a woman at the time.

From *A Wheel within a Wheel: How I Learned to Ride the Bicycle, with Some Reflections by the Way* (1895)

From my earliest recollections, and up to the ripe age of fifty-three, I had been an active and diligent worker in the world. This sounds absurd; but having almost no toys except such as I could manufacture, my first plays were but the outdoor work of active men and women on a small scale. Born with an inveterate opposition to staying in the house, I very early learned to use a carpenter's kit and a gardener's tools, and followed in my mimic way the occupations of the poulterer and the farmer, working my little field with a wooden plow of my own making, and felling saplings with an ax rigged up from the old iron of the wagon-shop. Living in the country, far from the artificial restraints and conventions by which most girls are hedged from the activities that would develop a good physique, and endowed with the companionship of a mother who let me have my own sweet will, I "ran wild" until my sixteenth birthday, when the hampering long skirts were brought, with their accompanying corset and high heels; my hair was clubbed up with pins, and I remember writing in my journal, in the first heartbreak of a young human colt taken from its pleasant pasture, "Altogether, I recognize that my occupation is gone."

From that time on I always realized and was obedient to the limitations thus imposed, though in my heart of hearts I felt their unwisdom even more than their injustice. My work then changed from my beloved and breezy outdoor world to the indoor realm of study, teaching, writing, speaking, and went on almost without a break or pain until my fifty-third year, when the loss of my mother accentuated the strain of this long period in which mental and physical life were out of balance, and I fell into a mild form of what is called nerve-wear by the patient and nervous prostration by the lookers-on. Thus ruthlessly thrown out of the usual lines of reaction on my environment, and sighing for new worlds to conquer, I determined that I would learn the bicycle.

An English naval officer had said to me, after learning it himself, "You women have no idea of the new realm of happiness which the bicycle has opened to us men." Already I knew well enough that tens of thousands who could never afford to own, feed, and stable a horse, had by this bright invention enjoyed the swiftness of motion which is perhaps the most fascinating feature of material life, the charm of a wide outlook upon the natural world, and that sense of mastery which is probably the greatest attraction in horseback-riding. But the steed that never tires, and is "mettlesome" in the fullest sense of the word, is full of tricks and capers, and to hold his head steady and make him prance to suit you is no small accomplishment. I had often mentioned in my temperance writings that the bicycle was perhaps our strongest ally in winning young men away from public-houses, because it afforded them a pleasure far more enduring, and an exhilaration as much more delightful as the natural is than the unnatural. From my observation of my own brother and hundreds of young men who have been my pupils, I have always held that a boy's heart is not set in him to do evil any more than a girl's, and that the reason our young men fall into evil ways is largely because we have not had the wit and wisdom to provide them with amusements suited to their joyous youth, by means of which they could invest their superabundant animal spirits in ways that should harm no one and help themselves to the best development and the cleanliest ways of living. So as a temperance reformer I always felt a strong attraction toward the bicycle, because it is the vehicle of so much harmless pleasure, and because the skill required in handling it obliges those who mount to keep clear heads and steady hands. Nor could I see a reason in the world why a woman should not ride the silent steed so swift and blithesome. I knew perfectly well that when, some ten or fifteen years ago, Miss Bertha von Hillern, a young German artist in America, took it into her head to give exhibitions of her skill in riding the bicycle she was thought by some to be a sort of semi-monster; and liberal as our people are in their views of what a woman may undertake, I should certainly have felt compromised, at that remote and benighted period, by going to see her ride, not because there was any harm in it, but solely because of what we call in homely phrase "the speech of people." But behold! it was long ago conceded that women might ride the tricycle—indeed, one had been presented to me by my friend Colonel Pope, of Boston, a famous manufacturer of these swift roadsters, as far back as 1886; and I had swung around the garden-paths upon its saddle a few minutes every evening when work was over at my Rest Cottage home. I had even hoped to give an impetus among conservative women to this new line of physical development and outdoor happiness; but that is quite another story and will come in later. Suffice it for the present that it did me good, as it doth the upright in heart, to notice recently that the Princesses Louise and Beatrice both ride the tricycle at Balmoral; for I know that with the great mass of feminine humanity this precedent will have exceeding weight and where the tricycle prophesies the bicycle shall ere long preach the gospel of outdoors.

For we are all unconsciously the slaves of public opinion. When the hansom first came on London streets no woman having regard to her social state and standing would have dreamed of entering one of these pavement gondolas unless accompanied by a gentleman as her escort.

But in course of time a few women, of stronger individuality than the average, ventured to go unattended; later on, use wore off the glamour of the traditions which said that women must not go alone, and now none but an imbecile would hold herself to any such observance.

A trip around the world by a young woman would have been regarded a quarter of a century ago as equivalent to social outlawry; but now young women of the highest character and talent are employed by leading journals to whip around the world "on time," and one has done so in seventy-three, another in seventy-four days, while the young women recently sent out by an Edinburgh newspaper will no doubt considerably contract these figures.

As I have mentioned, Fräulein von Hillern is the first woman, so far as I know, who ever rode a bicycle, and for this she was considered to be one of those persons who classified nowhere, and who could not do so except to the injury of the feminine guild with which they were connected before they "stepped out"; but now, in France, for a woman to ride a bicycle is not only "good form," but the current craze among the aristocracy.

Since Balaam's beast there has been but little authentic talking done by the four-footed; but that is no reason why the two-wheeled should not speak its mind, and the first utterance I have to chronicle in the softly flowing vocables of my bicycle is to the following purport. I heard it as we trundled off down the Priory incline at the suburban home of Lady Henry Somerset, Reigate, England; it said: "Behold, I do not fail you; I am not a skittish beastie, but a sober, well-conducted roadster. I did not ask you to mount or drive, but since you have done so you must now learn the laws of balance and exploitation. I did not invent these laws, but I have been built conformably to them, and you must suit yourself to the unchanging regulations of gravity, general and specific, as illustrated in me. Strange as the paradox may seem, you will do this best by not trying to do it at all. You must make up what you are pleased to call your mind—make it up speedily, or you will be cast in yonder mud-puddle, and no blame to me and no thanks to yourself. Two things must occupy your thinking powers to the exclusion of every other thing: first, the goal; and, second, the momentum requisite to reach it. Do not look down like an imbecile upon the steering-wheel in front of you—that would be about as wise as for a nauseated voyager to keep his optical instruments fixed upon the rolling waves. It is the curse of life that nearly every one looks down. But the microscope will never set you free; you must glue your eyes to the telescope for ever and a day. Look up and off and on and out; get forehead and foot into line, the latter acting as a rhythmic spur in the flanks of your equilibriated equine; so shall you win, and that right speedily.

"It was divinely said that the kingdom of God is within you. Some make a mysticism of this declaration, but it is hard common sense; for the lesson you will learn from me is this: every kingdom over which we reign must be first formed within us on what the psychic people call the 'astral plane,' but what I as a bicycle look upon as the common parade-ground of individual thought."

From *Do Everything: A Handbook for the World's White Ribboners* (1895)

PREFACE

When we began the delicate, difficult, and dangerous operation of dissecting out the alcohol nerve from the body politic, we did not realize the intricacy of the undertaking nor distances that must be traversed by the scalpel of investigation and research. More than twenty years have elapsed since the call to battle sounded its bugle note among the homes and hearts of Hills, Ohio. One thought, sentiment, and purpose animated those saintly "Praying Bands," whose name will never die out from human history: "Brothers, we beg of you not to drink, and not to sell!" This was the single wailing note of these moral Paganinis, playing on one string. It caught the universal ear, and set the key of that mighty orchestra, organized with so much toil and hardship, in which the tender and exalted strain of the Crusade violin still soars aloft, but upborne now by the clanging cornets of science, the deep trombones of legislation, and the thunderous drums of politics and parties. The "Do Everything Policy" was not of our choosing, but is an evolution, as inevitable as any traced by the naturalist, or described by the historian. Woman's genius for details, and her patient steadfastness in following the enemies of those she loves "through every lane of life," have led her to antagonize the alcohol habit, and the liquor traffic, just where they are, wherever that may be. If she does this, since they are everywhere, her policy will be, "Do Everything."

A one-sided movement makes one-sided advocates. Virtues, like hounds, hunt in packs. Total abstinence is not the crucial virtue in life that excuses financial crookedness, defamation of character, or habits of impurity. The fact that one's father was, and one's self is, a bright and shining light in the total abstinence galaxy, does not give one a vantage ground for high behavior toward those who have not been trained to the special virtue that forms the central idea of the Temperance Movement. We have known persons who, because they had "never touched a drop of liquor," set themselves up as if they belonged to a royal line, but whose tongues were as biting as alcohol itself, and whose narrowness had no competitor, save a straight line. An all-round movement can only be carried forward by all advocates; a scientific age requires the study of every subject in its correlations. It was once supposed that light, heat, and electricity were wholly separate entities; it is now believed, and practically proved, that they are but different modes of motion. Standing in the valley, we look up and think we see an isolated mountain; climbing to its top, we see that it is but one member of a range of mountains, many of them of well-nigh equal altitude.

Some bright women who have opposed the "Do Everything Policy," used as their favorite illustration, a flowing river and expatiated on the ruin that would follow if that river (which represents their Do One Thing Policy) were diverted into many channels; but it should be remembered that the most useful of all rivers is the Nile, and that the agricultural economy of Egypt consists in the effort to spread its waters upon as many fields as possible. It is not for the river's sake that it flows through the country, but for the sake of the fertility it can bring upon the adjoining fields, and this is pre-eminently true of the Temperance Reform.

Let us not be disconcerted, but stand bravely by that blessed trinity of movements, Prohibition, Woman's Liberation, and Labor's Uplift.

Everything is not in the Temperance Reform, but the Temperance Reform should be in everything.

"Organized Mother Love," is the best definition of the White Ribbon Movement,[1] and it can have no better motto than: "Make a chain, for the land is full of bloody crimes and the city of violence."

If we can remember this simple rule, it will do much to unravel the mystery of the much controverted "Do Everything Policy," viz.: that every question of practical philanthropy or reform has its temperance aspect, and with that we are to deal.

FRANCES E. WILLARD.

Eastnor Castle, Ledbury, England.

June 15, 1895.

CHAPTER II. The Name

When the women of the Crusade met in 1874, they determined to organize their work in a systematic and permanent manner. And the first question was, What shall we call the new Society?

First of all it was formed exclusively of women, because they felt that if men had an equal place in its councils their greater knowledge of Parliamentary usage, and their more aggressive nature would soon place women in the background, and deprive them of the power of learning by experience, so that in some future day they might be true co-partners with their brothers in an organized effort to help the world to loftier heights of purity in conduct and character.

The word Temperance must come into the name as a matter of course. To them it meant the moderate use of all things good, and total abstinence from all things questionable or harmful. And as their knowledge grew it came to mean the total prohibition of the liquor traffic, the opium trade, the gambling den, the haunt of infamy; and in later times it came to mean also alliance with the great labor movement for purposes of mutual defense, and the enfranchisement of woman, that her influence might be brought to bear at the point where an opinion passes into a ballot and a conviction is wrought into a law.

The word Union had acquired new meanings to the Crusaders who went outside denominational hedges upon the broad highways of humanity. It was a revelation of the man-made qualities of sectarianism in every form, so that the crusade women extended their hands to grasp any that were held out to them in loyalty to the Gospel of peace and good-will, no matter whether the woman thus coming to the rescue was Protestant, Catholic, or a member of no church whatever. The Crusaders believed that it was for them to pass along "like bread at sacrament," the blessed cause to which they had pledged their utmost devotion, and that whoever came into this circle of organized motherhood could not fail to come nearer to Him who said, "If I be lifted up I will draw all men unto me."

The word Christian was the only one about which there was debate. Some said that if we incorporated it into our Society "we should shut out the Jews." But others insisted that since we had no creed test this result need not be feared. Some said if we nailed the flag of Christ to the masthead of the new ship which we were launching in a stormy sea, "we should not have so large a following." But the great majority declared that we did not come together to seek a following, but to lift up an ensign with the motto, "Falter who must; follow who dare." Quality not quantity was what we sought, and all those like-minded with the women, who by this Union endeavored to protect the home, were welcome to its fireside and its altar. When the vote was taken on including the word Christian, the affirmative was supported with practical unanimity.

CHAPTER III. The Polyglot Petition for Home Protection

To the Governments of the World (Collectively and Severally).

Honored Rulers, Representatives, and Brothers,—We, your petitioners, although belonging to the physically weaker sex, are strong of heart to love our homes, our native land, and the world's family of nations. We know that clear brains and pure hearts make honest lives and happy homes, and that by these the nations prosper and the time is brought nearer when the world shall be at peace. We know that indulgence in Alcohol and Opium, and in other vices which disgrace our social life, makes misery for all the world, and most of all for us and for our children. We know that stimulants and opiates are sold under legal guarantees which make the governments partners in the traffic, by accepting as revenue a portion of the profits, and we know with shame that they are often forced by treaty upon populations either ignorant or unwilling. We know that the law might do much now left undone to raise the moral tone of society and render vice difficult. We have no power to prevent these great iniquities, beneath which the whole world groans, but you have power to redeem the honor of the nations from an indefensible complicity. We, therefore, come to you with the united voices of representative women of every land, beseeching you to raise the standard of the law to that of Christian morals, to strip away the safeguards and sanctions of the State from the drink traffic and the opium trade, and to protect our homes by the total prohibition of these curses of civilization throughout all the territory over which your Government extends.

According to my best recollection this Petition was written in the year 1884 in my workshop at Rest Cottage, Evanston, Ill., after reading a book on current reforms, in which the evils of the opium trade were set forth with remarkable clearness and power. Its first presentation to a Convention was by Mrs. Mary Bannister Willard, at the International Temperance Congress at Antwerp, Belgium, September 12th, 1885.

It was festooned in Faneuil Hall, Boston, at the first World's W.C.T.U. Convention, November, 1891, and in Tremont Temple, in the same city, at the Annual Meeting of the W.C.T.U. which immediately followed. It was first publicly presented in Washington, D.C., February 15th, 1895, where it decorated the great "Convention Hall," holding 7,000 people.

[. . .]

CHAPTER V. The Power of the Press

The way to make a thing known is—to make it known. This is the alpha and omega of success in the Press department, but all along my way in life I have found a great variety of men and women who seem to feel that to make things known is somehow or other to make a great mistake, even to commit a mild form of crime. My own nature and outlook are wholly different. I believe that the shades are so heavy over the earth that we have seen the merest glint of light through some chink, and we who hold up the sun of our individuality catch the glint of that and flash it round in every direction to the utmost of our power. There is nothing so very private after all; the secrets are all open secrets, everybody reads between the lines the things one has left out. Whoever minimizes mystery has helped to brighten knowledge. Why should we make so much ado about the trifling little things we hoard? Are they really worth the hoarding? God is light, and in Him there is no darkness at all. Love and light and life seem to be largely interchangeable. The more a Society is pure and good the less mystery and secrecy there will be in it. Let us then tell all the good things we may, and think as little evil as we can, that we may have little to tell but good, and then let us tell it out and keep on telling it.

In every village, town and city of the world in these days, there is, as a rule, some sort of newspaper to establish which cost the proprietor a snug sum of money. To keep it going makes a constant demand upon his purse.

We women could no more have started these papers than we could have made a world, but if we have the tact and talent, or to state it more correctly, the good common sense to put a mortgage on a few square inches every week in the columns of these papers, it is just as well as if we owned that amount of space which, if paid for at the advertising rates, would cost an incalculable amount of money.

There is not another line of work except that of Gospel meetings which our women have taken up with so much alacrity, for they are quick enough to see that there is not in the world another power where we can bring to a focus so much influence for the spread of Temperance principles and Temperance practice as the newspapers, because they go everywhere and are read by all people.

The voice that speaks dies on the air almost before its echoes reach us, but the firm types and black ink hold through months and years. The newspapers that issue from the press in New York city may be read in Yokohama, Melbourne, St. Petersburg, and in the Islands of the Sea.

When you have got a thought into "cold type," it is there "for keeps." There is no magician in this age like the clear-headed, far-sighted man or woman who impresses the thoughts that he believes are winged with God's truth, upon the printed page.

But unhappily, the powers of darkness are more alert as yet to use this printed page for selfish purposes than the powers of life are intent to gain it for purposes of blessing; still, I have always felt that women when once their attention had been strongly impressed were so gifted in carrying out details, that if we could only make our press department seem as important to our great home cause as it actually is, they would make it hum like a top in every locality where the mother heart has come to the front to guard its little ones, and twenty years of experience since this department was organized in Cleveland, O., at the first National Convention have confirmed me in this belief.

The universal complaint concerning our Local Press Superintendents is that while they "run well for a season" they are apt to "grow weary in well doing," and seem to forget that it is "in due season" that "we shall reap if we faint not." Innumerable editors have said to me, "I gave a quarter of a column" (or half, as the case may be) "to your Superintendent, and she sent me material to fill it for a month, three months, six months, or possibly a year, and then the whole thing dropped." Other editors have said, "If we could count upon the copy as a certainty, and that it would not come in too late, we would set aside space, but the women do not seem to understand that an hour, or even a moment, makes all the difference in a newspaper office between having what is sent put in the paper or in the waste-paper basket."

Verily we must be up to the time as well as up to date if we expect to inspire the confidence of that much tormented dignitary, the editor.

Another mistake that we sometimes make is to devote our attention wholly to the local editor. A paper of importance is divided into departments, each of which is under the care of some one member of the staff, and an ingenious Press Superintendent will try not only to secure the insertion of local news on the city page, but will furnish every now and then a story, a bit of verse, an anecdote, a pithy paragraph for the home column or the scientific selections; indeed, there is hardly a subdivision of the paper for which an ingenious woman would not be able to find, from time to time, appropriate and attractive selections.

One of the most neglected fields is reporting the sermons and addresses of temperance men and women. Many a time and oft have found in the local press some account of where we had come from and were going to, some account of our general appearance or manners, some friendly hope expressed, or adverse prophecy, but almost never any setting forth of what we had said.

If our press superintendents in the cities and large towns could secure stenographic reports at least of the leading addresses made, in the course of the year they would be furnishing to the public the latest and best facts and illustrations of those who are constantly studying the movement, and whose method of presenting it to the public has proved so satisfactory that a large audience is assured to them wherever they go.

A ready lead pencil is the magic wand of power to a press superintendent whether she be national, state, or local. To catch an expression on the fly is an art for which women are peculiarly adapted by reason of their quick thought and quicker sympathy. If we learn to be on the alert for the department under our care we shall constantly be hearing or seeing something that helps to illustrate and extend its influence. It is practically impossible for two or three White Ribbon comrades to come together without developing experiences, incidents or arguments that would be most helpful to that larger number whom the reformer must constantly have in mind, for as the material of the sculptor is marble on which he works untiringly with hammer and chisel, so people form the material of the Temperance apostle, upon which he is steadily trying to make the impress of his own thoughts and convictions.

The bright sayings of children as well as "grown ups," the reminiscences, statistics, illustrations and arguments that we all have stored up in our minds and with which we are wont to regale one another, would, if brought out upon the printed page, be transferred to tens of thousands of brains as readily as a single electrotype makes its impress upon a thousand pieces of paper. Doubtless the process is just as scientific as it would be to take a photograph or stamp with a stencil plate, and not until we have received as clear an impression of what we are capable of doing and called to do in the press department as a photographer has of the impress to be made by the plate in his hand, or the printer by the type between his fingers, have we measured up at all to the boundless possibilities and importance of the work that has come to our hands in connection with the press.

It is true now as it was when the words were uttered first, "My people perish for lack of knowledge." The reason why our young folks go their way into wrong is largely because they have not been trained in a better way. A mother's hand smoothing the wrappings around her little child to protect and shelter him, is not more worthily engaged than a woman hand that pens high and holy thoughts, which passing under the eye of untaught childhood and youth produce that arrest of attention in the mind from which every good cause has everything to hope. For this reason there is to my mind nothing secular but everything sacred in the contemplation of the press department through which we have as White Ribbon women, spread the pure light of a pure life over the nations fast and far.

We should be grateful to those friendly men who have opened to us the use of their columns, and we should do our utmost to win and hold their respect not only for our intentions but our clear practical sagacity in furnishing them suitable material with which to occupy the space they have kindly given. We are nearer now to victory than when we first believed; the day begins to dawn and the shadows flee away.

SOURCES

Willard, Frances. *Do Everything: A Handbook for the World's White Ribboners*, 4–6, 19–20, 23–24, 71–76. Chicago: Miss Ruby I. Gilbert, 1895.

———. *A Wheel within a Wheel: How I Learned to Ride the Bicycle, with Some Reflections by the Way*, 9–18. New York: Fleming H. Revell, 1895.

NOTE

1. "White ribboners" are members of the Woman's Christian Temperance Union.

Sarah Winnemucca

ca. 1844–1891

SARAH WINNEMUCCA was born into a family of Northern Paiute leaders in Humboldt Sink, Mexico (now Nevada). She was an educator, lecturer, tribal leader, and writer best known for her book *Life among the Piutes, Their Wrongs and Claims* (1883). Winnemucca tried to operate as a peacemaker for decades, using her language skills to work as an interpreter for the U.S. Army. When the Bannock War broke out in 1878, she volunteered to serve as a scout, freeing her father and other captives. Her fame grew, and she even obtained promises from President

Rutherford B. Hayes and his interior secretary that her tribe would be able to return to the Malheur Reservation. Despite the passage of legislation enabling the return of the Paiute land, it was never enacted.

From *Life among the Piutes,* *Their Wrongs and Claims* (1883)

CHAPTER I. First Meeting of Piutes and Whites

I was born somewhere near 1844, but am not sure of the precise time. I was a very small child when the first white people came into our country. They came like a lion, yes, like a roaring lion, and have continued so ever since, and I have never forgotten their first coming. My people were scattered at that time over nearly all the territory now known as Nevada. My grandfather was chief of the entire Piute nation, and was camped near Humboldt Lake, with a small portion of his tribe, when a party travelling eastward from California was seen coming. When the news was brought to my grandfather, he asked what they looked like? When told that they had hair on their faces, and were white, he jumped up and clasped his hands together, and cried aloud,—

"My white brothers,—my long-looked for white brothers have come at last!"

He immediately gathered some of his leading men, and went to the place where the party had gone into camp. Arriving near them, he was commanded to halt in a manner that was readily understood without an interpreter.

Grandpa at once made signs of friendship by throwing down his robe and throwing up his arms to show them he had no weapons; but in vain,— they kept him at a distance. He knew not, what to do. He had expected so much pleasure in welcoming his white brothers to the best in the land, that after looking at them sorrowfully for a little while, he came away quite unhappy. But he would not give them up so easily. He took some of his most trustworthy men and followed them day after day, camping near them at night, and travelling in sight of them by day, hoping in this way to gain their confidence. But he was disappointed, poor dear old soul!

I can imagine his feelings, for I have drank deeply from the same cup. When I think of my past life, and the bitter trials I have endured, I can scarcely believe I live, and yet I do; and, with the help of Him who notes the sparrow's fall, I mean to fight for my down-trodden race while life lasts.

Seeing they would not trust him, my grandfather left them, saying, "Perhaps they will come again next year." Then he summoned his whole people, and told them this tradition:—

"In the beginning of the world there were only four, two girls and two boys. Our forefather and mother were only two, and we are their children. You all know that a great while ago there was a happy family in this world. One girl and one boy were dark and the others were white. For a time they got along together without quarrelling, but soon they disagreed, and there was trouble. They were cross to one another and fought, and our parents were very much grieved. They prayed that their children might learn better, but it did not do any good; and afterwards the whole household was made so unhappy that the father and mother saw that they must separate their children; and then our father took the dark boy and girl, and the white boy and girl, and asked them, 'Why are you so cruel to each other?' They hung down their heads, and would not speak. They were ashamed. He said to them, 'Have I not been kind to you all, and given you everything your hearts wished for? You do not have to hunt and kill your own game to live upon. You see, my dear children, I have power to call whatsoever kind of game we want to eat; and I also have the power to separate my dear children, if they are not good to each other.' So he separated his children by a word. He said, 'Depart from each other, you cruel children;—go across the mighty ocean and do not seek each other's lives.'

"So the light girl and boy disappeared by that one word, and their parents saw them no more, and they were grieved, although they knew their children were happy. And by-and-by the dark children grew into a large nation; and we believe it is the one we belong to, and that the nation that sprung from the white children will some time send some one to meet us and heal all the old trouble. Now, the white people we saw a few days ago must certainly be our white brothers, and I want to welcome them. I want to love them as I love all of you. But they would not let me; they were afraid. But they will come again, and I want you one and all to promise that, should I not live to welcome them myself, you will not hurt a hair on their heads, but welcome them as I tried to do."

How good of him to try and heal the wound, and how vain were his efforts! My people had never seen a white man, and yet they existed, and were a strong race. The people promised as he wished, and they all went back to their work.

[...]

CHAPTER II. Domestic and Social Moralities

Our children are very carefully taught to be good. Their parents tell them stories, traditions of old times, even of the first mother of the human race; and love stories, stories of giants, and fables; and when they ask if these last stories are true, they answer, "Oh, it is only coyote," which means that they are make-believe stories. Coyote is the name of a mean, crafty little animal, half wolf, half dog, and stands for everything low. It is the greatest term of reproach one Indian has for another. Indians do not swear,—they have no words for swearing till they learn them of white men. The worst they call each is bad or coyote; but they are very sincere with one another, and if they think each other in the wrong they say so.

We are taught to love everybody. We don't need to be taught to love our fathers and mothers. We love them without being told to. Our tenth cousin is as near to us as our first cousin; and we don't marry into our relations. Our young women are not allowed to talk to any young man that is not their cousin, except at the festive dances, when both are dressed in their best clothes, adorned with beads, feathers or shells, and stand alternately in the ring and take hold of hands. These are very pleasant occasions to all the young people.

Many years ago, when my people were happier than they are now, they used to celebrate the Festival of Flowers in the spring. I have been to three of them only in the course of my life.

Oh, with what eagerness we girls used to watch every spring for the time when we could meet with our hearts' delight, the young men, whom in civilized life you call beaux. We would all go in company to see if the flowers we were named for were yet in bloom, for almost all the girls are named for flowers. We talked about them in our wigwams, as if we were the flowers, saying, "Oh, I saw myself today in full bloom!" We would talk all the evening in this way in our families with such delight, and such beautiful thoughts of the happy day when we should meet with those who admired us and would help us to sing our flower-songs which we made up as we sang. But we were always sorry for those that were not named after some flower, because we knew they could not join in the flower-songs like ourselves, who were named for flowers of all kinds.[1]

At last one evening came a beautiful voice, which made every girl's heart throb with happiness. It was the chief, and every one hushed to hear what he said to-day.

"My dear daughters, we are told that you have seen yourselves in the hills and in the valleys, in full bloom. Five days from to-day your festival day will come. I know every young man's heart stops beating while I am talking. I know how it was with me many years ago. I used to wish the Flower Festival would come every day. Dear young men and young women, you are saying, 'Why put it off five days?' But you all know that is our rule. It gives you time to think, and to show your sweetheart your flower."

All the girls who have flower-names dance along together, and those who have not go together also. Our fathers and mothers and grandfathers and grandmothers make a place for us where we can dance. Each one gathers the flower she is named for, and then all weave them into wreaths and crowns and scarfs, and dress up in them.

Some girls are named for rocks and are called rock-girls, and they find some pretty rocks which they carry; each one such a rock as she is named for, or whatever she is named for. If she cannot, she can take a branch of sage-brush, or a bunch of rye-grass, which have no flower.

They all go marching along, each girl in turn singing of herself; but she is not a girl any more,—she is a flower singing. She sings of herself, and her sweetheart, dancing along by her side, helps her sing the song she makes.

I will repeat what we say of ourselves. "I, Sarah Winnemucca, am a shell-flower, such as I wear on my dress. My name is Thocmetony. I am so beautiful! Who will come and dance with me while I am so beautiful? Oh, come and be happy with me! I shall be beautiful while the earth lasts. Somebody will always admire me; and who will come and be happy with me in the Spirit-land? I shall be beautiful forever there. Yes, I shall be more beautiful than my shell-flower, my Thocmetony! Then, come, oh come, and dance and be happy with me!" The young men sing with us as they dance beside us.

Our parents are waiting for us somewhere to welcome us home. And then we praise the sage-brush and the rye-grass that have no flower, and the pretty rocks that some are named for; and then we present our beautiful flowers to these companions who could carry none. And so all are happy; and that closes the beautiful day.

My people have been so unhappy for a long time they wish now to *disincrease* instead of multiply. The mothers are afraid to have more children, for fear they shall have daughters, who are not safe even in their mother's presence.

The grandmothers have the special care of the daughters just before and after they come to womanhood. The girls are not allowed to get married until they have come to womanhood; and that period is recognized as a very sacred thing, and is the subject of a festival, and has peculiar customs. The young woman is set apart under the care of two of her friends, somewhat older, and a little wigwam, called a teepee, just big enough for the three, is made for them, to which they retire. She goes through certain labors which are thought to be strengthening, and these last twenty-five days. Every day, three times a day, she must gather, and pile up as high as she can, five stacks of wood. This makes fifteen stacks a day. At the end of every five days the attendants take her to a river to bathe. She fasts from all flesh-meat during these twenty-five days, and continues to do this for five days in every month all her life. At the end of the twenty-five days she returns to the family lodge, and gives all her clothing to her attendants in payment for their care. Sometimes the wardrobe is quite extensive.

It is thus publicly known that there is another marriageable woman, and any young man interested in her, or wishing to form an alliance, comes forward. But the courting is very different from the courting of the white people. He never speaks to her, or visits the family, but endeavors to attract her attention by showing his horsemanship, etc. As he knows that she sleeps next to her grandmother in the lodge, he enters in full dress after the family has retired for the night, and seats himself at her feet. If she is not awake, her grandmother wakes her. He does not speak to either young woman or grandmother, but when the young woman wishes him to go away, she rises and goes and lies down by the side of her mother. He then leaves as silently as he came in. This goes on sometimes for a year or longer, if the young woman has not made up her mind. She is never forced by her parents to marry against her wishes. When she knows her own mind, she makes a confidant of her grandmother, and then the young man is summoned by the father of the girl, who asks him in her presence, if he really loves his daughter, and reminds him, if he says he does, of all the duties of a husband. He then asks his daughter the same question, and sets before her minutely all her duties. And these duties are not slight. She is to dress the game, prepare the food, clean the buckskins, make his moccasins, dress his hair, bring all the wood,—in short, do all the household work. She promises to "be himself," and she fulfils her promise. Then he is invited to a feast and all his relatives with him. But after the betrothal, a teepee is erected for the presents that pour in from both sides.

At the wedding feast, all the food is prepared in baskets. The young woman sits by the young man, and hands him the basket of food prepared for him with her own hands. He does not take it with his right hand; but seizes her wrist, and takes it with the left hand. This constitutes the marriage ceremony, and the father pronounces them man and wife. They go to a wigwam of their own, where they live till the first child is born. This event also is celebrated. Both father and mother fast from all flesh, and the father goes through the labor of piling the wood for twenty-five days, and assumes all his wife's household work during that time. If he does not do his part in the care of the child, he is considered an outcast. Every five days his child's basket is changed for a new one, and the five are all carefully put away at the end of the days, the last one containing the navel-string, carefully wrapped up, and all are put up into a tree, and the child put into a new and ornamented basket. All this respect shown to the mother and child makes the parents feel their responsibility, and makes the tie between parents and children very strong. The young mothers often get together and exchange their experiences about the attentions of their husbands; and inquire of each other if the fathers did their duty to their children, and were careful of their wives' health. When they are married they give away all the clothing they have ever worn, and dress themselves anew. The poor people have the same ceremonies, but do not make a feast of it, for want of means.

Our boys are introduced to manhood by their hunting of deer and mountain-sheep. Before they are fifteen or sixteen, they hunt only small game, like rabbits, hares, fowls, etc. They never eat what they kill themselves, but only what their father or elder brothers kill. When a boy becomes strong enough to use larger bows made of sinew, and arrows that are ornamented with eagle-feathers, for the first time, he kills game that is large, a deer or an antelope, or a mountain-sheep. Then he brings home the hide, and his father cuts it into a long coil which is wound into a loop, and the boy takes his quiver and throws it on his back as if he was going on a hunt, and takes his bow and arrows in his hand. Then his father throws the loop over him, and he jumps through it. This he does five times. Now for the first time he eats the flesh of the animal he has killed, and from that time he eats whatever he kills but he has always been faithful to his parents' command not to eat what he has killed before. He can now do whatever he likes, for now he is a man, and no longer considered a boy. If there is a war he can go to it; but the Piutes, and other tribes west of the Rocky Mountains, are not fond of going to war. I never saw a war-dance but once. It is always the whites that begin the wars, for their own selfish purposes. The government does not take care to send the good men; there are a plenty who would take pains to see and understand the chiefs and learn their characters, and their good will to the whites. But the whites have not waited to find out how good the Indians were, and what ideas they had of God just like those of Jesus, who called him Father, just as my people do, and told men to do to others as they would be done by, just as my people teach their children to do. My people teach their children never to make fun of any one, no matter how they look. If you see your brother or sister doing something wrong, look away, or go away from them. If you make fun of bad persons, you make yourself beneath them. Be kind to all, both poor and rich, and feed all that come to your wigwam, and your name can be spoken of by every one far and near. In this way you will make many friends for yourself. Be kind both to bad and good, for you don't know your own heart. This is the way my people teach their children. It was handed down from father to son for many generations. I never in my life saw our children rude as I have seen white children and grown people in the streets.[2]

The chief's tent is the largest tent, and it is council-tent, where every one goes who wants advice. In the evenings the head men go there to discuss everything, for the chiefs do not rule like tyrants; they discuss everything with their people, as a father would in his family. Often they sit up all night. They discuss the doings of all, if they need to be advised. If a boy is not doing well they talk that over, and if the women are interested they can share in the talks. If there is not room enough inside, they all go out of doors, and make a great circle. The men are in the inner circle, for there would be too much smoke for the women inside. The men never talk without smoking first. The women sit behind them in another circle, and if the children wish to hear, they can be there too. The women know as much as the men do, and their advice is often asked. We have a republic as well as you. The council-tent is our Congress, and anybody can speak who has anything to say, women and all. They are always interested in what their husbands are doing and thinking about. And they take some part even in the wars. They are always near at hand when fighting is going on, ready to snatch their husbands up and carry them off if wounded or killed. One splendid woman that my brother Lee married after his first wife died, went out into the battle-field after her uncle was killed, and went into the front ranks and cheered the men on. Her uncle's horse was dressed in a splendid robe made of eagles' feathers and she snatched it off and swung it in the face of the enemy, who always carry off everything they find, as much as to say, "You can't have that—I have it safe"; and she staid and took her uncle's place, as brave as any of the men. It means something when the women promise their fathers to make their husbands *themselves*. They faithfully keep with them in all the dangers they can share. They not only take care of their children together, but they do everything together; and when they grow blind, which I am sorry to say is very common, for the smoke they live in destroys their eyes at last, they take sweet care of one another. Marriage is a sweet thing when people love each other. If women could go into your Congress I think justice would soon be done to the Indians. I can't tell about all Indians; but I know my own people are kind to everybody that does not do them harm; but they will not be imposed upon, and when people are too bad they rise up and resist them. This seems to me all right. It is different from being revengeful. There is nothing cruel about our people. They never scalped a human being.

SOURCE

Hopkins, Sarah Winnemucca. *Life among the Piutes: Their Wrongs and Claims*, edited by Mrs. Horace Mann, 5–7, 45–54. Boston: G. P. Putnam's Sons, 1883.

NOTES

Chapter opening photo: Sarah Winnemucca, 1883. National Portrait Gallery, Smithsonian Institution.

1. [Source editor's note.] Indian children are named from some passing circumstance; as, for instance, one of Mrs. Hopkins' brothers was named Black-eye,

because when a very small child, sitting in a sister's lap, who had beautiful black eyes, he said, "What beautiful black eyes you have!" If they observed the flight of a bird, or an animal, in short, anything striking that became associated with them, that would be their appellation.

2. [Source editor's note.] In one of her lectures, Mrs. Hopkins spoke of other refinements and manners that the Indian mother teaches her children; and it is worthy the imitation of the whites. Such manners in the children account for their behavior to each other in manhood, their self-respect, and respect for each other. The Indian children really get education in heart and mind, such as we are beginning to give now to ours for the first time. They are taught a great deal about nature; how to observe the habits of plants and animals. It is not unlikely that when something like a human communication is established between the Indians and whites, it may prove a fair exchange, and the knowledge of nature which has accumulated, for we know not how long, may enrich our early education as much as reading and writing will enrich theirs. The fact that the Indian children are not taught English, makes the provision for education made by our government nugatory. Salaries are paid teachers year after year, who sit in the school-rooms (as Mrs. Hopkins says) and read dime novels, and the children play round, and learn nothing from them, except some few hymns *by rote*, which when visitors come they sing, without understanding one word of it. It is not for the advantage of the agents to civilize and teach the Indians. And by means of necessary interpreters there is constant mutual misunderstanding. Indians are made to sign papers that have very different contents from what they are told. The late William B. Ogden, of Chicago, who has always maintained that the Indians ought to have citizens' rights, and be represented in Congress, founding his opinion on his life-long knowledge of the high-toned morality of Indians who wore blankets, said to my sister in 1853, that it was the stereotyped lie of the fur-traders (whose interest it was) that they could not be civilized; and the late Lewis Cass was their attorney, writing in the North American Review about it, for his fortune came largely through the fur-interests. We know from H. H.'s "Century of Dishonor," that from the beginning the Christian bigots who peopled America looked upon the Indians as heathen, to be dealt with as Moses commanded Joshua to deal with the heathen of Syria, who "passed their children through the fire to Moloch," and the services of whose temples were as licentious as they were cruel. Thus Christendom missed the moral reformation it might have had, if they had become acquainted with the noble Five Nations, and others whom they have exterminated. But, "it is never too late to mend," as, at last, the country is beginning to see.

Victoria Woodhull

1838–1927

VICTORIA WOODHULL, born in Homer, Ohio, was a white activist and leader of the U.S. suffrage movement. She was an advocate for "free love": the right to marry, divorce, and bear children without government interference. She and her sister were the first women to operate a brokerage firm on Wall Street, opening their business in 1870. With the profits they founded a women's rights and reform newspaper, *Woodhull & Claflin's Weekly*, which printed the first English version of the *Communist Manifesto* and endorsed causes such as a single moral standard for men and women, dress reform, and legalized prostitution. In 1871, Woodhull argued before the House Judiciary Committee that the Fourteenth and Fifteenth Amendments had already given women the right to vote, as they guaranteed the right to all U.S. citizens. In 1872, she was the Equal Rights Party's presidential candidate. She was the first woman to run for president, although legally she was not old enough to do so.

To the Women of the South (1870)

Your precedents show that you are equal to all emergencies. Born and reared in the lap of luxury, never having known what responsibilities were, never sinking under the weight of care nor striving to fulfill onerous duties—it was scarcely to be expected that you could bear with dignity the reverses which the war developed for you.

Whatever of right or wrong there may have been in the causes which led to the war, does not add to or detract from the measure of your conduct. It came upon you, was waged with stern determination by both sides, and ended by depriving you of the means of returning to your previous modes of life. The deprivations of personal comforts and luxuries which you suffered throughout the continuance of the conflict, were only exceeded in degree by your devotion to the cause which you made your own. It was paramount to everything you had been called upon to endure, and has rendered you famous in history—the honored of all who can appreciate true nobility of soul, and the revered of those to whom your conduct imparted new hope, enlarged courage and unyielding valor when the dark clouds of battle hung heavily over them.

The careful student of that conduct and of the talents which made it possible, finds therein so much capacity, adaptability and application, that he naturally asks—how can such talents be made available to the country, now that the circumstances which developed them and under which they were displayed no longer exist? Can they not be turned into some channels presenting wider ranges for activity and use?

It is a great loss to the world and a great mistake to yourselves that they should remain inactive and surely sink into dormancy. Life is for action—is action—and he or she lives the best who make the most and best use of all their powers and capabilities. The richest legacy we can possess when the duties of this sphere are about to close, is the record of a well spent life; one that has been productive of general benefit. There are other riches than gold and silver and houses and lands; indeed, these should be counted as the least to be desired species of wealth. Wealth of mind, riches of soul and breadth of heart give caste or position after purely material objects become of no avail.

The capacities for these more desirable forms of wealth are possessed by you to an extent rarely equaled by the women of our Northern country and never excelled. You have the common feminine characteristic—a quick, piercing perception, and to this I add rare judgment, extraordinary discretion and firmness of purpose. This combination of qualities is possessed by men in exceptional cases only. It makes you, as a class, what it makes those very rare men who possess it—great. As such you have experienced the extremes of the vicissitudes of life and in all you have shown yourselves superior. Are you content to settle again into that condition from which the terrors of war alone could arouse you? Are you willing to let the fires of devotion die out upon the altar of your souls? Will you rest satisfied to stifle growing capabilities just as they have developed into great possibilities? Can you now retire to a condition of nonentity?

You may reply that such questions are superfluous, nay, preposterous, since there no longer exists any opportunity for the application of your talents. That is just the point of which I would make you conscious, and then I would ask, do you desire a remedy for submission to existing conditions?

The war could not have been conducted so long as it was without your much needed assistance. Husbands, fathers and brothers would have been helpless without you. And they need you just as much now, but of this they remain to be convinced. Be it now yours to do, and then yours to convict your fellow-sufferers of a stupid lack of appreciation in not extending to you the means of being what the circumstances of that dire struggle made possible and permitted. They do not seem to realize that your former servants are now your political masters. Do you remember and understand this fact, and, doing so, will you remain under the obvious imputation?

Women of the North have many and weighty reasons for demanding a voice in making and administering the laws. Possessing an equality of interests in the results of government, they demand an equality of privileges in its formation and maintenance. Yet all upon which they base their claim is but chaff when considered as convincing arguments, and compared to the merits of your demand. You have earned your right and proved your capacity. Unchivalrous indeed will those be for whom you have done so much should they deny you. But they will not deny you. Ask, and the way will be opened by them.[1] You can then take your stand by and with them, and prove yourselves as useful in peace as you were necessary in war.

SOURCE

Woodhull, Victoria. "To the Women of the South." *Atlanta Constitution*, July 14, 1870, 6.

NOTE

Chapter opening photo: Victoria Woodhull, ca. 1866–73. Courtesy of Special Collections, Fine Arts Library, Harvard University.

1. A reference to Matthew 7:7: "Ask, and it shall be given you; seek, and ye shall find; knock, and it shall be opened unto you."

Zitkala-Sa

1876–1938

ZITKALA-SA (Lakota: "Red Bird") was a Yankton Dakota Sioux writer and reformer born on the Yankton Reservation in South Dakota. She was also known by her missionary-given name, Gertrude Simmons Bonnin. When she was eight, she was taken by Quaker missionaries to a boarding school. As an adult, she wrote several works on the oppression of Native Americans at the hands of the church and the state, as well as her struggles with cultural identity caused by forced assimilation. She also published many of the traditional oral stories she had heard growing up, making them available to an English-speaking audience for the first time. In addition, she wrote the first Native American opera, *Sun Dance Opera* (1913). She was cofounder and president of the National Council of American Indians, which lobbied for Native Americans' right to citizenship and other civil rights that they had long been denied. She was one of the foremost Native American activists of the twentieth century.

From *The School Days of an Indian Girl* (1900)

I.

The Land of Red Apples.

There were eight in our party of bronzed children who were going East with the missionaries. Among us were three young braves, two tall girls, and we three little ones, Judéwin, Thowin, and I.

We had been very impatient to start on our journey to the Red Apple Country, which, we were told, lay a little beyond the great circular horizon of the Western prairie. Under a sky of rosy apples we dreamt of roaming as freely and happily as we had chased the cloud shadows on the Dakota plains. We had anticipated much pleasure from a ride on the iron horse, but the throngs of staring palefaces disturbed and troubled us.

On the train, fair women, with tottering babies on each arm, stopped their haste and scrutinized the children of absent mothers. Large men, with heavy bundles in their hands, halted near by, and riveted their glassy blue eyes upon us.

I sank deep into the corner of my seat, for I resented being watched. Directly in front of me, children who were no larger than I hung themselves upon the backs of their seats, with their bold white faces toward me. Sometimes they took their forefingers out of their mouths and pointed at my moccasined feet. Their mothers, instead of reproving such rude curiosity, looked closely at me, and attracted their children's further notice to my blanket. This embarrassed me, and kept me constantly on the verge of tears.

I sat perfectly still, with my eyes downcast, daring only now and then to shoot long glances around me. Chancing to turn to the window at my side, I was quite breathless upon seeing one familiar object. It was the telegraph pole which strode by at short paces. Very near my mother's dwelling, along the edge of a road thickly bordered with wild sunflowers, some poles like these had been planted by white men. Often I had stopped, on my way down the road, to hold my ear against the pole, and, hearing its low moaning, I used to wonder what the paleface had done to hurt it. Now I sat watching for each pole that glided by to be the last one.

In this way I had forgotten my uncomfortable surroundings, when I heard one of my comrades call out my name. I saw the missionary standing very near, tossing candies and gums into our midst. This amused us all, and we tried to see who could catch the most of the sweetmeats.

Though we rode several days inside of the iron horse, I do not recall a single thing about our luncheons.

It was night when we reached the school grounds. The lights from the windows of the large buildings fell upon some of the icicled trees that stood beneath them. We were led toward an open door, where the brightness of the lights within flooded out over the heads of the excited palefaces who blocked the way. My body trembled more from fear than from the snow I trod upon.

Entering the house, I stood close against the wall. The strong glaring light in the large whitewashed room dazzled my eyes. The noisy hurrying of hard shoes upon a bare wooden floor increased the whirring in my ears. My only safety seemed to be in keeping next to the wall. As I was wondering in which direction to escape from all this confusion, two warm hands grasped me firmly, and in the same moment I was tossed high in mid-air. A rosy-cheeked paleface woman caught me in her arms. I was both frightened and insulted by such trifling. I stared into her eyes, wishing her to let me stand on my own feet, but she jumped me up and down with increasing enthusiasm. My mother had never made a plaything of her wee daughter. Remembering this I began to cry aloud.

They misunderstood the cause of my tears, and placed me at a white table loaded with food. There our party were united again. As I did not hush my crying, one of the older ones whispered to me, "Wait until you are alone in the night."

It was very little I could swallow besides my sobs, that evening.

"Oh, I want my mother and my brother Dawée! I want to go to my aunt!" I pleaded; but the ears of the palefaces could not hear me.

From the table we were taken along an upward incline of wooden boxes, which I learned afterward to call a stairway. At the top was a quiet hall, dimly lighted. Many narrow beds were in one straight line down the entire length of the wall. In them lay sleeping brown faces, which peeped just out of the coverings. I was tucked into bed with one of the tall girls, because she talked to me in my mother tongue and seemed to soothe me.

I had arrived in the wonderful land of rosy skies, but I was not happy, as I had thought I should be. My long travel and the bewildering sights had exhausted me. I fell asleep, heaving deep, tired sobs. My tears were left to dry themselves in streaks, because neither my aunt nor my mother was near to wipe them away.

II.

The Cutting of My Long Hair.

The first day in the land of apples was a bitter-cold one; for the snow still covered the ground, and the trees were bare. A large bell rang for breakfast, its loud metallic voice crashing through the belfry overhead and into our sensitive ears. The annoying clatter of shoes on bare floors gave us no peace. The constant clash of harsh noises, with an undercurrent of many voices murmuring an unknown tongue, made a bedlam within which I was securely tied. And though my spirit tore itself in struggling for its lost freedom, all was useless.

A paleface woman, with white hair, came up after us. We were placed in a line of girls who were marching into the dining room. These were Indian girls, in stiff shoes and closely clinging dresses. The small girls wore sleeved aprons and shingled hair. As I walked noiselessly in my soft moccasins, I felt like sinking to the floor, for my blanket had been stripped from my shoulders. I looked hard at the Indian girls, who seemed not to care that they were even more immodestly dressed than I, in their tightly fitting clothes. While we marched in, the boys entered at an opposite door. I watched for the three young braves who came in our party. I spied them in the rear ranks, looking as uncomfortable as I felt.

A small bell was tapped, and each of the pupils drew a chair from under the table. Supposing this act meant they were to be seated, I pulled out mine and at once slipped into it from one side. But when I turned my head, I saw that I was the only one seated, and all the rest at our table remained standing. Just as I began to rise, looking shyly around to see how chairs were to be used, a second bell was sounded. All were seated at last, and I had to crawl back into my chair again. I heard a man's voice at one end of the hall, and I looked around to see him. But all the others hung their heads over their plates. As I glanced at the long chain of tables, I caught the eyes of a paleface woman upon me. Immediately I dropped my eyes, wondering why I was so keenly watched by the strange woman. The man ceased his mutterings, and then a third bell was tapped. Every one picked up his knife and fork and began eating. I began crying instead, for by this time I was afraid to venture anything more.

But this eating by formula was not the hardest trial in that first day. Late in the morning, my friend Judéwin gave me a terrible warning. Judéwin knew a few words of English, and she had overheard the paleface woman talk about cutting our long, heavy hair. Our mothers had taught us that only unskilled warriors who were captured had their hair shingled by the enemy. Among our people, short hair was worn by mourners, and shingled hair by cowards!

We discussed our fate some moments, and when Judéwin said, "We have to submit, because they are strong," I rebelled.

"No, I will not submit! I will struggle first!" I answered.

I watched my chance, and when no one noticed I disappeared. I crept up the stairs as quietly as I could in my squeaking shoes,—my moccasins had been exchanged for shoes. Along the hall I passed, without knowing whither I was going. Turning aside to an open door, I found a large room with three white beds in it. The windows were covered with dark green curtains, which made the room very dim. Thankful that no one was there, I directed my steps toward the corner farthest from the door. On my hands and knees I crawled under the bed, and cuddled myself in the dark corner.

From my hiding place I peered out, shuddering with fear whenever I heard footsteps near by. Though in the hall loud voices were calling my name, and I knew that even Judéwin was searching for me, I did not open my mouth to answer. Then the steps were quickened and the voices became excited. The sounds came nearer and nearer. Women and girls entered the room. I held my breath, and watched them open closet doors and peep behind large trunks. Some one threw up the curtains, and the room was filled with sudden light. What caused them to stoop and look under the bed I do not know. I remember being dragged out, though I resisted by kicking and scratching wildly. In spite of myself, I was carried downstairs and tied fast in a chair.

I cried aloud, shaking my head all the while until I felt the cold blades of the scissors against my neck, and heard them gnaw off one of my thick braids. Then I lost my spirit. Since the day I was taken from my mother I had suffered extreme indignities. People had stared at me. I had been tossed about in the air like a wooden puppet. And now my long hair was shingled like a coward's! In my anguish I moaned for my mother, but no one came to comfort me. Not a soul reasoned quietly with me, as my own mother used to do; for now I was only one of many little animals driven by a herder.

From *An Indian Teacher among Indians* (1900)

II.

A Trip Westward.

One sultry month I sat at a desk heaped up with work. Now, as I recall it, I wonder how I could have dared to disregard nature's warning with such recklessness. Fortunately, my inheritance of a marvelous endurance enabled me to bend without breaking.

Though I had gone to and fro, from my room to the office, in an unhappy silence, I was watched by those around me. On an early morning I was summoned to the superintendent's office. For a half-hour I listened to his words, and when I returned to my room I remembered one sentence above the rest. It was this: "I am going to turn you loose to pasture!" He was sending me West to gather Indian pupils for the school, and this was his way of expressing it.

I needed nourishment, but the mid-summer's travel across the continent to search the hot prairies for overconfident parents who would intrust their children to strangers was a lean pasturage. However, I dwelt on the hope of seeing my mother. I tried to reason that a change was a rest. Within a couple of days I started toward my mother's home.

The intense heat and the sticky car smoke that followed my homeward trail did not noticeably restore my vitality. Hour after hour I gazed upon the country which was receding rapidly from me. I noticed the gradual expansion of the horizon as we emerged out of the forests into the plains. The great high buildings, whose towers overlooked the dense woodlands, and whose gigantic clusters formed large cities, diminished, together with the groves, until only little log cabins lay snugly in the bosom of the vast prairie. The cloud shadows which drifted about on the waving yellow of long-dried grasses thrilled me like the meeting of old friends.

At a small station, consisting of a single frame house with a rickety board walk around it, I alighted from the iron horse, just thirty miles from my mother and my brother Dawée. A strong hot wind seemed determined to blow my hat off, and return me to olden days when I roamed bareheaded over the hills. After the puffing engine of my train was gone, I stood on the platform in deep solitude. In the distance I saw the gently rolling land leap up into bare hills. At their bases a broad gray road was winding itself round about them until it came by the station. Among these hills I rode in a light conveyance, with a trusty driver, whose unkempt flaxen hair hung shaggy about his ears and his leather neck of reddish tan. From accident or decay he had lost one of his long front teeth.

Though I call him a paleface, his cheeks were of a brick red. His moist blue eyes, blurred and bloodshot, twitched involuntarily. For a long time he had driven through grass and snow from this solitary station to the

Indian village. His weather-stained clothes fitted badly his warped shoulders. He was stooped, and his protruding chin, with its tuft of dry flax, nodded as monotonously as did the head of his faithful beast.

All the morning I looked about me, recognizing old familiar sky lines of rugged bluffs and round-topped hills. By the roadside I caught glimpses of various plants whose sweet roots were delicacies among my people. When I saw the first cone-shaped wigwam, I could not help uttering an exclamation which caused my driver a sudden jump out of his drowsy nodding.

At noon, as we drove through the eastern edge of the reservation, I grew very impatient and restless. Constantly I wondered what my mother would say upon seeing her little daughter grown tall. I had not written her the day of my arrival, thinking I would surprise her. Crossing a ravine thicketed with low shrubs and plum bushes, we approached a large yellow acre of wild sunflowers. Just beyond this nature's garden we drew near to my mother's cottage. Close by the log cabin stood a little canvas-covered wigwam. The driver stopped in front of the open door, and in a long moment my mother appeared at the threshold.

I had expected her to run out to greet me, but she stood still, all the while staring at the weather-beaten man at my side. At length, when her loftiness became unbearable, I called to her, "Mother, why do you stop?"

This seemed to break the evil moment, and she hastened out to hold my head against her cheek.

"My daughter, what madness possessed you to bring home such a fellow?" she asked, pointing at the driver, who was fumbling in his pockets for change while he held the bill I gave him between his jagged teeth.

"Bring him! Why, no, mother, he has brought me! He is a driver!" I exclaimed.

Upon this revelation, my mother threw her arms about me and apologized for her mistaken inference. We laughed away the momentary hurt. Then she built a brisk fire on the ground in the tepee, and hung a blackened coffeepot on one of the prongs of a forked pole which leaned over the flames. Placing a pan on a heap of red embers, she baked some unleavened bread. This light luncheon she brought into the cabin, and arranged on a table covered with a checkered oilcloth.

My mother had never gone to school, and though she meant always to give up her own customs for such of the white man's ways as pleased her, she made only compromises. Her two windows, directly opposite each

other, she curtained with a pink-flowered print. The naked logs were un-
stained, and rudely carved with the axe so as to fit into one another. The
sod roof was trying to boast of tiny sunflowers, the seeds of which had
probably been planted by the constant wind. As I leaned my head against
the logs, I discovered the peculiar odor that I could not forget. The rains
had soaked the earth and roof so that the smell of damp clay was but the
natural breath of such a dwelling.

"Mother, why is not your house cemented? Do you have no interest in a
more comfortable shelter?" I asked, when the apparent inconveniences of
her home seemed to suggest indifference on her part.

"You forget, my child, that I am now old, and I do not work with beads
any more. Your brother Dawée, too, has lost his position, and we are left
without means to buy even a morsel of food," she replied.

Dawée was a government clerk in our reservation when I last heard
from him. I was surprised upon hearing what my mother said concerning his lack of employment. Seeing the puzzled expression on my face,
she continued: "Dawée! Oh, has he not told you that the Great Father at
Washington sent a white son to take your brother's pen from him? Since
then Dawée has not been able to make use of the education the Eastern
school has given him."

I found no words with which to answer satisfactorily. I found no reason
with which to cool my inflamed feelings.

Dawée was a whole day's journey off on the prairie, and my mother did
not expect him until the next day. We were silent.

When, at length, I raised my head to hear more clearly the moaning
of the wind in the corner logs, I noticed the daylight streaming into the
dingy room through several places where the logs fitted unevenly. Turning to my mother, I urged her to tell me more about Dawée's trouble, but
she only said: "Well, my daughter, this village has been these many win-
ters a refuge for white robbers. The Indian cannot complain to the Great
Father in Washington without suffering outrage for it here. Dawée tried
to secure justice for our tribe in a small matter, and today you see the
folly of it."

Again, though she stopped to hear what I might say, I was silent.

"My child, there is only one source of justice, and I have been praying
steadfastly to the Great Spirit to avenge our wrongs," she said, seeing I did
not move my lips.

My shattered energy was unable to hold longer any faith, and I cried out desperately: "Mother, don't pray again! The Great Spirit does not care if we live or die! Let us not look for good or justice: then we shall not be disappointed!"

"Sh! my child, do not talk so madly. There is Taku Iyotan Wasaka, to which I pray," she answered, as she stroked my head again as she used to do when I was a smaller child.

III.

My Mother's Curse upon White Settlers.

One black night mother and I sat alone in the dim starlight, in front of our wigwam. We were facing the river, as we talked about the shrinking limits of the village. She told me about the poverty-stricken white settlers, who lived in caves dug in the long ravines of the high hills across the river.

A whole tribe of broad-footed white beggars had rushed hither to make claims on those wild lands. Even as she was telling this I spied a small glimmering light in the bluffs.

"That is a white man's lodge where you see the burning fire," she said. Then, a short distance from it, only a little lower than the first, was another light. As I became accustomed to the night, I saw more and more twinkling lights, here and there, scattered all along the wide black margin of the river.

Still looking toward the distant firelight, my mother continued: "My daughter, beware of the paleface. It was the cruel paleface who caused the death of your sister and your uncle, my brave brother. It is this same paleface who offers in one palm the holy papers, and with the other gives a holy baptism of firewater. He is the hypocrite who reads with one eye, 'Thou shalt not kill,' and with the other gloats upon the sufferings of the Indian race." Then suddenly discovering a new fire in the bluffs, she exclaimed, "Well, well, my daughter, there is the light of another white rascal!"

She sprang to her feet, and, standing firm beside her wigwam, she sent a curse upon those who sat around the hated white man's light. Raising her right arm forcibly into line with her eye, she threw her whole might into her doubled fist as she shot it vehemently at the strangers. Long she held her outstretched fingers toward the settler's lodge, as if an invisible power passed from them to the evil at which she aimed.

IV.

Retrospection.

Leaving my mother, I returned to the school in the East. As months passed over me, I slowly comprehended that the large army of white teachers in Indian schools had a larger missionary creed than I had suspected.

It was one which included self-preservation quite as much as Indian education. When I saw an opium-eater holding a position as teacher of Indians, I did not understand what good was expected, until a Christian in power replied that this pumpkin-colored creature had a feeble mother to support. An inebriate paleface sat stupid in a doctor's chair, while Indian patients carried their ailments to untimely graves, because his fair wife was dependent upon him for her daily food.

I find it hard to count that white man a teacher who tortured an ambitious Indian youth by frequently reminding the brave changeling that he was nothing but a "government pauper."

Though I burned with indignation upon discovering on every side instances no less shameful than those I have mentioned, there was no present help. Even the few rare ones who have worked nobly for my race were powerless to choose workmen like themselves. To be sure, a man was sent from the Great Father to inspect Indian schools, but what he saw was usually the students' sample work *made* for exhibition. I was nettled by this sly cunning of the workmen who hoodwinked the Indian's pale Father at Washington.

My illness, which prevented the conclusion of my college course, together with my mother's stories of the encroaching frontier settlers, left me in no mood to strain my eyes in searching for latent good in my white co-workers.

At this stage of my own evolution, I was ready to curse men of small capacity for being the dwarfs their God had made them. In the process of my education I had lost all consciousness of the nature world about me. Thus, when a hidden rage took me to the small white-walled prison which I then called my room, I unknowingly turned away from my one salvation.

Alone in my room, I sat like the petrified Indian woman of whom my mother used to tell me. I wished my heart's burdens would turn me to unfeeling stone. But alive, in my tomb, I was destitute!

For the white man's papers I had given up my faith in the Great Spirit. For these same papers I had forgotten the healing in trees and brooks.

On account of my mother's simple view of life, and my lack of any, I gave her up, also. I made no friends among the race of people I loathed. Like a slender tree, I had been uprooted from my mother, nature, and God. I was shorn of my branches, which had waved in sympathy and love for home and friends. The natural coat of bark which had protected my oversensitive nature was scraped off to the very quick.

Now a cold bare pole I seemed to be, planted in a strange earth. Still, I seemed to hope a day would come when my mute aching head, reared upward to the sky, would flash a zigzag lightning across the heavens. With this dream of vent for a long-pent consciousness, I walked again amid the crowds.

At last, one weary day in the schoolroom, a new idea presented itself to me. It was a new way of solving the problem of my inner self. I liked it. Thus I resigned my position as teacher; and now I am in an Eastern city, following the long course of study I have set for myself. Now, as I look back upon the recent past, I see it from a distance, as a whole. I remember how, from morning till evening, many specimens of civilized peoples visited the Indian school. The city folks with canes and eyeglasses, the countrymen with sunburnt cheeks and clumsy feet, forgot their relative social ranks in an ignorant curiosity. Both sorts of these Christian palefaces were alike astounded at seeing the children of savage warriors so docile and industrious.

As answers to their shallow inquiries they received the students' sample work to look upon. Examining the neatly figured pages, and gazing upon the Indian girls and boys bending over their books, the white visitors walked out of the schoolhouse well satisfied: they were educating the children of the red man! They were paying a liberal fee to the government employees in whose able hands lay the small forest of Indian timber.

In this fashion many have passed idly through the Indian schools during the last decade, afterward to boast of their charity to the North American Indian. But few there are who have paused to question whether real life or long-lasting death lies beneath this semblance of civilization.

SOURCES

Zitkala-Sa (Gertrude Bonnin). "An Indian Teacher among Indians," *Atlantic Monthly* 85 (March 1900), 381–87.
———. "The School Days of an Indian Girl," *Atlantic Monthly* 85 (February 1900): 18–94.

Acknowledgments

We would like to acknowledge the following people and institutions for permitting us to reprint texts or images found among their holdings: Canada's Early Women Writers, SFU Library Digital Collections, Simon Fraser University; the Emily Dickinson Collection, Amherst College, Archives and Special Collections; Harvard University Press; John O'Connor and Jack Watson of the Dialectic and Philanthropic Societies of the University of North Carolina; the National Museum of American History, Smithsonian Institution; the National Urban League; University of Massachusetts Press; and University of Nebraska Press. Our own institutions, the Universities of Iowa and Idaho, deserve thanks as well for supporting our work over the past year, particularly the University of Idaho's Center for Digital Inquiry and Learning, whose resources, staff, and Digital Scholarship Fellowship helped make this anthology possible.

We would also like to offer our deepest gratitude to Roxane Gay and Katha Pollitt, for their words and their wisdom—it has been the opportunity of a lifetime to work with you and benefit from your insights and expertise. We are grateful for all of the work that you share with the world, and your fearless advocacy on behalf of women; you are the modern-day counterparts to the women we celebrate here.

Thanks, too, are owed to professor emerita Ellen DuBois, for pointing us to Elizabeth Cady Stanton's, Susan B. Anthony's, and Matilda Joslyn Gage's landmark introduction to *History of Woman Suffrage, Volume 1*; as well as to Linda Chamberlin, Alan Chamberlin, and David Chamberlin, great-grandchildren of Charlotte Perkins Gilman, for generously granting us permission to reprint "The Right to Die" and a passage from *The Living of Charlotte Perkins Gilman*. The work of their great-grandmother is indeed a blessing to humanity; we are glad to be able to help continue her legacy.

We also wish to express our gratitude and appreciation to everyone at the University of Iowa Press who made this project possible, especially

James McCoy, Jacob Roosa, Susan Hill Newton, Karen Copp, Allison Means, Sara Hales-Brittain, Suzanne Glémot, and Angela Dickey, as well as copyeditor extraordinaire Carolyn Brown. You're not only the crafters of important books but also great souls and good friends.

Finally, in a time when we are reminded daily and hourly of the debts we owe to activists, journalists, and truth-tellers of the past and present, debts we will never be able to repay—thank you to the women whose words make up these volumes.